The Good Book

OWNER

Owner's Name

The above-signed owner undertakes to identify all of the words that are, for certain, true about themselves starting with the Positive Adjectives and highlighting, underlineing, circling, or checking all certainly true words. A personal *Ideal* can thereafter be set in Chapter 2.

CONTENTS

Introduction

INTRODUCTION

Inherent in omnipresent existence, as prepotent as the laws of physical science, are motivational touchstones that guide, and ultimately impel us towards our personal and collective moral and spiritual evolution. These can be identified and pragmatically utilized via our daily use of language.

This is intended primarily as a personal workbook, or reference book for practical betterment. But it's also a writing resource of the upper spectrum of the English lexicon useful for everything from birthdays to eulogies.

Positive words, and their accompanying thoughts, fortified by every positive emotion from ability to zing, can elevate us from the abyss of despair, up through reason, compassion, and all the way to ecstatic gramercy.

Know yourself. This book helps a person find, and underline or otherwise identify, their best personal characteristics. Beyond that, these words can be used to describe the attributes of someone's adversary, co-worker, family, friend, lover, or spouse.

The Universal Laws are listed here as well as the related *Fruits of the Spirit* that are the personal characteristics imperative for psychological and spiritual advancement. Also listed are many of the motivational *Gifts of the Spirit*; each one as miraculous as ESP, that are the rewards for spiritual advancement. To this end it helps to choose a single Personal Ideal to consistently work towards from the many options presented herein.

Word lists, even a list as remarkable *The Universal Laws* can seem a little wooden and pedantic. The way to bring them to life and invigorate them with the energy of the living world, is to bring them to life by acting act on them.

Contemplating some of the good words found here for an extended period of time can have a remarkable effect. Thinking about the meaning of a word, like 'synchronicity', for example, over-and-over, while out moving among people, can make it happen. Alternatively, thinking about the meaning of a particular word throughout the day can cause fantastic, good-feeling, or instructive dreams to result. And some of the most remarkable nature-based miracles can occur while jogging out in nature thinking about these words assisted by the emotional inspiration of a pumping heart, lungs, arms and legs of the exercise.

Have you ever wanted Grace? This comes from cultivating *The Fruits of the Spirit.*

"There is a river whose streams make glad the city of God, the Holy Place where the most high dwells" – Psalm 46-4

These positive words increase, and flow with, the current.

The spiritual foundation underlying this book is by virtue of American prophet Edgar Cayce. His New Age Christian outlook isn't the only spiritual framework but it's among those oft proven true and accurate.

Edgar Cayce stated that the "I Am" is of the ego and also that there is *"no other way than the 'I Am'"*; a noteworthy imperative. Evidently the ego isn't merely something that needs to be overcome via suppression. The ego is intended to be directed towards "Oneness", "Love", "Patience", "Compassion", "Joy", and more.

Don't fail to sign the Owner's page and take the time to identify all the true words about yourself to know for a rainy day. Choose an ideal for your life and aspire to it throughout your day-to-day decisions.

"Know thyself" means more than knowing one's limitations. The words found here can help take the "I Am" and answer the question "what?"

Yours,

Marty Ozols

Chapter 1

THE NATURE OF GOOD

"Keep thy faith in that which is good for good alone lives, ever."
(Edgar Cayce Reading 2537-1)

Everyone wants a high quality of life into the future and the primary way of achieving that good life, in all of mortal orbific creation, is to think about positive things first. In accordance with *The Universal Laws of Attraction*; if you want good, be good. The nature of good is defined by adjectives, nouns, and adverbs:

GOOD

Adj. 1.to be desired or approved of
2. having the qualities desired for a particular role

N. 1. that which is morally right; righteousness
2. of benefit or advantage
3. both 1&2

Adv. Well *Informal*
ex. "My mother never used to cook this good."

Adjective: 1. To be **desired or approved of** or 2. Having **the qualities required for a particular role**: A comprehensive list of these can be found in the *Positive Adjectives* in Chapter 3.

Noun: 1. That which is **morally right**; **righteousness**: Aegis, Afflatus, Agape, Agapism, Aid, Alignment, Amour-propre, Application, Appreciation, Aroha, Assiduity, Assiduousness, Assistance, Awareness, Balance, Beneficence, Benevolence, Brotherly love, Buoyancy, Compassion, Consonance, Constancy, Diligence, Earnestness, Encouragement, Enlightenment, Ethicality, Faith,

Fellowship, Forbearance, Friendship, Generosity, Gentleness, Giving, Good, Goodness, Gramercy, Happiness, Harmony, Help, Helping, Honesty, Honour, Humaneness, Indubitableness, Integrity, Intent, Joy, Judiciousness, Kindliness, Kindness, Knowledge, Leading/Administrating diligently, Lightheartedness, Longanimity, Long-suffering, Love, showing Mercy cheerfully, Morality, Niceness, Obedience, Optimism, Patience, Peace, Peacefulness, Politeness, Positiveness, Probity, Rectitude, Respect, Righteousness, Rightness, Sagacity, Sedulousness, Self-control, Self-sacrifice, Service, Seva, Solicitude, Steadiness, Sureness, Surety, Teaching, Thaumaturgy, Thoughtfulness, Tolerance, Tranquility, Truth, Truthfulness, Uprightness, Understanding, Unicity, Unity, Values, Vigilance, Virtue, Virtuousness, Wholesomeness, Wisdom, Worthiness

2. That which is a **benefit** or **advantage** to someone or something: Abundance, Activity, Acumen, Adroitness, Advantage, Aegis, Afflatus, Aid, Alignment, Amour propre, Aplomb, Apotheosis, Apperception, Application, Appreciation, Approbation, Arrival, Assurance, Attention, Attentiveness, Awakening, Awareness, Balance, Beneficence, Benefit, Benevolence, Blissfulness, Bounteousness, Bountifulness, Brotherly love, Buoyancy, Certainty, Clarity, Compassion, Confidence, Consonance, Delight, Discernment, Discretion, Ease, Economy, Encouragement, Energy, Engagement, Enjoyment, Enlightenment, Esteem, Eudaimonia, Exactitude, Faith, Favour, Fellowship, Forbearance, Foresight, Forethought, Fortune, Freedom, Friendship, Fun, Gain, Gentleness, Grace, Gramercy, Happiness, Harmony, Health, Heedfulness, Help, Industry, Indubitableness, Intent, Interest, Inspiration, Intrigue, Joy, Joyfulness, Judiciousness, Kindness, Keenness, Knowingness, Knowledge, Lightheartedness, Love, Luxury, Mercy, Merit, Mindfulness, Niceness, Nobleness, Nourishment, Obligingness, Optimism, Patience, Peace, Peacefulness, Pleasure, Politeness, Positiveness, Possibility, Potential, Precision, Profit, Progress, Promise, Prosperity, Providence, Prudence, Purpose, Quality, Quickness, Reasoning, Refreshment, Relief, Repletion, Respect, Revelation, Sagacity, Sangfroid, Satisfaction, Security,

Serendipity, Service, Self-control, Spirit, Staunchness, Steadiness, Suffisance, Supply, Sureness, Surety, Synchronicity, Thaumaturgy, Thoughtfulness, Tolerance, Tranquility, Truth, Understanding, Unicity, Utopia, Values, Vigour, Virtuosity, Vivacity, Watchfulness, Wealth, Welfare, Well-being, Wisdom, Worthiness
Find more synonyms in *The Positive Emotions* in Chapter 9.

3. That which is both **righteous** and **beneficial**: Aegis, Afflatus, Aid, Alignment, Application, Appreciation, Assistance, Awareness, Balance, Beneficence, Benevolence, Brotherly love, Buoyancy, Care, Certainty, Compassion, Consonance, Encouragement, Enlightenment, Faith, Fellowship, Forbearance, Friendship, Gramercy, Happiness, Harmony, Help, Indubitableness, Intent, Joy, Judiciousness, Kindliness, Kindness, Lightheartedness, Love, Mercy, Niceness, Nobleness, Optimism, Patience, Peace, Peacefulness, Politeness, Positiveness, Respect, Sagacity, Self-control, Service, Steadiness, Sureness, Surety, Thaumaturgy, Thoughtfulness, Tolerance, Tranquility, Truth, Understanding, Unicity, Values, Wisdom, Worthiness

That which is both righteous and beneficial can increase over time in sync with increased awareness. For example the realization of how holistic love, or being a pure channel of blessing, in service, in being essentially omni-beneficial, is also acutely self-beneficial.

Adverb: informal **Well** "My mother could never cook this good" Ably, Admirably, Adroitly, Agreeably, Aptly, Appositely, Appropriately, Capably, Competently, Decently, Deftly, Desirably, Excellently, Expertly, Exquisitely, Finely, Fittingly, Obligingly, Perfectly, Pertinently, Pleasingly, Precisely, Relevantly, Satisfactorily, Skillfully, Suitably

In a reincarnate model, with *Universal Laws* in place, only good lasts.

So far, so good.

Chapter 2

THE UNIVERSAL LAWS

"Then condemn none. For, there are universal and spiritual laws that are a part of the self as well as of the universal consciousness."
(Edgar Cayce Reading 2560-1)

Dating back into prehistory *The Universal Laws* reflect fundamental biological imperatives. These are known as the **Laws of Self: Physical Preservation** and **Perpetuation of Self via Procreation.** As we advance with these laws they become less and less limited to self.

Everything in the universe is governed by *The Universal Laws* which are active in the physical, mental and spiritual worlds. The **Law of Cause & Effect**, for example, is well-known in Newtonian physics and thereby enters the sphere of the "As you sow, so shall you reap" realm of interpersonal justice. When it transcends lifetimes, it becomes the **Laws of Karma & Grace.**

Many of *The Universal Laws* merge into each other. For example the **Law of Cause & Effect** which includes "For every effect there is a cause" is also related to "Like Begets Like" of **The Laws of Attraction** which also includes the famous "Like Attracts Like" and, conversely, "Opposites Repel". These are also related to the **Law of Recompense.**

In light of **The Law of One**; "We are One", the practicality of the **Law of Love;** "Love is Law" only makes sense. These two laws are foundational. The selfless *Law of Love*, is 'giving in action'.

The Whole Law: *"Love the Lord, eschew evil, do good to thy fellow man; this is the whole law."* (Edgar Cayce Reading 2733-2)

In the context of physics **The Law of Relativity** includes the physical relationships in everything from atoms to planets including chemical, temporal, and energy-related phenomena. Individually we are locally proximal and cleansing our Earthly interpersonal relationships while being one with every force in the Universe and seeking to know our relative relationship of unicity to the conditions upon which all life giving forces depend. *We seek and find unicity with the Source of life via knowing relativity.*

The First Lesson: *"There is so much good in the worst of us, and so much bad in the best of us, it doesn't behoove any of us to speak evil of the rest of us."* (Edgar Cayce Reading *3063-1)* Until an individual learns this they won't go very far in spiritual or soul development.

Law of Mercy: Never put off or hesitate to ease the mind of another.

Law of Increase: The Spirit of your actions multiplies the result. God alone gives the increase.

The Law of Faith is both a *Universal Law* and *Fruit of the Spirit. The Power of Expectancy* is related to the Law of Faith and gives energy to, or expecting less takes energy from, creative power. If you ask and expect not, you set a barrier. The Laws of Increase and Faith affect the Laws of Attraction

Individuals will be subject to *The Universal Laws* until they become *The Law*, in a constructive way, in their thought, intent and purpose. As individuals apply the laws, are under them, and become them with no doubt, fear, or animosity, selfless in God's purpose, they become equal with the law, as Christ did, and thereby become it. This overcomes all material law including gravity, and supply, and all phases of Earthly experience.

Timed Law of Attraction Slideshow

THE LAWS OF ATTRACTION

1. Like attracts like   2. Like begets like   3. Opposites repel

These three *Laws of Attraction* assert that we must feel a thing in order to attract it. The premise is that feelings such as "allowing" and "enjoyment" are important and necessary in leading to the recipience of popular qualities such as 'prosperity' and 'abundance'. If a positive thought, such as 'satisfaction', can be sustained for a long enough duration, a secondary, fortifying, vibratory force is said to form to compound with it into the future.

An interest in personal prosperity is a popular economic motivator for study and practice of these laws. This perspective has its practical merits but is limited in that it disregards many other *Universal Laws* and *Fruits of the Spirit*. It's a focus on love of self and things without much regard for all other living things where most of love resides.

'Amour propre' is "the appropriate love of self". All the positive things that go into it rank more highly on the Power vs. Force scale, relative to anger, as an alternative way to overcome low self-esteem. The forthcoming words are well deployed when used to out-talk our inner critical voice.

Timed Thoughts to Create a New Reality

Choosing just one word per day, how long/often can feeling its meaning be sustained throughout the day?

Simply closing our eyes and holding the thought will sustain the feeling for as long as desired. If there's a stopwatch app handy then benefit can be found in timing these thoughts and comparing the times. These word meanings can also be contemplated while out among people or even pumped while jogging.

In addition to frequency and duration, momentum can be gained via increasing enthusiasm. Energizing words are included for that purpose. *See also the Positive Emotions, Chapter 9*

Nouns

Abundance, Advancement, Advantage, Agacerie, Alignment, Allure, Amour propre, Amusement, Anticipation, Appreciation, Arrival, Attraction, Awakening, Balance, Beauty, Blissfulness, Bounteousness, Bountifulness, Buoyancy, Calling, Certainty, Clarity, Coincidence, Confidence, Consonance, Delectation, Delight, Draw, Eagerness, Ease, Energy, Engagement, Enjoyment, Enlightenment, Enthrallment, Enthusiasm, Eudaimonia, Evocation, Exhilaration, Fellowship, Flow, Fortune, Friendship, Freedom, Fun, Gentleness, Good, Grace, Gramercy, Gratification, Gravy, Harmony, Increase, Indulgence, Inspiration, Intrigue, Invigoration, Joy, Jubilance, Knowingness, Light-heartedness, Lodestone, Love, Luxury, Magnetism, Magnetization, Optimism, Passion, Peace, Pizazz, Pleasure, Possibility, Potential, Prevision, Progress, Promise, Prosperity, Purpose, Quality, Ravishment, Receiving, Recipient, Refreshment, Relish, Repletion, Responsiveness, Revelation, Sangfroid, Satisfaction, Security, Serendipity, Serenity, Spirit, Suffisance, Supply, Surety, Synchronicity, Tantalization, Understanding, Unicity, Utopia, Vehemence, Vigour, Vivacity, Wellbeing, Whole-spiritedness, Worthiness, Wow, Zestfulness

Adverb: Freely

Verbs
Accepting, Allowing, Basking, Rising, Summoning, Thriving

Exclamations

Aaah! (Satisfaction), Excellent!, Cool!, Gramercy!, Hallelujah! Hurray!, Joy!, *Mmmmm...*, Oooo!, Whee!, Woo-Hoo!, Yay!, Yes!, Yippy!

Above and beyond our personal interests every individual benefits by magnifying *The Fruits of the Spirit* as much as possible because they are *The Universal Laws* as applied within self.

THE FRUITS OF THE SPIRIT

"THESE make for the awareness in the soul of its relationship to the Creative Force that is manifest in self, in the ego, in the I AM of each soul, and of I AM THAT I AM."
(Edgar Cayce Reading 378-14)

Edgar Cayce's statement that the ways of man are via power whereas the ways of God are via *The Fruits of the Spirit* is consistent with the biblical 'Meek inheriting the Earth' phrase as well as with the eastern 'Seva' concept. *The Fruits of the Spirit* are:

Brotherly love, Compassion, Fellowship, Friendship, Gentleness, Hope, Joy, Kindness, Long-suffering, Love, Nobleness, Obedience, Patience, Peace, Self-sacrifice, Tolerance and Truth. In addition to these **Goodness, Faith, Meekness, Self-control,** and **Temperance** are also mentioned in Galatians 5:22-23.

Meditate on The Fruits of the Spirit in the inner secrets of the consciousness, and the cells in the body become aware of the awakening of the life in their activity through the body. In the mind, the cells of the mind become aware of the life in the spirit.
(Edgar Cayce Reading 5752-3)

This requisite study of every soul in its own consciousness is helpful to everyone.

Hope/Faith, Joy, Love, and **Peace** are also among the energizing, well-directed, and great-feeling top *Positive Emotions* in Chapter 9.

THE GIFTS OF THE SPIRIT

"It isn't the great things... It is just being kind, just being gentle, just being patient, FIRST with self and self's relationships to thy fellow man." (Edgar Cayce Reading 416-7)

The Gifts of the Spirit are all highly personalized supernatural growth incentives such as **Healing ability, Prophetic ability, Spirit communication, Faith that moves mountains** and other miraculous powers. These include more commonly familiar areas such as:

**Knowledge   Wisdom   Serving   Teaching
Encouraging   Giving   Leading Diligently
Showing Mercy Cheerfully...**

Gifts of the Spirit can also be myriads of other talents including the **Workings of Miracles, Different Kinds of Tongues**, and **Interpretation of Tongues** as identified in 1 Corinthians 12.

All of these must be accompanied by love.

The Gifts of the Spirit are granted for realizing *The Fruits of the Spirit* and *The Fruits of the Spirit* are *The Universal Laws* personally applied.

*"When you choose the paradigm of service,
it turns everything you do from a job into a gift."*
- Oprah Winfrey

IDEALS

"For it is the spirit, the purpose, the ideal with which ye think, ye speak, ye act, that will determine what the fruit of thy life, of thy thoughts, will be." (Edgar Cayce Reading 3459-1)

An ideal is a guiding star that has a Spiritual, Mental, and Physical component.

A spiritual ideal is the highest spiritual quality or attainment that we could hope to have motivating us in our lives right now. It determines the possibilities for the related mental attitudes and physical activities.

My Spiritual Ideal

Example: LOVE See *The Fruits of the Spirit,* a few pages back, for particularly good recommendations or find other alternatives in the Positive Adjective and Noun chapters.

My Spiritual Ideal is

_____
_____
_____
_____
_____

It doesn't always but an Ideal could last a lifetime. Write yours above. Then consistently act on it, and live, as if it's real whenever possible.

"O that all would realize, come to the consciousness that what we are, in any given experience or time, is the result of what we have done about the ideals that we have set".
(Edgar Cayce Reading 1549-1)

Chapter 3

POSITIVE ADJECTIVES

"There is no way to be pointed out save [except] the 'I AM'. It is the birth of the spirit." (Edgar Cayce Reading 262-10)

Know Thyself: Circle, underline, or otherwise identify, the truth about you.

... "I am..."

A-1, A-OK, A-one, Abiding, Able, Able-bodied, Abloom, Abounding, Above, Aboveboard, Absolute, Absolved, Abundant, Accelerated, Acceptable, Accepted, Accepting, Accessible, Acclaimed, Accommodating, Accommodative, Accomplished, Accordant, Accountable, Accredited, Accurate, Accustomed, Ace, Aces, Acknowledged, Acquainted, Active, Actual, Actualized, Acuminate, Acuminous, Adaptable, Adaptive, Adept, Adequate, Adjusted, Admirable, Admired, Admissible, Adonic, Adorable, Adored, Adoring, Adroit, Advanced, Advantaged, Advantageous, Adventuresome, Adventurous, Advisable, Advocative, Ae, Aeonian, Aesthetic, Aesthetical, Affable, Affectionate, Affective, Affiliated, Affine, Affined, Affirming, Afflated, Afflating, Affluencial, Affluent, Affordable, Agapeistic, Ageless, Agile, Aglitter, Aglow, Agreeable, Airy, Alacritous, Alaudine, Alert, Alfresco, Alimental, Alimentary, Alive, All ears, All heart, All right, All set, All systems go, All there, Allegiant, Allied, All-important, Allowing, Alluring, Altruistic, Alright, Amaranthine, Amazed, Amazing, Ambidextrous, Ambitious, Ambrosial, Ambrosian, Ameliorative, Amelioratory, Amenable, Amiable, Amicable, Ample, Amoroso, Amused, Amusing, Anamnestic, Angelic, Animastic, Animated, Anodyne, Anointed, Anthophilous, Aperitive, Aplenty, Apodictic, Apollonian, Apparent, Appealing, Appeasing, Appetent, Appetizing, Applauded, Apposite, Appreciated, Appreciative,

Apprehensible, Approachable, Approbative, Appropriate, Approving, Apropos, Apt, Arcadian, Archangelic, Ardent, Argus-eyed, Aristocratic, Aromatic, Aroused, Arousing, Arresting, Artful, Articulate, Artisanal, Artistic, Ascendant, Ascending, As it ought to be, As it should be, Aspirant, Aspiring, Assertive, Assiduous, Assistive, Associated, Associative, Assured, Assurgent, Assuring, Astonishing, Astounding, Astral, Astute, At ease, At hand, At leisure, Athletic, At one's disposal, Attainable, At the ready, Attentive, Attractive, Atypical, Au fait, August, Auriferous, Auroral, Auspicious, Authentic, Authenticated, Authoritative, Authorized, Autodidactic, Autonomous, Available, Avant-garde, Avid, Awaited, Awake, Awakening, Aware, Awesome, Axiological, Axiomatic

Assertions, as advanced abstractions, alter actions. Actions ascertain an aggressive anima, or alternatively, admirable attributes. Actions also animate and alter authentic affections. The active articles among abstraction and action are assertions. Acceptable assertions are abiding, accomplished, admirable, altruistic and absolutely appealing.

Baconian, Balanced, Ball of fire, Balmy, Baronial, Beaming, Beamish, Beatific, Beauteous, Beautified, Beautiful, Becoming, Bedazzling, Beefy, the Bee's knees, Befriended, Believable, Beloved, Benedictive, Benedictory, Benefic, Beneficent, Beneficial, Beneficiary, Benevolent, Benign, Benignant, Besotted, Best, Best-loved, Better, Better-than-before, Bewitching, Beyond compare, Big, Biggest, Big league, Big-hearted, Big-time, Bijou, Biophilic, Blameless, Blazing, Blessed, Blissful, Blithe, Blithesome, Blockbuster, Blooming, Blossoming, Blue-ribbon, Bodacious, Boffo, Boisterous, Bold, Bonafide, Bonny, Bonza/Bonzer, Boolean, Boss, Bounteous, Bountiful, Brainy, Brave, Brawny, Breathtaking, Breezy, Breviloquent, Brief, Bright, Brill, Brilliant, Brimming, Brisk, Broadminded, Brobdingnagian, Brotherly, Bubbly, Buccal, Bucolic, Budding, Buff, Bulletproof, Bullish, Buoyant, Burgeoning, Business-like, Bustling, Busy, By the numbers

Calm, Calmative, Calming, Candescent, Can do, Canny, Canorous, Cantier, Cantiest, Canty, Capable, Capital, Captivating, Cared for, Carefree, Careful, Caretaking, Caring, Casual, Categorical, Causal, Causative, Celebrated, Celebratory, Celeritous, Celestial, Centered, Central, Cerebral, Certain, Champion, Changeable, Changeless, Chaplinesque, Charismatic, Charitable, Charmed, Charming, Cheerful, Cheery, Cherishable, Cherished, Cherry, Chic, Chief, Childlike, Chipper, Chirpiest, Chirpy, Chivalrous, Chocolatey, Choice, Choicest, Chosen, Chummy, Civic, Civil, Civilized, Clairvoyant, Classic, Classical, Classy, Clean, Cleansing, Clear, Clearcut, Clear-eyed, Clearheaded, Clear-sighted, Clement, Clever, Climactic, Clinquant, Close, Coadjutant, Cock-a-hoop, Coequal, Cogent, Cogitabund, Cognizant, Coherent, Cohortative, Collaborative, Collected, Collegial, Collegiate, Colossal, Colourful, Coltish, Columbine, Come-at-able, Comely, Comfortable, Comforting, Comic, Comical, Commanding, Commendable, Commendatory, Commiserative, Committed, Commodious, Commonsensical, Communal, Communicative, Commutual, Companionable, Compassionate, Compatible, Compelling, Compendious, Competent, Complaisant, Complete, Completed, Complimentary, Composed, Comprehensive, Concentrated, Conceptual, Conciliatory, Concise, Conclusive, Concordant, Concrete, Condolatory, Conducive, Confelicitous, Conferrable, Confident, Confirmed, Congenial, Congruent, Congruous, Conjugate, Connected, Conquering, Conscientious, Conscious, Consecrated, Consensual, Consentaneous, Consentient, Consequential, Considerable, Considerate, Consistent, Consolidated, Consonant, Constitutional, Constitutive, Constructive, Consubstantial, Contemplative, Contemporary, Content, Contiguous, Continuous, Contributive, Convenient, Conversant, Convictive, Convincing, Convivial, Cooking with gas, Cool, Cooperative, Coordinated, Copacetic, Copious, Cordial, Corking, Correct, Correlative, Coruscant, Cosmic, Cosmopolitan, Cosy, Courageous, Courteous, Courtly, Couthie, Cozy, Crack, Crackerjack, Cranked, Cream of the crop, Creamy, Creative, Credential, Credible, Creditable, Credited, Crepuscular, Crisp, Crowd-pleasing, Crucial, Crystal (clear), Cuddly, Culminating, Cultivated, Cultured, Curative, Curious, Current, Curvaceous, Curvy, Cushy, Cute, Cutting-edge

Daedal, Dainty, Dandy, Dapatical, Dapper, Daring, Darling, Dashing, Dauntless, Dazzled, Dazzling, Dear, Dearest, Debonair, Decent, Deciding, Decisive, Decorous, Dedicated, Deductive, Deep, Defiant, Definite, Definitive, Deft, Delectable, Deliberate, Delicate, Delicious, Delighted, Delightful, Delish, Deluxe, Democratic, Demonstrative, Demulcent, Dependable, Deserving, Designer, Desirable, Desired, Desirous, Destined, Determinant, Determined, Developed, Developing, Devoted, Devotional, Devout, Dexterous, Dialectical, Didactic, Didascalic, Diehard, Different, Dignified, Diligent, Dinkum, Diplomatic, Direct, Disarming, Discerning, Disciplined, Discreet, Discriminating, Dispassionate, Distinct, Distinctive, Distinguished, Diverse, Diverting, Divine, Doable, Dominant, Doted on, Doting, Doubtless, Doughty, Dovelike, Down-to-earth, Doxological, Dreamy, Driven, Driving, Droll, Ducky, Dulcet, Durable, Dutiful, Dynamic, Dynamite

Eager, Earnest, Earthy, Easy, Easygoing, Easy-peasy, Easy to approach, Easy to reach, Easy to talk to, Easy to understand, Ebullient, Ecclesiastical, Echt, Eclectic, Economic, Economical, Ecstatic, Ecumenical, Edified, Edifying, Educated, Educational, Effective, Effectual, Effervescent, Efficacious, Efficient, Efflorescent, Effortless, Effulgent, Elated, Elating, Electric, Electrifying, Eleemosynary, Elegant, Elemental, Elevated, Elevating, Eleutherian, Eligible, Eloquent, Emergent, Eminent, Empathetic, Empathic, Employable, Empowered, Empowering, Empyreal, Empyrean, Emulated, Enabled, Enamoured, Enamouring, Enchanted, Enchanting, Encouraged, Encouraging, Endeared, Endearing, Endless, Endorsed, Endorsing, Endowed, Enduring, Energetic, Energizing, Engaged, Engaging, Engrossed, Engrossing, Enhanced, Enjoyable, Enjoyed, Enlightened, Enlightening, Enlivened, Enlivening, Ennobled, Ennobling, Enophilic, Enormous, Enough, Enrapturing, En règle, Enriched, Enriching, Ensuring, Enterprising, Entertaining, Enthralled, Enthralling, Enthusiastic, Enticed, Enticing, Entranced, Entrancing, Entrepreneurial, Entrusted, Epic, Epicurean, Epideictic, Epididactic, Epigrammatic, Epinician, Equable, Equal, Equalized, Equanimous, Equiparent, Equipollent, Equiponderant,

Equiponderate, Equipped, Equitable, Erogenous, Erotic, Erudite, Especial, Essential, Established, Esteemed, Esthetic, Esthetical, Eternal, Ethereal, Ethical, Eudaimonistic, Eudaimonistical, Eupeptic, Euphonic, Euphonious, Euphoric, Eurythmic, Even-handed, Eventful, Evident, Eviternal, Evocative, Evolved, Evolving, Exact, Exalted, Exalting, Exceeding, Excellent, Excelling, Excelsior, Exceptional, Excited, Exciting, Exclusive, Executive, Exemplary, Exhaustive, Exhilarated, Exhilarating, Exhortative, Exhortatory, Expansive, Expectant, Expedient, Expeditious, Expeditive, Expergefacient, Expensive, Experienced, Expert, Explorative, Expressive, Exquisite, Exotic, Extra, Extra-, Extraordinaire, Extraordinary, Exuberant, Exultant, Exulting, Eyesome, Eye-catching

Fab, Fabulous, Facilitative, Factual, Facund, Facundious, Fain, Fair, Faithful, Famed, Familial, Familiar, Family, Famous, Fancy, Fancy-free, Fanciful, Fantabulous, Fantastic, Far-out, Far-reaching, Far-sighted, Fascinated, Fascinating, Fashionable, Fast, Fatherly, Faultless, Favourable, Favoured, Favourite, Fearless, Feasible, Featous, Fecund, Feelgood, Felicitous, Feminine, Fertile, Feracious, Fervent, Festal, Festive, Fetching, Fidelitous, Fiery, Filial, Filled, Filling, Filigreed, Fine, Finer, Finest, Firm, First, First-class, First-order, First-rate, Fit, Fitting, Five-star, Flamboyant, Flashy, Flavoured, Flavourful, Flavoursome, Flawless, Fleek, Fleet, Flexible, Flourishing, Flowing, Fluent, Fly (chiefly British), Flying, Focused, Fond, Foolproof, Forbearant, Forbearing, Forceful, Foremost, Foresighted, Forgivable, Forgiving, Formidable, For real, Forthcoming, Forthright, Fortified, Fortifying, Fortuitous, Fortunate, Forward-thinking, Foundational, Foundationary, Four-star, Foxy, Frabjous, Fragrant, Frank, Fraternal, Free, Freethinking, Fresh, Friendly, Frisky, Frolicsome, Front-page, Fruitful, Fulgent, Full, Fun, Fundamental, Funny, Futuristic

Gainful, Gallant, Galore, Galvanized, Galvanizing, Game, Gamesome, Gargantuan, Gastronomic, Gay, Gelastic, Gelogenic, Generative, Generous, Genial, Genteel, Gentle, Gentlemanly, Genuine, Germane, Get-at-able, Gettable, Gifted, Giggly, Giving, Glabrous, Glad, Glamorous, Gleaming, Gleeful, Glistening, Glorified, Glorious, Glowing, Gnarly, Gnomic, Goal-oriented,

Godlike, Godly, Golden, Good, Goodhearted, Good-feeling, Good-humoured, Good-looking, Goodly, Good-natured, Gorgeous, Graced, Graceful, Gracile, Gracious, Gradely, Graith, Graithly, Grand, Grateful, Gratified, Gratifying, Gratis, Great, Greatest, Great-hearted, Gregarious, Groovy, Grounded, Growing, Grown, Gruntled, Guaranteed, Gubernatorial, Guided, Guiding, Guileless, Guilt-free, Guiltless, Gumptious, Gustatory, Gung ho, Gutsy, Gymnastic

Halcyon, Hale, Haloed, Hallowed, Handsome, Handy, Happening, Happy, Happy-go-lucky, Hard-working, Hardy, Harmless, Harmonic, Harmonious, Harmonizable, Haunting, Head, Healing, Healthful, Healthy, Heartfelt, Heart-to-heart, Heartsome, Heart-stopping, Heartwarming, Hearty, Heavenly, Heavyweight, Heedful, Henotic, Helped, Helpful, Helping, Hep, Heralded, Heroic, Heuristic, High calibre, High-class, High-demand, High-minded, High-power, High-powered, High-principled, High-priority, High-quality, High-reaching, High-spirited, Highest, Highly regarded, Highly seasoned, Highly valued, Hilarious, Hip, Holy, Honest, Honeyed, Honorary, Honourable, Honoured, Hopeful, Hortative, Hortatory, Hospitable, Hot, Hot off the fire, Hot off the press, Hotshot, Huge, Huggy, Huggable, Human, Humane, Humanistic, Humanitarian, Humble, Humorous, Hunky, Hunky-dory, Hygeian, Hygienic, Hypersonic, Hypnotic

Ideal, Idealistic, Idiosyncratic, Idolized, Idoneous, Illecebrous, Illimitable, Illuminable, Illuminated, Illuminating, Illustrious, Imaginative, Imitable, Immaculate, Immarcescible, Immeasurable, Immediate, Immense, Immortal, Immune, Impartial, Impassioned, Impavid, Impeccable, Impeccant, Imperturbable, Impetrative, Impetratory, Impish, Important, Impressive, Improved, Improvisational, In, In 7th heaven, Inaurate, Incandescent, Incisive, Included, Inclusive, Incomparable, Incomplex, Incontestable, Incontrovertible, Incorrupt, Incorruptible, Incredible, Inculpable, Indefatigable, In demand, Independent, Indestructible, Indispensable, Indisputable, Individual, Individualistic, Indivisible, Indomitable, Indubitable, Industrious, Inebriating, Ineffable, Inerrant, Inexhaustible, Infallible, Infatuated, Infatuating, In favour, In fine fettle (good spirits),

Infinite, Influential, Informative, Informed, Ingenious, In good health, Inimitable, Initiative, Innate, Innocent, Innocuous, Innovative, In love, In one's grasp, In one's power, In order, Innoxious, Inquisitive, In readiness, In seventh Heaven, Insightful, Insouciant, Inspirational, Inspired, Inspiring, Inspirited, Inspiriting, Instantaneous, Instinctive, Instructive, Instrumental, Integral, Integrated, Integrative, Intellectual, Intelligent, Intemerate, Intense, Intent, Interactive, Interconnected, Interconnective, Interested, Interesting, Internal, International, Intertwined, In the bag, In the groove, In the mainstream, In the moment, In the now, In the pink, In the saddle, In the swim, Intimate, Intoxicating, Intrepid, Intrigued, Intriguing, Intrinsic, Introspective, Inventive, Invigorated, Invigorating, Invincible, Inviolable, Inviting, In vogue, Irenic, Iridescent, Iridine, Irrefragable, Irrefutable, Irreplaceable, Irrepressible, Irreproachable, Irresistible, Irrevincible, Isonomic, Isonomous

Jam-packed, Jaunty, Jazzed, Jazzy, Jestful, Jeweled, Jiggish, Jim-dandy, Jimp (Scot. and N. English), Jocose, Jocoserious, Jocular, Joculatory, Jocund, Joint, Jointed, Jolif, Jolly, Jovial, Joyful, Joyous, Joysome, Jubilant, Judicious, Juicy, Junoesque, Just, Justified, Just right, Juvenescent

Keen, Kempt, Key, Kind, Kind-hearted, Kindly, Kindred, Kinetic, Kingly, Kissable, Knightly, Knowable, Knowing, Knowledgeable, Known, Kooky, Kosher

Ladylike, Laid-back, Lambent, Large, Largifical, Lasting, Latitudinarian, Laudable, Laudatory, Laureate, Lautitious, Lavish, Law-abiding, Lawful, Leading, Leading-edge, Learned, Legal, Legendary, Legible, Legit, Legitimate, Leisured, Leisurely, Lenient, Leonine, Lepid, Lettered, Level-headed, Liberal, Liberated, Liberating, Libertarian, Liefly, Light, Light-hearted, Likable, Liked, Likely, Like-minded, Limber, Limpid, Lionhearted, Lionized, Lissome, Literary, Literate, Lithe, Lithesome, Littoral, Live, Lively, Living, Logical, Longanimous, Long-established, Long-lived, Long-standing, Lordly, Lousy with love, Lovable, Loved, Lovely, Loving, Loyal, Lucent, Lucid, Luciferous, Lucky,

Lucrative, Lucriferous, Luculent, Ludibund, Ludic, Luminous, Luscious, Lush, Lusory, Lustrous, Lusty, Luxuriant, Luxurious, Lyric, Lyrical

Mabsoot, Macrobian, Made (...of money, have it...), Magical, Magistral, Magnanimous, Magnetic, Magnificent, Maiden, Main, Mainstream, Majestic, Major, Major league, Malleable, Manageable, Managerial, Manifest, Manly, Mannerly, Many, Margaric, Margaritiferous, Marketable, Marmoreal, Marmorean, Marvelous, Masculine, Massagable, Massive, Master, Masterful, Masterly, Matchless, Maternal, Matter-of-fact, Mature, Maxed, Maximal, Maximum, Meaningful, Measured, Mediagenic, Meditative, Meek, Meet, Melioristic, Mellifluent, Mellifluous, Melliloquent, Mellisonant, Mellow, Melodious, Memorable, Merciful, Meritable, Meritorious, Merry, Mesmerizing, Metaphysical, Meteoric, Methodical, Methodological, Meticulous, Mettlesome, Mickle, Mighty, Mind-blowing, Mindful, Minikin, Ministerial, Mint, Miraculous, Mirific, Mirthful, Mischievous, Mitigative, Mitigatory, Model, Modern, Modernist, Modern-istic, Modest, Momentous, Moneyed, Monumental, Moon-struck, Moral, More, Most, Most excellent, Motherly, Motivated, Motivational, Mouthwatering, Moved, Moving, Mucho, Muliebral, Muliebrile, Muliebrous, Multicultural, Multidimensional, Multidisciplined, Multifaceted, Multifarious, Multilingual, Munificent, Muscular, Musical, Mutual, Mycophilic

Nailed down, Naissant, Nanophilic, Nascent, Natalitial, National, Nationwide, Native, Natty, Natural, Near to one's heart, Nearby, Neat, Necessary, Needed, Negentropic, Neighbourly, Neoteric, Neutral, Never-failing, New, Newborn, New-fashioned, Next, Nice, Nifty, Nimble, Nimble-witted, Nitid, Nobiliary, Nobilitate, Noble, Nobody's fool, Noctiflorous, No dummy, No end, No end of, Noetic, Nonchalant, Nonpareil, Normal, Normative, No strings attached, Notable, Not born yesterday, Noteworthy, Not tied down, Not unlikely, Nourished, Nourishing, Novel, Now, Nubigenous, Nubile, Number 1, Number one, Numero uno, Nurtured, Nurturing, Nutrimental, Nutritional, Nutritious

Objective, Obliging, Observant, Obtainable, Oecumenical, Oeno-philic, OK, Okay, Okayed, Olympian, Omnifarious, Omnipotent, Omnipresent, On, On Cloud Nine, On hand, On one's toes, On target, On the ball, On the beam, On the button, On the job, On the money, On the move, On the nose, On the outlook, On the qui vive, One, One and only, Oneiric, Open, Open-handed, Open-hearted, Open-minded, Opinable, Opportune, Optimal, Optimistic, Optimum, Opulent, Orbific, Orderly, Organic, Organized, Oriented, Original, Ornamental, Orphean, Oscular, Outdoorsy, Outgoing, Out-of-sight, Out-of-this-world, Outspoken, Outstanding, Over-flowing, Overjoyed, Overjoying, Overriding, Overruling, Overt

Pabulous, Pacific, Paciferous, Pacifistic, Painstaking, Palatable, Pally, Palmarian, Palmary, Panglossian, Pansophical, Pansophistical, Paradisaic, Paradisaical, Paradisal, Paradisiac, Paramount, Pardon-able, Parental, Par excellence, Parnassian, Parthenian, Participative, Participatory, Particular, Passionate, Paternal, Patient, Peaceable, Peaceful, Peachy, Peachy keen, Peak, Pecuniary, Peerless, Pellucid, Penetrating, Peppy, Perceptive, Perceptual, Percipient, Perdurable, Peregal, Perennial, Perfect, Perfectible, Perfective, Perky, Perma-nent, Permissive, Perpetual, Perseverant, Persevering, Persistent, Personable, Perspicacious, Perspicuous, Persuasive, Pert, Pertinent, Pet, Petite, Pharaonic, Phenomenal, Philanthropic, Philodemic, Philoprogenitive, Philosophical, Philoxenial, Phlegmatic, Picked, Picturesque,   Piece of cake,   Pierian,   Pioneering,   Pious, Piquant, Pithy, Pivotal, Placid, Planetary, Plausible, Playful, Pleasant, Pleased, Pleasing, Pleasurable, Plenary, Plenteous, Plen-tiful, Pliable, Plucky, Plum, Plummy, Pluperfect, Poetic, Poignant, Poised, Polished, Polite, Pollent, Popular, Posh, Positive, Possible, Potable, Potent, Potential, Powerful, Practicable, Practical, Prac-ticed, Pragmatic, Praised, Praiseworthy, Prayerful, Precious, Precise, Precocious, Predominant, Preeminent, Preemptory, Preferable, Preferred, Prefulgent, Premier, Premium, Prepared, Preponderant, Prepossessing, Prepotent, Prescient, Present, Presentable, Presidential, Prestigious, Pretty, Prevalent, Prevailing, Prevenient, Prevoyant, Priceless, Primal, Primary, Prime, Primed, Primo, Princely, Principal, Principled, Priority, Pristine, Privileged,

Prized, Prize-winning, Pro, Proactive, Probable, Probative, Procinct, Procurable, Prodigious, Productive, Professional, Proficient, Profitable, Profound, Profulgent, Profuse, Progressive, Proleptic/Proleptical, Prolific, Prominent, Promising, Promoted, Prompt, Proper, Propertied, Propitiable, Propitiative, Propitious, Prophetic, Prospective, Prospering, Prosperous, Protean, Protected, Protective, Proto-, Providential, Provocative, Proud, Proven, Prudent, Psyched up, Psychic, Public-spirited, Puissant, Pulchritudinous, Pukka, Pumped, Pumped up, Punchy, Punctual, Pure, Purified, Purifying, Purposeful, Purposive

Quaint, Quantifiable, Qualified, Qualitative, Quality, Queenly, Quemeful, Quick, Quickened, Quick on the draw, Quick on the uptake, Quick-witted, Quiet, Quietsome, Quintessential, Quixotic, Quotable

Racy, Rad, Radiant, Rapid, Rapt, Rapturous, Rare, Rascally, Rathe, Ratiocinative, Rational, Ravishing, Razor-sharp, Reachable, Readied, Ready, Real, Realistic, Realizable, Reasonable, Reassuring, Recherche', Recognizable, Receiving, Receptive, Recipient, Reciprocal, Recognized, Recommendable, Recommended, Recuperative, Red-carpet, Redolent, Refined, Refreshed, Refreshing, Refulgent, Regal, Regnant, Regular, Rejoicing, Rejuvenating, Rejuvenescent, Related, Relative, Relaxed, Relaxing, Relevant, Reliable, Relieved, Remarkable, Remissive, Renascent, Renewable, Renewing, Renewed, Renowned, Replete, Reputable, Resilient, Resolute, Resolved, Resounding, Resourceful, Respectable, Respected, Respectful, Resplendent, Responsible, Responsive, Rested, Restful, Restorative, Retentive, Revealing, Revelational, Revered, Reverent, Revitalized, Revitalizing, Revived, Reviviscent, Revivifying, Rewardable, Rewarded, Rewarding, Rhapsodic, Riant, Rich, Rident, Ridibund, Right, Righteous, Rightful, Right neighbourly, Risible, Risorial, Robust, Rock solid, Rollicking, Romantic, Rosy, Roused, Rousing, Ruling, Rutilant

Sacred, Sacrosanct, Safe, Sagacious, Sage, Saintly, Salubrious, Salutary, Salutatory, Salutiferous, Salvific, Sanative, Sanatory, Sanctified, Sanctiloquent, Sanctioned, Sanguine, Sanitary, Sapid, Sapiential, Sapient, Saporific, Saporous, Sartorial, Sassy, Satisfactory, Satisfied, Satisfying, Sative, Saucy, Saved, Savoury, Savvy, Scented, Scholarly, Scientific, Scintillant, Scintillated, Scintillating, Scintillescent, Scrumptious, Scrupulous, Seamless, Seasoned, Second-to-none, Secure, Secured, Sedulous, Seemly, Select, Self-accepting, Self-assertive, Self-assured, Self-confident, Self-disciplined, Self-expressive, Self-governing, Selfless, Self-made, Self-sacrificing, Self-starting, Self-sufficient, Self-taught, Sempiternal, Sensate, Sensational, Sensible, Sensitive, Sentimental, Seraphic, Serendipitous, Serene, Service-minded, Service-oriented, Sesquipedalian, Set, Settled, Settling, Shapely, Sharing, Sharp, Sharp-eyed, Sharp-witted, Shining, Shiny-eyed, Shipshape, Showy, Shrewd, Sightly, Significant, Simple, Sincere, Sinewy, Singular, Sisterly, Sizable, Skilled, Skillful, Skookum, Slamin', Sleek, Slick, Smart, Smashing, Smiley, Smiling, Smitten, Smooth, Snazzy, Snappy, Snod (Scot. and N. England), Snug, Snugly, Soaring, Sociable, Social, Societal, Soft-hearted, Soigne, Solacious, Solar, Sole, Solid, Solid gold, Solomon-like, Something else, Sonorous, Sonsy, Sooth, Soothed, Soothfast, Soothing, Sophic, Sophisticated, Sought, Sought-after, Soulful, Sound, Souped up, Sovereign, Spacious, Spanking, Sparkling, Sparkly, Special, Spectacular, Speedy, Spellbinding, Spicy, Spiffy, Spirited, Spiritual, Splendent, Splendid, Splendiferous, Splendorous, Spontaneous, Sponsal, Sporting, Sportive, Sportsmanlike, Sporty, Spotless, Spot on, Sprauncy, Sprightly, Spruce, Spruced up, Sprucest, Spry, Spunky, Square, Stable, Staid, Stainless, Stalwart, Stand-up, Star, Stately, State-of-the-art, Statuesque, Staunch, Steadfast, Steady, Stellar, Sterling, Sthenic, Stick-to-itive, Still, Stimulated, Stimulating, Stimulative, Stimulatory, Stipendiary, Stirred, Stirring, Stoic, Stonking, Storied, Stouthearted, Straightforward, Straight out, Strapping, Strategic, Street smart, Streetwise, Striking, Strong, Strong-willed, Studious, Stunning, Stupendous, Sturdy, Stylish, Suasive, Suave, Suaveloquent, Suaveolens/Suaveolent, Sublime, Substant, Substantial, Substantive, Subtle, Successful, Succinct, Succulent, Sufficient, Sui generis, Suitable, Suited, Summary, Summery, Sumptuous,

Sunny, Super, Superabundant, Super-angelic, Superb, Superconscious, Super-duper, Supercalifragilisticexpialidocious, Super-civilized, Super-eminent, Super-ethical, Super-excellent, Superior, Superlative, Supernal, Super-popular, Supersensible, Supersonic, Supple, Supported, Supporting, Supportive, Supraliminal, Supreme, Sure, Sure-fire, Sure-footed, Sure-handed, Surpassing, Surprised, Surprising, Sustainable, Sustained, Sustaining, Sustentative, Svelte, Swank, Swaying, Sweeping, Sweet, Sweet-smelling, Swell, Swift, Sybaritic, Sylvan, Symbiotic, Symmetrical, Sympathetic, Synergistic, Systematic

Tachytelic, Tactful, Tailor-made, Take-charge, Talented, Tall, Tangible, Tantalizing, Tasteful, Tasty, Taught, Teachable, Telegenic, Teleorganic, Tempean, Temperate, Tempestive, Tenable, Tenacious, Tender, Tender-hearted, Terrific, Thankful, Thankworthy, Thaumatological, Theanthropic, Theophilanthropic, Theopneustic, Therapeutic, There, Thorough, Thoroughgoing, Thoughtful, Thrilled, Thrilling, Thriving, Tickety-Boo, Tickled, Tidy, Tight, Tight with, Time-honoured, Timeless, Timely, Timeous, Time-saving, Tip-top, Tireless, Titanic, Titillating, Titivated, Today, Together, Tolerant, Tonic, Tony, Toothsome, Topical, Top, Top drawer, Topnotch, Tops, Totally-tubular, To the max, Touched, Touching, Tough, Touted, Traditive, Trailblazing, Tranquil, Transcendent, Transcendental, Transformable, Transformative, Transparent, Transpicuous, Transporting, Traveled, Treasurable, Treasured, Tremendous, Tretis, Trim, Triumphant, True, True-blue, Trusted, Trustful, Trusting, Trustworthy, Trusty, Truthful, Tuneful, Tutelary, Twenty-first century, Twenty-four carat, Twitterpated, Tympanic

Uber, Ubiquitous, Ultimate, Ultra-precise, Unabashed, Unadulterated, Unaffected, Unafraid, Unalloyed, Unambiguous, Unanimous, Unarguable, Unassuming, Unattached, Unbeatable, Unbeaten, Unbiased, Unbigoted, Unblemished, Unbroken, Uncensurable, Uncommon, Uncomplicated, Uncompromising, Unconditional, Unconditionally loving, Uncontestable, Unconventional, Uncorrupted, Undamaged, Undauntable, Undaunted, Undefeated, Undefiled, Undeniable, Under control, Understandable, Understanding, Understood, Undesigning, Undiminished,

Undisputed, Undivided, Undoubted, Unencumbered, Unequalled, Unequivocable, Unequivocal, Unerring, Unfailing, Unfaltering, Unfaultable, Unfeigned, Unfettered, Unflagging, Unflappable, Unforgettable, Ungrudging, Unhampered, Unharmed, Unhesitating, Unhurt, Unified, Unimpaired, Unimpeachable, Unimpeded, Unique, Unisonal, Unisonant, Unisonous, United, Universal, Univocal, Unlimited, Unmistakable, Unmitigated, Unobjectionable, Unobstructed, Unobtrusive, Unopposed, Unparalleled, Unprejudiced, Unpretentious, Unquestionable, Unrefuted, Unreserved, Unrivalled, Unruffled, Unselfish, Unshakable, Unshaken, Unspoiled, Unspoilt, Unstoppable, Unsullied, Unsurpassed, Untarnished, Untiring, Untouched, Untroubled, Unusual, Unwavering, Unwithdrawing, Up, Up-and-coming, Upbeat, Upbuilding, Upcoming, Updated, Up front, Uplifted, Uplifting, Uppermost, Upright, Upstanding, Up to code, Up-to-date, Up to par, Up to snuff, Up to speed, Up-to-the-minute, Uptown, Upward, Upwardly, Urbane, Usable, Useful, User-friendly, Utile, Utile dulci, Utilitarian, Utilizable, Utmost, Utopian, Utopic, Uxorial

Valiant, Valid, Validating, Validatory, Valorous, Valuable, Valued, Vast, Vatic, Vaticinal, Vegetarian, Vegete, Vehement, Velocious, Venerable, Venerated, Venial, Ventorious, Venturesome, Venust, Veracious, Verdant, Verdurous, Verecund, Veridical, Veridicous, Verifiable, Verified, Veriloquent, Veritable, Vernal, Versatile, Versed, Vespertine, Veteran, Viable, Vibrant, Vibratile, Victorious, Vigilant, Vigorous, Viparious, Virile, Virtuous, Visionary, Vital, Vitalizing, Vitative, Vivacious, Vivid, Vivifying, Vocal, Vogue, Volable, Volant, Volcanic, Volitional, Voluptuary, Voluptuous, Vulnerary

Waggish, Wanted, Warm, Warm-hearted, Warranted, Wealthy, Weighty, Welcome, Welcomed, Welcoming, Weleful, Welfaring, Well, Well-arranged, Well-behaved, Well-built, Well-disposed, Well-done, Well-established, Well-founded, Well-grounded, Well-informed, Well-intentioned, Well-known, Well-liked, Well-made, Well-meaning, Well-planned, Well-proportioned, Well-read, Well-received, Well-spoken, Well-suited, Well-timed, Welsome, Whimsical, Whiz-bang, Whole, Wholehearted,

Wholesome, Wide-awake, Widely used, Wight, Willing, Winnable, Winged, Winning, Winsome, Wired, Wise, Within reach, With it, Without equal, Without error, Without limit, Witty, Wizardly, Wonderful, Wonderstruck, Wonder-working, Wondrous, Workable, Working, World class, Worldly, Worldly-wise, Worshipful, Worshipped, Worthwhile, Worthy

Xenial, Xenodocial

Yare, Yern, Young-at-Heart, Youthful, Yummy

Zany, Zappy, Zazzy, Zealed, Zealous, Zero cool, Zestful, Zesty, Zippy, Zoetic

If someone is smart, strong, or kind they remain so no matter what else happens, even on their worst day. Once the foregoing words have been highlighted, underlined or circled then they can be used as a pick-me-up whenever needed. Positive adjectives also have significant potential to beneficially affect all parties involved in an exchange.

Positive Adjective Graphic Definitions

Following are five positive adjective subsets; Masculine, Feminine, Romantic and Business.

POSITIVE MASCULINE ADJECTIVES

Positive Words to Describe your Father, Son, Husband, Lover, or Boyfriend

"And by keeping a record of self - not as a diary, but thy purposes, what you have thought, what you have desired, the good that you have done - we will find this will bring physical and mental reactions that will be in keeping with the purposes for which soul enters a material manifestation." (Edgar Cayce Reading 830-3)

"He is..."

A-1, A-OK, A-one, Abiding, Able, Able-bodied, Aboveboard, Abundant, Accelerated, Accepting, Accessible, Accommodating, Accommodative, Accomplished, Accordant, Accountable, Accurate, Ace, Aces, Active, Actual, Acuminous, Adaptable, Adapted, Adaptive, Adept, Admirable, Admired, Adonic, Adorable, Adoring, Adroit, Advanced, Advantaged, Advantageous, Adventuresome, Adventurous, Advocative, Affable, Affectionate, Affective, Affiliated, Affined, Affirming, Afflated, Affluent, Agile, Agreeable, Alacritous, Alert, All heart, All right, All set, All systems go, All there, Allegiant, Allied, Allowing, Alluring, Alright, Altruistic, Amazing, Ambitious, Amenable, Amiable, Amicable, Amoroso, Ample, Amusing, Apollonian, Appealing, Apposite, Appreciated, Appreciative, Approachable, Appropriate, Approving, Apropos, Apt, Ardent, Argus-eyed, Aristocratic, Arresting, Artful, Articulate, Artisanal, Ascendant, Assertive, Assiduous, Assistive, Associated, Associative, Assured, Assuring, Astute, At ease, At hand, At leisure, Athletic, At one's disposal, At the ready, Attentive, Attractive, Atypical, Au fait, August, Auspicious, Authentic, Authoritative, Autodidactic, Autonomous, Available, Avid, Awaited, Aware, Awesome, Axiological

Balanced, Baronial, Becoming, Beefy, Believable, Beloved, Benefic, Beneficent, Beneficial, Benevolent, Benignant, Better, Better-than-before, Best, Best-loved, Beyond compare, Big, Big league, Biggest, Big-hearted, Big-time, Blameless, Blessed, Bold, Bonafide, Boss, Bounteous, Bountiful, Brainy, Brave, Brawny, Brief, Bright, Brilliant, Brisk, Broadminded, Brotherly, Bullish, Buoyant, Business-like, Busy, By the numbers

Calm, Calming, Calmative, Can do, Canny, Capable, Capital, Captivating, Cared for, Carefree, Careful, Caring, Caretaking, Casual, Categorical, Causal, Causative, Centered, Central, Cerebral, Certain, Champion, Changeable, Changeless, Charismatic, Charitable, Charmed, Charming, Cheerful, Cherishable, Cherished, Cherry, Chief, Chipper, Chivalrous, Choice, Choicest, Chummy, Civic, Civil, Civilized, Classic, Classical, Classy, Clean, Clear, Clear-cut, Clear-eyed, Clearheaded, Clear-sighted, Clement, Clever, Climactic, Close, Cogent, Cognizant, Coherent, Cohortative, Collaborative, Collected, Collegial, Colourful, Come-at-able, Comfortable, Comforting, Comical, Commanding, Commendable, Commendatory, Commiserative, Committed, Commodious, Commonsensical, Communicative, Commutual, Companionable, Compassionate, Compatible, Compelling, Competent, Complete, Completed, Complimentary, Composed, Comprehensive, Concentrated, Conciliatory, Concise, Conclusive, Concordant, Concrete, Condolatory, Conferrable, Confident, Confirmed, Congenial, Connected, Conquering, Conscientious, Conscious, Consensual, Consentaneous, Consentient, Consequential, Considerable, Considerate, Consistent, Consonant, Constructive, Contemplative, Contemporary, Content, Contributive, Convenient, Conversant, Convictive, Convincing, Convivial, Cooking with fire/gas, Cool, Cooperative, Coordinated, Copacetic, Cordial, Correct, Correlative, Courageous, Courteous, Courtly, Couthie, Cozy, Crack, Crackerjack, Creative, Credential, Credible, Creditable, Credited, Crowd-pleasing, Crucial, Crystal (clear), Cuddly, Cultivated, Cultured, Cunning, Curative, Curious, Current, Cute

Daedal, Dapper, Daring, Dashing, Dauntless, Dazzling, Dear, Dearest, Debonair, Decent, Decisive, Decorous, Dedicated, Deductive, Deep, Definite, Definitive, Deft, Delectable, Deliberate, Deluxe, Democratic, Demonstrative, Dependable, Desired,

Desirable, Destined, Determinant, Determined, Developed, Devoted, Devout, Dexterous, Dialectical, Didactic, Didascalic, Diehard, Different, Dignified, Diligent, Diplomatic, Direct, Disarming, Discerning, Disciplined, Discreet, Discriminating, Distinct, Distinctive, Distinguished, Diverse, Diverting, Dominant, Doted on, Doting, Doubtless, Doughty, Down-to-earth, Dreamy, Driven, Durable, Dutiful, Dynamic, Dynamite

Eager, Earnest, Earthy, Easy, Easygoing, Easy to approach, Easy to reach, Easy to talk to, Easy to understand, Echt, Economical, Edified, Edifying, Educated, Educational, Effective, Effectual, Efficacious, Efficient, Effortless, Elating, Electric, Electrifying, Eleemosynary, Eleutherian, Elevated, Elevating, Eligible, Eloquent, Emerging, Eminent, Empathetic, Employed, Empowered, Empowering, Enamouring, Enchanting, Encouraging, Endearing, Endorsing, Enduring, Energetic, Energizing, Engaged, Engaging, Enhanced, Enjoyable, Enjoyed, Enlightened, Enlightening, Enlivened, Enlivening, Ennobled, Ennobling, En règle, Enriched, Enriching, Ensured, Enterprising, Entertaining, Enthusiastic, Enthralling, Enticed, Enticing, Entrepreneurial, Entrusted, Epic, Equable, Equanimous, Equiparent, Equiponderant, Equiponderate, Equipped, Equitable, Erudite, Essential, Established, Esteemed, Ethical, Eudaimonistic, Eudaimonistical, Even-handed, Evocative, Evolved, Evolving, Exact, Excellent, Excelling, Exceptional, Exciting, Exclusive, Executive, Exemplary, Exhilarating, Expeditious, Expeditive, Experienced, Expert, Explorative, Expressive, Exhortative, Exhortatory, Exquisite, Extraordinary, Exultant

Facilitative, Factual, Fain, Fair, Faithful, Familial, Fantastic, Far-reaching, Far-sighted, Fascinating, Fatherly, Faultless, Favourable, Favoured, Favourite, Fearless, Feasible, Fecund, Feelgood, Felicitous, Feracious, Fertile, Fervent, Festive, Fetching, Fidelitous, Fiery, Filigreed, Fine, Finer, Finest, Firm, First, First-class, First-order, First-rate, Fit, Fitting, Five-star, Flawless, Flexible, Flourishing, Fluent, Focused, Fond, Forceful, Foremost, Foresighted, Forgivable, Forgiving, Formidable, For real, Forthcoming, Forthright, Fortified, Fortifying, Fortuitous, Fortunate, Forward-thinking,

Foundational, Foundationary, Four-star, Frank, Fraternal, Free, Freethinking, Friendly, Frisky, Front-page, Fruitful, Fulfilled, Fulfilling, Fun, Fundamental, Funny

Gainful, Gallant, Galore, Game, Gamesome, Generative, Generous, Genial, Genteel, Gentle, Gentlemanly, Genuine, Germane, Get-at-able, Gifted, Giving, Glad, Gnarly, Goal-oriented, Godly, Golden, Good, Goodhearted, Good-feeling, Good-humoured, Good-looking, Good-natured, Graceful, Gracious, Grand, Grateful, Gratified, Gratifying, Great, Greatest, Greathearted, Gregarious, Grounded, Growing, Gruntled, Guaranteed, Gubernatorial, Guiding, Guileless, Gumptious, Gung ho, Gutsy, Gymnastic

Hale, Handsome, Handy, Happening, Happy, Hard-working, Hardy, Harmless, Harmonic, Harmonious, Harmonizable, Head, Healthy, Heartfelt, Heartsome, Heart-to-heart, Heartwarming, Hearty, Heavyweight, Helpful, Helping, Henotic, Heroic, High calibre, High-class, High-demand, Highly regarded, Highly seasoned, Highly valued, High-minded, High-power, High-powered, High-quality, High-reaching, High-spirited, Hilarious, Honest, Honourable, Honoured, Hortative, Hortatory, Hospitable, Hot, Huggy, Huggable, Human, Humane, Humanistic, Humanitarian, Humble, Humorous, Hunky, Hygienic, Hypnotic

Ideal, Idealistic, Idiosyncratic, Idoneous, Illimitable, Illuminating, Imaginative, Imitable, Immaculate, Immeasurable, Impartial, Impassioned, Impavid, Impeccable, Impeccant, Imperturbable, Impish, Important, Impressive, Improvisational, Incisive, Inclusive, Incomparable, Incomplex, Incontestable, Incontrovertible, Incorrupt, Incorruptible, Indefatigable, In demand, Independent, Indestructible, Indispensable, Indomitable, Indubitable, Industrious, Inexhaustible, Infallible, Infatuated, Infatuating, In fine fettle (good spirits), Influential, Informative, Informed, Ingenious, In good health, Inimitable, Innate, Innovative, In love, Inquisitive, In readiness, Insightful, Inspirational, Inspired, Inspiring, Inspirited, Instinctive, Instructive, Instrumental, Integral, Integrated, Integrative, Interconnected, Interconnective, Intellectual, Intelligent, Intense, Intent, Interactive,

Interested, Interesting, International, Intertwined, In the moment, In the now, In the pink, In the saddle, In the swim, Intimate, Intrepid, Intrigued, Intriguing, Introspective, Inventive, Invigorated, Invigorating, Invincible, Inviolable, Inviting, Irenic, Irrefutable, Irrefragable, Irreplaceable, Irrepressible, Irreproachable, Irresistible

Jaunty, Jazzy, Jocose, Jocular, Jocund, Jolly, Jovial, Joyful, Joyous, Jubilant, Judicious, Juicy, Just, Justified, Just right, Juvenescent

Keen, Key, Kind, Kind-hearted, Kindly, Kingly, Kissable, Knightly, Knowable, Knowing, Knowledgeable

Laid-back, Lasting, Latitudinarian, Laudable, Lavish, Lawful, Law-abiding, Leading, Leading-edge, Learned, Learning, Legal, Legit, Legitimate, Leisurely, Lenient, Leonine, Lepid, Lettered, Level-headed, Liberal, Liberated, Liberating, Libertarian, Lighthearted, Likable, Liked, Like-minded, Limber, Lionhearted, Lionized, Literate, Lithe, Lithesome, Lively, Logical, Longanimous, Long-lived, Long-standing, Lordly, Lovable, Loved, Loving, Loyal, Lucid, Lucky, Lucrative, Luculent, Luminous, Luscious, Luxurious

Mabsoot, Magistral, Magical, Magnanimous, Magnetic, Magnificent, Main, Majestic, Major, Major league, Making a difference, Manageable, Managerial, Malleable, Manly, Mannerly, Marmoreal, Marmorean, Marvelous, Masculine, Massagable, Masterful, Masterly, Matchless, Matter-of-fact, Mature, Maximal, Maximum, Meaningful, Measured, Meditative, Melioristic, Mellow, Memorable, Merciful, Meritable, Meritorious, Merry, Mesmerizing, Meteoric, Methodical, Methodological, Meticulous, Mettlesome, Mindful, Mirthful, Mischievous, Mitigative, Mitigatory, Model, Modest, Moneyed, Moral, More, Most excellent, Motivated, Motivational, Moving, Mucho, Multidimensional, Multidisciplined, Multifaceted, Munificent, Muscular

Natty, Natural, Near to one's heart, Nearby, Neat, Necessary, Needed, Neighbourly, Never-failing, Nice, Nifty, Nimble, Nimble-witted, Noble, Nobody's fool, No dummy, Noetic, No strings attached, Nonchalant, Nonpareil, Not born yesterday, Not tied down, Not unlikely, Nourished, Nourishing, Now, Nubile, Number 1, Number one, Numero uno, Nurtured, Nurturing, Nutrimental

Objective, Obliging, Observant, Obtainable, Olympian, On hand, On one's toes, On target, On the ball, On the beam, On the button, On the job, On the money, On the move, On the nose, On the outlook, One, Oneiric, Open, Open-handed, Open-hearted, Open-minded, Opportune, Optimal, Optimistic, Optimum, Opulent, Orderly, Organic, Organized, Oriented, Original, Ornamental, Outgoing, Out-of-sight, Out-of-this-world, Outspoken, Outstanding, Overflowing, Overjoyed, Overriding, Overruling, Overt

Pabulous, Pacific, Pacifistic, Pally, Panglossian, Paramount, Pardonable, Parental, Par excellence, Participative, Participatory, Particular, Passionate, Paternal, Patient, Peaceable, Peaceful, Peak, Pecuniary, Peerless, Peppy, Penetrating, Perceptive, Perceptual, Percipient, Perdurable, Perennial, Perfect, Perfective, Perky, Permanent, Permissive, Perpetual, Perseverant, Persistent, Personable, Perspicacious, Perspicuous, Persuasive, Pertinent, Pharaonic, Phenomenal, Philanthropic, Philoprogenitive, Philosophical, Phlegmatic, Picked, Pioneering, Pithy, Pivotal, Placid, Playful, Pleasant, Pleased, Pleasing, Pleasurable, Plenteous, Plentiful, Plummy, Pluperfect, Poignant, Poised, Polished, Polite, Pollent, Popular, Posh, Positive, Possible, Potent, Potential, Powerful, Practicable, Practical, Practiced, Pragmatic, Praiseworthy, Precious, Precise, Predominant, Preeminent, Pre-emptive, Preferred, Premier, Premium, Prepared, Preponderant, Prepotent, Present, Presentable, Presidential, Prevalent, Prevailing, Prevenient, Priceless, Primal, Primary, Prime, Primed, Primo, Princely, Principal, Principled, Priority, Privileged, Prized, Prize-winning, Pro, Proactive, Probable, Probative, Procurable, Prodigious, Productive, Professional, Proficient, Profound, Profuse, Progressive, Prolific, Prominent, Promising, Promoting, Prompt, Proper, Propitious, Prospective, Prosperous, Protective, Proto-, Proud, Prudent, Public-spirited, Puissant, Pumped up, Punctual, Pure, Purifying, Purposeful, Purposive

Qualified, Qualitative, Quality, Quemeful, Quick, Quickened, Quick on the uptake, Quick-witted, Quiet, Quintessential, Quixotic

Rad, Rapt, Rapturous, Rare, Rascally, Rational, Ravishing, Razor-sharp, Reachable, Ready, Real, Reassuring, Receiving, Receptive, Reciprocal, Recommendable, Recommended, Red-carpet, Refined, Refreshing, Regal, Rejuvenating, Related, Relaxed, Relaxing, Reliable, Relished, Remarkable, Renewed, Renewing, Resourceful, Respectable, Respected, Respectful, Rested, Restful, Restorative, Revitalized, Revitalizing, Revived, Revivifying, Rewarding, Rhapsodic, Riant, Rich, Rident, Right, Righteous, Right neighbourly, Robust, Rollicking, Rousing

Safe, Salubrious, Salutiferous, Sanguine, Sapient, Sapiential, Sartorial, Satisfactory, Satisfied, Satisfying, Savvy, Scholarly, Scientific, Scintillated, Scintillating, Scrumptious, Scrupulous, Seamless, Seasoned, Second-to-none, Secure, Sedulous, Seemly, Select, Selected, Self-accepting, Self-assured, Self-confident, Self-disciplined, Self-expressive, Self-governing, Selfless, Self-made, Self-sacrificing, Self-starting, Self-sufficient, Self-taught, Sensational, Sensible, Sensitive, Sensuous, Sensual, Sentimental, Serendipitous, Serene, Service-minded, Service-oriented, Settled, Settling, Sharing, Sharp, Sharp-eyed, Sharp-witted, Sheltering, Shiny-eyed, Shipshape, Shrewd, Sightly, Significant, Simple, Sincere, Sinewy, Sizable, Skillful, Skilled, Skookum, Sleek, Smart, Smashing, Smiley, Smiling, Smitten, Smooth, Snazzy, Snappy, Snugly, Sociable, Social, Societal, Soft-hearted, Soigne, Solid, Solid gold, Solomon-like, Something else, Soothfast, Soothing, Sophic, Sophisticated, Sought, Sought-after, Soulful, Sound, Sovereign, Sparkling, Special, Spectacular, Spellbinding, Spicy, Spiffy, Spirited, Spiritual, Splendent, Splendid, Sponsal, Spontaneous, Sporting, Sportive, Spotless, Sprauncy, Sprightly, Spruce, Spruced up, Spry, Square, Stable, Staid, Stainless, Stalwart, Stand-up, Star, Stately, State-of-the-art, Statuesque, Staunch, Steadfast, Steady, Stellar, Sterling, Sthenic, Stick-to-itive, Stimulating, Stimulative, Stimulatory, Stirring, Stoic, Storied, Stouthearted, Straightforward, Straight out, Strapping, Strategic, Street smart, Streetwise, Striking, Strong, Strong-willed, Studious, Stunning, Stupendous, Sturdy,

Stylish, Suasive, Suave, Sublime, Substantial, Substantive, Subtle, Successful, Succinct, Sufficient, Suitable, Suited, Sunny, Super, Superb, Super-duper, Super-civilized, Super-ethical, Super-excellent, Superior, Superlative, Supersonic, Supple, Supported, Supportive, Sure, Sure-fire, Sure-footed, Sure-handed, Surpassing, Surprising, Sustentative, Swank, Swaying, Sweeping, Sweet, Symbiotic, Symmetrical, Sympathetic, Synergistic, Systematic

Tactful, Tailor-made, Take-charge, Talented, Tangible, Tantalizing, Tasteful, Taught, Teachable, Teaching, Teleorganic, Temperate, Tenable, Tenacious, Tender, Tender-hearted, Terrific, Thankful, Thankworthy, Therapeutic, There, Thorough, Thoroughgoing, Thoughtful, Thrilled, Thrilling, Thriving, Tickled, Tidy, Timely, Time-honoured, Timeless, Time-saving, Tip-top, Tireless, Titanic, Titillating, Today, Together, Tolerant, Tonic, Topical, Top, Top drawer, Top-notch, Tops, Totally-tubular, To the max, Touching, Tough, Trailblazing, Traditive, Tranquil, Transcendent, Transcendental, Transformable, Transformative, Transparent, Transpicuous, Traveled, Treasurable, Treasured, Tremendous, Trim, Triumphant, True, True-blue, Trusted, Trustful, Trusting, Trustworthy, Trusty, Truthful, Tuneful, Tutelary, Twenty-first century, Twenty-four carat, Tympanic

Unabashed, Unaffected, Unafraid, Unambiguous, Unassuming, Unattached, Unbiased, Unbigoted, Uncommon, Uncomplicated, Uncompromising, Unconditional, Unconditionally loving, Unconventional, Uncorrupted, Undauntable, Undaunted, Understandable, Understanding, Understood, Under control, Undesigning, Undiminished, Undisputed, Undivided, Undoubted, Unencumbered, Unequalled, Unequivocable, Unequivocal, Unfailing, Unfaltering, Unfeigned, Unfettered, Unflagging, Unflappable, Unhesitating, Unified, Unimpeachable, Unimpeded, Unique, Unisonous, United, Unlimited, Unobjectionable, Unparalleled, Unprejudiced, Unpretentious, Unquestionable, Unreserved, Unrivalled, Unruffled, Unselfish, Unshakable, Unshaken, Unstoppable, Unsurpassed, Untiring, Unwavering, Up, Up-and-coming, Upbeat, Upbuilding, Upcoming, Up front, Uplifting, Upright, Upstanding, Up-to-date, Up to par, Up to snuff, Up to speed, Uptown, Urbane, Utilitarian

Valiant, Valid, Validating, Validatory, Valorous, Valuable, Valued, Vast, Vegete, Vehement, Venerable, Venerated, Venial, Ventorious, Venturesome, Veracious, Verecund, Veridical, Veridicous, Verified, Veriloquent, Veritable, Versatile, Versed, Veteran, Viable, Vibrant, Victorious, Vigilant, Vigorous, Viparious, Virtuous, Virile, Visionary, Vital, Vitative, Vivacious, Vivid, Vivifying, Vocal, Vogue, Volcanic, Volitional

Wanted, Warm, Warm-hearted, Wealthy, Weighty, Welcome, Welcoming, Well, Well-arranged, Well-behaved, Well-built, Well-disposed, Well-established, Well-founded, Well-grounded, Well-informed, Well-intentioned, Well-liked, Well-made, Well-meaning, Well-proportioned, Well-read, Well-received, Well-spoken, Well-suited, Well-timed, Whimsical, Wholehearted, Wholesome, Wide-awake, Willing, Winged, Winnable, Winning, Wired, Wise, With it, Within reach, Without equal, Without limit, Witty, Wizardly, Woke, Wonderful, Wondrous, Working, World class, Worldly, Worldly-wise, Worthy

Xenial, Xenodochial

Yummy

Zany, Zealous, Zestful, Zoetic

Happy Birthday
Adjectives & Synonyms

POSITIVE FEMININE ADJECTIVES
Especially Words Describing Mom

"That is the law of love. Giving in action, without the force felt, expressed, manifested, shown, desired or reward for that given."
(Edgar Cayce Reading 3744-4)

"She is..."

Abiding, Able, Aboveboard, Abundant, Accepting, Accessible, Accommodating, Accommodative, Acknowledging, Active, Actual, Adaptable, Adept, Admirable, Admired, Adored, Adoring, Advocative, Affable, Affectionate, Affective, Alimentary, All heart, Allegiant, All-important, Altruistic, Amazing, Ameliorative, Amelioratory, Amenable, Amiable, Amicable, Amusing, Appeasing, Appreciated, Approachable, Appropriate, Approving, Apt, Assertive, Assiduous, Assistive, Associative, Assuring, At hand, At the ready, Attentive, Autodidactic, Atypical, August, Authentic, Authoritative, Available, Awaited, Aware, Awesome

Balanced, Beaming, Beautiful, Believable, Belonging, Beneficent, Benevolent, Benignant, Better, Best, Beyond compare, Big-hearted, Blue-ribbon, Bright, Buoyant, Bustling, Busy

Calm, Calming, Calmative, Can do, Canny, Capable, Cared for, Careful, Caring, Casual, Celebrated, Celebratory, Centered, Central, Certain, Changeless, Charitable, Charming, Cheerful, Cherishable, Cherished, Cherishing, Chosen, Chummy, Classic, Classy, Clean, Clear, Clear-cut, Clearheaded, Clear-sighted, Clement, Close, Collaborative, Colourful, Comfortable, Comforting, Commanding, Commiserative, Committed, Commodious, Commonsensical, Communal, Communicative, Commutual, Companionable, Compassionate, Competent, Complete, Complimentary, Composed, Conciliatory, Condolatory, Confident, Congenial, Conscientious, Consentient, Considerable, Considerate, Consistent, Constructive, Contemplative, Conversant, Convivial, Cooking with gas, Cool,

Copacetic, Cordial, Correct, Correlative, Courteous, Cozy, Crackerjack, Creative, Credible, Creditable, Credited, Cultured, Curative

Dapatical, Dauntless, Dear, Decent, Decisive, Dedicated, Deductive, Definite, Deliberate, Delightful, Dependable, Deserving, Determined, Devoted, Didactic, Diehard, Dignified, Diligent, Diplomatic, Direct, Disarming, Discerning, Disciplined, Discreet, Distinguishing, Diverse, Doting, Doubtless, Doughty, Down-to-earth, Driven, Durable, Dutiful, Dynamic

Earnest, Earthy, Easy to approach, Easy to talk to, Echt, Economical, Edifying, Educational, Effective, Effectual, Efficient, Efflorescent, Elevating, Empathetic, Empowering, Enabling, Enchanting, Encouraging, Endearing, Endorsing, Enduring, Energetic, Energizing, Engaged, Engaging, Enjoyable, Enlightening, Enlivening, En règle, Enriched, Enriching, Enterprising, Entertaining, Enthusiastic, Entrusted, Equiponderant, Equiponderate, Equitable, Essential, Established, Esteemed, Ethical, Eudaimonistic, Eudaimonistical, Even-handed, Evocative, Evolved, Excellent, Exemplary, Exhortative, Exhortatory, Expeditious, Expeditive, Experienced, Extraordinary

Facilitative, Factual, Fair, Faithful, Familial, Familiar, Fantabulous, Fantastic, Far-sighted, Favourite, Feelgood, Felicitous, Fiery, Filigreed, Firm, First, First-class, First-order, First-rate, Five-star, Flavourful, Flavoursome, Focused, Fond, Forbearant, Forbearing, Foremost, Foresighted, Forgivable, Forgiving, Formidable, For real, Forthcoming, Forthright, Fortifying, Forward-thinking, Foundational, Foundationary, Four-star, Frank, Friendly, Fruitful, Fulfilling, Fundamental

Generative, Generous, Genial, Genteel, Gentle, Genuine, Germane, Giving, Goal-oriented, Good, Good-feeling, Goodhearted, Good-humoured, Goodly, Good-natured, Graceful, Gracious, Greathearted, Grounded, Guaranteed, Guiding, Guileless, Gumptious, Gung ho

Handy, Happy, Hard-working, Harmless, Harmonic, Harmonious, Head, Healing, Heartfelt, Heartsome, Heart-to-heart, Heartwarming,

Hearty, Heavenly, Helpful, Helping, Heroic, High calibre, High-demand, Highly valued, High-minded, High-quality, High-reaching, High-spirited, Honest, Honourable, Honoured, Hortative, Hortatory, Hospitable, Huggy, Huggable, Human, Humane, Humanistic, Humanitarian, Humble, Hygienic

Ideal, Idealistic, Illuminating, Imaginative, Imitable, Immaculate, Immeasurable, Immediate, Impartial, Impassioned, Impeccable, Imperturbable, Important, Improvisational, Incisive, Inclusive, Incomparable, Incontrovertible, Incomplex, Incorrupt, Incorruptible, Inculpable, Indefatigable, In demand, Indestructible, Indispensable, Indisputable, Indomitable, Indubitable, Industrious, Inexhaustible, In fine fettle (good spirits), Influential, Informative, Inimitable, Innovative, Inquisitive, Insightful, Inspirational, Inspiring, Inspiriting, Instinctive, Instructive, Integral, Integrated, Integrative, Interconnected, Interconnective, Intelligent, Intent, Interactive, Interested, Intertwined, Intrepid, Intrinsic, Inventive, Invigorated, Invigorating, Invincible, Inviting, Irenic, Irreplaceable, Irrepressible, Irreproachable

Jovial, Joyful, Joyous, Judicious, Junoesque, Just, Justified, Just right, Juvenescent

Keen, Key, Kind, Kind-hearted, Kindly, Knowable, Knowing, Knowledgeable, Known, Kosher

Ladylike, Laid-back, Laudable, Leading, Leisurely, Lenient, Level-headed, Liberal, Liberated, Liberating, Libertarian, Liefly, Light-hearted, Likable, Lively, Longanimous, Logical, Lovable, Loved, Lovely, Loving, Loyal

Magical, Magnanimous, Made a difference, Managerial, Mannerly, Matchless, Maternal, Matter-of-fact, Mature, Maximal, Meaningful, Measured, Meditative, Melioristic, Memorable, Merciful, Meritable, Meritorious, Merry, Methodical, Methodological, Meticulous, Mettlesome, Mindful, Miraculous, Mitigative, Mitigatory, Model, Modest, Moral, Motherly, Motivating, Motivational, Moving, Muliebral, Muliebrile, Muliebrous, Multidimensional, Multi-disciplined, Multifaceted, Munificent

Natural, Near to one's heart, Nearby, Neat, Necessary, Needed, Neighbourly, Never-failing, Nice, Noble, Nobody's fool, No dummy, No strings attached, Nonchalant, Nonpareil, Normal, Normative, Not born yesterday, Nourishing, Number 1, Number one, Numero uno, Nurturing, Nutrimental

Objective, Obliging, Observant, OK, Okay, On hand, On the ball, On the beam, On the job, On the outlook, On the money, On the move, Open, Open-handed, Open-hearted, Open-minded, Optimal, Optimistic, Optimum, Orderly, Organic, Organized, Original, Outgoing, Outspoken, Outstanding, Overflowing, Overriding, Overruling, Overt

Pabulous, Pacific, Pacifistic, Painstaking, Pally, Parental, Par excellence, Participative, Participatory, Particular, Patient, Peaceable, Peaceful, Pecuniary, Peerless, Penetrating, Perceptive, Perceptual, Perennial, Permissive, Perseverant, Persevering, Persistent, Personable, Persuasive, Pertinent, Philanthropic, Philosophical, Pious, Placid, Pleasing, Plenteous, Plentiful, Plucky, Poignant, Poised, Pollent, Polite, Positive, Potent, Powerful, Practicable, Practical, Practiced, Pragmatic, Praiseworthy, Prayerful, Precious, Preemptory, Prepared, Preponderant, Prepotent, Present, Presentable, Prevalent, Prevailing, Priceless, Primary, Principled, Proactive, Probative, Productive, Proficient, Progressive, Promotional, Prompt, Proper, Propitious, Protective, Proud, Prudent, Puissant, Punctual, Pure, Purifying, Purposeful, Purposive

Qualified, Qualitative, Quality, Queenly, Quemeful, Quick, Quickened, Quick on the draw, Quick-witted, Quiet, Quintessential

Rare, Rational, Razor-sharp, Reliable, Reachable, Ready, Real, Reassuring, Receptive, Reciprocal, Recommendable, Rejuvenating, Related, Relative, Relaxed, Relaxing, Relished, Remarkable, Renewing, Renewed, Resourceful, Respectable, Respected, Respectful, Restorative, Revitalized, Revitalizing, Revivifying, Rewarded, Rewarding, Right, Righteous, Right neighbourly

Sacrosanct, Safe, Salubrious, Sapient, Sapiential, Satisfying, Saucy, Savoury, Savvy, Scrupulous, Seasoned, Second-to-none, Secure, Secured, Sedulous, Self-assured, Self-confident, Self-disciplined, Self-expressive, Self-governing, Selfless, Self-made, Self-sacrificing, Self-starting, Self-taught, Sensible, Sensitive, Sentimental, Serene, Service-minded, Service-oriented, Settling, Sharing, Sharp, Sharp-eyed, Sharp-witted, Sheltering, Shrewd, Significant, Simple, Sincere, Skillful, Skilled, Smart, Sociable, Social, Societal, Soft-hearted, Solid, Solid gold, Solomon-like, Soothing, Soulful, Sound, Special, Spicy, Spiffy, Spirited, Spiritual, Splendid, Sponsal, Spontaneous, Spotless, Square, Stable, Staid, Stainless, Stalwart, Stand-up, Stately, Staunch, Steadfast, Steady, Stellar, Sterling, Sthenic, Stick-to-itive, Still, Stimulative, Stouthearted, Straightforward, Straight out, Strategic, Strong, Strong-willed, Suasive, Substantial, Substantive, Succinct, Super, Superabundant, Superb, Super-ethical, Super-excellent, Superlative, Supporting, Supportive, Sure, Sure-fire, Sure-footed, Sure-handed, Surpassing, Sustaining, Sustentative, Sweet, Swell, Sympathetic, Synergistic, Systematic

Tactful, Take-charge, Talented, Taught, Teaching, Temperate, Tenacious, Tender-hearted, Terrific, Therapeutic, There, Thorough, Thoughtful, Thriving, Tidy, Tight, Timeless, Time-saving, Tip-top, Tireless, Together, Tolerant, Tonic, Top, Top drawer, Top-notch, Tops, Touching, Tough, Traditive, Trailblazing, Tranquil, Transformative, Transpicuous, Treasurable, Treasured, True, True-blue, Trusted, Trustful, Trusting, Trustworthy, Trusty, Truthful, Tutelary, Twenty-four carat

Unabashed, Unafraid, Unambiguous, Unassuming, Unbeatable, Unbeaten, Unbiased, Unblemished, Unbroken, Uncensurable, Uncommon, Uncomplicated, Uncompromising, Unconditional, Unconditionally loving, Unconventional, Uncorrupted, Undauntable, Undaunted, Undeniable, Understandable, Understanding, Understood, Undisputed, Undivided, Undoubted, Unequalled, Unequivocable, Unequivocal, Unfaltering, Unfaultable, Unfeigned, Unflagging, Unflappable, Unhesitating, Unimpaired, Unimpeachable, Unimpeded, Unique, Unisonous, Unobtrusive, Unparalleled, Unpretentious, Unquestionable, Unrefuted, Unreserved, Unrivalled,

Unselfish, Unshakable, Unshaken, Unstoppable, Unsurpassed, Untarnished, Untiring, Unwavering, Upbeat, Up front, Uplifting, Upright, Upstanding, User-friendly, Utilitarian, Uxorial

Validating, Valued, Veracious, Veridical, Versatile, Vibrant, Vigilant, Vigorous, Viparious, Virtuous, Vital, Vivacious, Vivid, Vivifying

Wanted, Warm, Warm-hearted, Watchful, Welcome, Welcoming, Well-behaved, Well-disposed, Well-established, Well-founded, Well-grounded, Well-informed, Well-intentioned, Well-liked, Well-meaning, Well-received, Well-spoken, Whiz-bang, Whole-hearted, Wholesome, Wise, Within reach, Without equal, Wonderful, Working, World class, Worthy

Xenial, Xenodocial

Young-at-Heart

Zealous, Zestful, Zesty, Zoetic

Did you know that the word for "Mother"
in virtually every language starts with the letter "M"?

The Cuddly Chronicles

ROMANTIC ADJECTIVES

"Give that of love, if ye would find love. Show thyself friendly and lovely if ye would have that love bestowed upon thee that brings peace and contentment." (Edgar Cayce Reading 2293-3)

"You are..."

Abiding, Abloom, Admirable, Admired, Adonic, Adorable, Adored, Adoring, Adventuresome, Ae, Affectionate, Afflated, Afflating, Ageless, Agile, Alacritous, Alaudine, All heart, All systems go, Alluring, Amazing, Ambrosial, Ambrosian, Amoroso, Ample, Angelic, Apollonian, Appetent, Ardent, Arresting, Astral, Attentive, Attracted, Attractive, Atypical, Auroral, Available, Avid, Awesome

Beaming, Beamish, Beauteous, Beautiful, Becoming, Bedazzling, Beloved, Best, Best-loved, Bewitching, Beyond compare, Blooming, Bonny, Bonzer, Breathtaking, Brilliant, Buccal, Buff, Buoyant

Candescent, Cantier, Cantiest, Canty, Captivating, Cared for, Caring, Celestial, Charmed, Charming, Cherishable, Cherished, Cherry, Choice, Choicest, Chosen, Classy, Clear-eyed, Cock-a-hoop, Coequal, Columbine, Comely, Comforting, Companionable, Compassionate, Compatible, Compelling, Commutual, Conjugate, Convivial, Copacetic, Coquettish, Coruscant, Cosmic, Courtly, Cozy, Coy, Crazy about, Cuddly, Cute

Dapatical, Dapper, Darling, Dashing, Dazzling, Dear, Dearest, Debonair, Delicate, Delightful, Desirable, Desired, Devoted, Dewy, Disarming, Divine, Doted on, Doting, Dovelike, Dreamy, Dulcet, Dynamite

Eager, Easygoing, Easy to approach, Easy to talk to, Effervescent, Effulgent, Elated, Elating, Electric, Electrifying, Elegant, Eligible, Empyrean, Enamoured, Enamouring, Enchanted, Enchanting, Endeared, Endearing, Energizing, Engaging, Enjoyable, Enjoyed, Enlivened, Enlivening, Enough, Enrapturing, Enriching, Enthralling, Enticed, Enticing, Entrancing, Epic, Equal, Equiparent, Equipollent, Euphonious, Evocative, Exceptional, Exciting, Exhilarating, Exquisite, Exotic, Extraordinary, Eyesome, Eye-catching

Fab, Fabulous, Fair, Faithful, Fantastic, Fantabulous, Fascinating, Favoured, Favourite, Featous, Feelgood, Feline, Feminine, Fetching, Fiery, Filled, Fine, Finer, Finest, First-class, Five-star, Flawless, Flexible, Flirtatious, Flirty, Fond, Foxy, Frabjous, Fragrant, Fresh, Friendly, Frolicsome, Fulfilling, Fulgent, Full, Fun, Funny

Gallant, Game, Gamesome, Generous, Gentle, Gentlemanly, Genuine, Giving, Glabrous, Glamorous, Gleaming, Glistening, Glowing, Gnarly, Golden, Good, Goodhearted, Good-humoured, Good-looking, Gorgeous, Graceful, Gracile, Gracious, Gradely, Gratifying, Gymnastic

Handsome, Harmonious, Haunting, Heartfelt, Heart-stopping, Heartwarming, Heavenly, High-class, High quality, High-spirited, Honeyed, Honourable, Honoured, Hot, Huggy, Huggable, Hunky, Hypnotic

Ideal, Illecebrous, Illimitable, Immeasurable, Impassioned, Impeccable, Impish, Impressive, Incandescent, Incomparable, Indomitable, Inebriating, Ineffable, Infatuated, Infatuating, In fine fettle (good spirits), Infinite, Inimitable, In my heart, Inseparable, Inspiriting, Intemerate, Intense, Interconnected, Interesting, In the now, Intoxicating, Intriguing, Invigorating, Inviting, Irrepressible, Irresistible

Jimp, Joyful, Joyous, Joysome, Junoesque, Just right

Kind, Kind-hearted, Kissable

Ladylike, Laudable, Lepid, Liberating, Liefly, Likable, Liked, Like-minded, Light, Lovable, Loved, Lovely, Lovesick, Lovestruck, Loving, Loyal, Lusory

Mad about, Magical, Magnetic, Magnificent, Major league, Manly, Mannerly, Marmoreal, Masculine, Matchless, Maximal, Mellifluous, Melliloquent, Mellisonant, Memorable, Mesmerizing, Miraculous, Mirthful, Mischievous, Moonstruck, Most excellent, Moving, Muliebral, Muliebrile, Muliebrous, Multidimensional, Muscular, Mutual

Natty, Natural, Near to one's heart, Necessary, Needed, Neverfailing, Nice, Nifty, Nimble, Noctiflorous, Nonpareil, Nourishing, Number one, Numero uno, Nutty about, Nuts over

Obliging, Olympian, One and only, Oneiric, Open, Open-hearted, Open-minded, Optimal, Optimum, Orphean, Original, Oscular, Out-of-sight, Out-of-this-world, Outstanding, Overflowing

Paradisiacal, Partial, Passionate, Peach-like, Peachy, Peachy keen, Perfect, Perky, Personable, Personal, Pert, Petite, Phenomabomb (slang), Phenomenal, Picked, Picturesque, Pierian, Piquant, Playful, Pleasant, Pleasing, Poetic, Polite, Porcelain, Positive, Pouty, Precious, Preferred, Prefulgent, Premium, Prepossessing, Pretty, Priceless, Prime, Principled, Prized, Prize-winning, Profulgent, Promising, Pulchritudinous, Pukka, Pure

Qualitative, Quality, Quintessential, Quixotic

Rad, Radiant, Rare, Rascally, Rathe, Ravishing, Receptive, Recherché, Reciprocal, Redolent, Refreshing, Refulgent, Rejuvenating, Relaxing, Reliable, Relished, Remarkable, Respectable, Respected, Restorative, Revitalizing, Rewarding, Rhapsodic, Right on, Robust, Rollicking, Romantic, Rosy

Sanguine, Sassy, Saucy, Savoury, Scented, Scintillant, Scintillated, Scintillating, Scintillescent, Second-to-none, Select, Selected, Sensate, Sensational, Sentimental, Shapely, Shimmering, Shining, Shiny-eyed, Shipshape, Sightly, Silken, Silky, Sincere, Sleek, Smashing, Smiling, Smitten, Smooth, Snazzy, Snugly, Soft, Solid gold, Something else, Sonsy, Sought, Sparkling, Special, Spectacular, Spellbinding, Spicy, Spiffy, Spirited, Spiritual, Splendiferous, Sponsal, Sprightly, Spunky, Statuesque, Stellar, Sterling, Sthenic, Stimulating, Stimulative, Stimulatory, Stirring, Strapping, Striking, Stunning, Stylish, Suave, Suaviloquent, Sublime, Sufficient, Suitable, Suited, Sunny, Super, Super-angelic, Superb, Super-duper, Super-excellent, Superior, Superlative, Supernal, Supple, Supported, Supporting, Supportive, Supreme, Surpassing, Svelte, Swaying, Sweet, Sweet-smelling, Swell, Sybaritic, Synergistic

Tempean, Temperate, Terrific, There, Thoughtful, Thrilling, Ticklish, Tip-top, Toothsome, Top drawer, Tops, Totally-tubular, Touching, Transcendent, Transporting, Treasurable, Treasured, Tremendous, Trim, True, True-blue, Trusted, Trustworthy, Trusty, Twenty-four carat, Twitterpated, Twitterpating, Tympanic

Uncommon, Unconditionally loving, Unencumbered, Unequalled, Unfettered, Unified, Unifying, Unique, Unisonal, Unisonant, Unisonous, United, Uniting, Unlimited, Unparalleled, Unrivalled, Unsurpassed, Unwithdrawing, Upbuilding, Up front, Uplifting, Uxorial

Valuable, Valued, Vegete, Venerated, Venust, Vibrant, Vigorous, Vital, Vitalizing, Vitative, Vivacious, Vivifying

Wanted, Warm, Warm-hearted, Welcome, Welcoming, Well-built, Well-liked, Well-made, Well-proportioned, Well-received, Well-suited, Whimsical, Whiz-bang, Wholehearted, Wild, Wild about, Winning, Winsome, With it, Without equal, Womanly, Wonderful, Wondrous, World class, Worthy

Yummy

Zestful, Zesty and Zoetic

POSITIVE BUSINESS ADJECTIVES
Professional Adjectives for Business

"Look for good and ye will find it.
Search for it, for it is a pearl of great price."
(Edgar Cayce Reading 1776-1)

A-1, A-OK, A-one, Able, Abundant, Accelerating, Acceptable, Accepted, Accessible, Accommodating, Accomplished, Accredited, Accurate, Acknowledged, Active, Actual, Acuminate, Acuminous, Adaptable, Adept, Administrative, Admirable, Admired, Adroit, Advanced, Advantageous, Affiliated, Afflated, Afflating, Aggressive, Alacritous, Amalgamated, Ambitious, Ample, Analytic, Analytical, Apodictic, Appetent, Apposite, Appreciated, Approachable, Appropriate, Approved, Apt, Ardent, Argus-eyed, Arranged, Artful, Articulate, Ascendant, Aspirant, Aspiring, Assertive, Assiduous, Assistive, Assembled, Associated, Associative, Assured, Assurgent, Astute, At ease, At hand, At one's disposal, At the ready, Attentive, Atypical, Audited, Au fait, August, Auriferous, Auspicious, Authentic, Authenticated, Authoritative, Authorized, Avid, Aware, Axiomatic

Balanced, Ball of fire, Banzai, Benefic, Beneficent, Beneficial, Better, Beyond compare, Big, Biggest, Big league, Big-time, Blockbuster, Blue-ribbon, Bold, Boffo, Bonafide, Booming, Bounteous, Bountiful, Busy, Business-like, Brain wave, Brainy, Brassy, Brave, Breviloquent, Bright, Brilliant, Brimming, Budgetary, Built, Bulletproof, Bullish, Buoyant, Business-like, Bustling, Busy, By-the-book, By-the-numbers

Calm, Calmative, Calming, Can do, Canny, Capable, Capital, Careful, Celeritous, Centered, Central, Cerebral, Certain, Certified, Champion, Charismatic, Chief, Civic-minded, Civilized, Classic, Clean, Clear, Clear-cut, Clear-eyed, Clearheaded, Clear-sighted, Clement, Clever, Coadjutant, Coequal, Cogent, Cognizant, Coherent, Collaborative, Collated, Collected, Collegial, Coming on strong, Commanding, Commendable, Commercial, Committed, Commonsensical, Communicative, Community-minded,

Commutual, Compatible, Compelling, Compendious, Compensatory, Competent, Composed, Comprehensive, Concerted, Concise, Concordant, Conducive, Conferrable, Confident, Confirmed, Congenial, Congruous, Conjoint, Conjugate, Conjunctive, Connected, Conscientious, Consentaneous, Consentient, Considerable, Considerate, Consistent, Consolidated, Consonant, Constant, Constructive, Consumable, Contemporary, Continuous, Contributive, Contributory, Controlled, Conversant, Convictive, Convincing, Cooperative, Coordinated, Copacetic, Copious, Correct, Corroborated, Cosmopolitan, Cost-effective, Courageous, Courteous, Crack, Crackerjack, Creative, Credential, Credible, Credited, Cultivated, Cultured, Cumulative, Current, Cutting-edge, Cyclic

Daedal, Dauntless, Decent, Decisive, Dedicated, Deductive, Definite, Definitive, Deft, Departmental, Dependable, Deserved, Deserving, Designing, Desirable, Destined, Determined, Developed, Developing, Devoted, Dexterous, Diagnostic, Dialectical, Dignified, Diligent, Diplomatic, Direct, Disarming, Discerning, Disciplined, Discreet, Discrete, Discriminating, Dispassionate, Distinctive, Distinguished, Diverse, Doable, Dominant, Doubtless, Doughty, Down-to-earth, Driven, Driving, Durable, Dutiful, Dynamic, Dynamite

Eager, Earnest, Easygoing, Easy to approach, Easy to reach, Easy to talk to, Easy to understand, Eco-friendly, Economic, Economical, Edified, Edifying, Educated, Educational, Effective, Effectual, Efficacious, Efficient, Electric, Electrifying, Eleemosynary, Eloquent, Emerging, Eminent, Empirical, Employable, Enacted, Endorsed, Enduring, Energetic, Energizing, Energy-giving, Engaged, Engaging, Enlightened, Enlightening, Ennobled, Ennobling, En règle, Enriching, Ensured, Enterprising, Enthusiastic, Entrepreneurial, Entrusted, Environmental, Epinician, Equable, Equal, Equalized, Equal opportunity, Equanimous, Equipollent, Equiponderant, Equiponderate, Equitable, Erudite, Essential, Established, Esteemed, Estimable, Ethical, Evenhanded, Exact, Excellent, Excelling, Exceptional, Executive, Exemplary, Expedient, Expeditious, Experienced, Expert, Extensive, Extraordinary, Exuberant

Facilitative, Factual, Fair, Faithful, Far-reaching, Far-sighted, Fast, Faultless, Favourable, Favourite, Fearless, Feasible, Fecund, Feracious, Fertile, Figureoutable, Financial, Fine, Finer, Finest, Fireball, Firm, First-class, First-order, First-rate, Fiscal, Fitting, Five-star, Flawless, Flourishing, Fluent, Focused, Forceful, Forbearing, Foremost, Foresighted, Formal, Formidable, Forthcoming, Fortified, Fortifying, Forthright, Fortuitous, Fortunate, Forward-looking, Forward-thinking, Foundational, Foundationary, Founded, Four-star, Frank, Fresh, Friendly, Fruitful, Functional, Fundamental

Gainful, Galvanizing, Generative, Genuine, Gifted, Go-ahead, Goal-oriented, Go-getter, Go-getting, Going (concern) Golden, Good, Good at, Good for, Gratifying, Green, Growing, Guaranteed, Guiding, Guileless, Gumptious, Gung ho, Gutsy

Hallowed, Handy, Hardworking, Hard-driving, Hardy, Harmonious, Head, Hearty, Healthy, Heavyweight, Heedful, Helpful, Henotic, Heuristic, High calibre, High-class, High-demand, High-income, High-minded, High-power, High-powered, High-principled, High-priority, High-quality, High-reaching, High-spirited, Highest, Highly regarded, Highly seasoned, Highly valued, Honest, Honourable, Honoured, Hortative, Hortatory, Hot off the fire, Hot off the press, Hotshot, Huge, Humanitarian, Hungry, Hypersonic

Idoneous, Illimitable, Imaginative, Imitable, Immaculate, Immediate, Immense, Impartial, Impassioned, Impavid, Impeccable, Impeccant, Impellent, Imperative, Imperious, Imperturbable, Important, Impressive, Improved, Improving, Incisive, Inclusive, Incomparable, Incontestable, Incontrovertible, Incorporated, Incorrupt, Incorruptible, Increasing, Inculpable, Indefatigable, In demand, Independent, Indispensable, Indisputable, Indomitable, Indubitable, Industrious, Inerrant, Inexhaustible, Inferential, Influential, Informative, Informed, Ingenious, Inimitable, Initiative, Innate, Innovative, In order, Inquisitive, In readiness, Insightful, Inspirational, Inspirative, Inspired, Inspiring, Inspirited, Inspiriting, Institutional, Instructed, Instructive, Instrumental, Insured, Integral, Integrated, Integrative, Intellectual, Intelligent, Intense, Intent, Intensifying, Interconnected,

Interconnective, Internal, International, In the bag, In the black, In the mainstream, Intrepid, Intriguing, Intrinsic, Invaluable, Inventive, Investigative, Invigorating, Irrefragable, Irrefutable, Irreplaceable, Irrepressible, Irreproachable

Joint, Judicious, Just, Justifiable

Keen, Kempt, Key, Kinetic, Knowledgeable, Known

Laudable, Law-abiding, Lawful, Leading, Leading-edge, Leagued, Learned, Legal, Lettered, Level-headed, Likable, Like-minded, Logical, Longanimous, Long-established, Lucrative, Lucriferous, Luculent

Magistral, Magnetic, Main, Mainstream, Major, Major league, Manageable, Managerial, Manifest, Malleable, Marketable, Masterful, Masterly, Material, Matter-of-fact, Maximal, Maximum, Meaningful, Measured, Melioristic, Mercantile, Merchandising, Meritable, Meritorious, Meteoric, Methodic, Methodical, Methodized, Methodological, Meticulous, Mettlesome, Mindful, Mitigative, Mitigatory, Model, Modern, Monetary, Moneyed, Money-making, Moral, Moralistic, More, Motivated, Motivating, Motivational, Mutual

Nascent, Nailed down, National, Nationwide, Neat, Necessary, Needed, Neoteric, Never-failing, Nimble-witted, Noble, Noetic, Nonpareil, Notable, Noteworthy, Novel

Objective, Obliging, Observant, Official, Of good repute, Ongoing, On one's toes, On target, On the ball, On the beam, On the button, On the job, On the level, On the money, On the nose, On the qui vive, Open, Open-minded, Operative, Opportune, Opinable, Optimal, Optimistic, Optimum, Ordered, Orderly, Original, Originative, Organized, Outspoken, Outstanding

Painstaking, Paramount, Pardonable, Par excellence, Participative, Participatory, Particular, Patient, Peak, Pecuniary, Peerless, Penetrating, Perceptive, Percipient, Performable, Perseverant,

Persevering, Persistent, Personable, Perspicacious, Perspicuous, Persuasive, Pertinent, Philanthropic, Phlegmatic, Pioneering, Pivotal, Planned, Pleasant, Plenary, Plenteous, Plentiful, Plucky, Poised, Polished, Polite, Popular, Positive, Possible, Potent, Potential, Powerful, Practicable, Practical, Practiced, Pragmatic, Praiseworthy, Precise, Predominant, Preeminent, Preferable, Preferred, Premier, Premium, Prepared, Preponderant, Present, Presidential, Prevalent, Prevailing, Prevoyant, Primary, Prime, Primed, Primo, Principal, Principled, Priority, Pro, Proactive, Probable, Procurable, Prodigious, Productive, Professional, Proficient, Profitable, Pro forma, Progressive, Prolific, Promising, Promoted, Promoting, Promotional, Prompt, Proper, Propertied, Propitious, Propulsive, Prospective, Prospering, Prosperous, Protean, Protective, Proto-, Proud, Proven, Provisional, Prudent, Public-spirited, Punchy, Punctual, Punctilious, Pure, Purified, Purposeful, Purposive

Quantifiable, Qualified, Qualitative, Quality, Quick, Quick on the draw, Quick on the uptake, Quick-witted, Quiet, Quietsome

Rapid, Rathe, Ratified, Ratiocinative, Rational, Razor-sharp, Reachable, Ready, Realistic, Realizable, Reasonable, Reasoned, Reassuring, Receptive, Recipient, Reciprocal, Recognized, Recommendable, Recommended, Refined, Refining, Refreshing, Regular, Regulated, Relevant, Reliable, Remarkable, Remunerative, Replete, Reputable, Resilient, Resolute, Resolved, Resourceful, Respectable, Respected, Respectful, Responsible, Responsive, Retail, Retentive, Rewardable, Rewarded, Rewarding, Right, Righteous, Rightful, Right-minded, Rigorous, Robust, Rock solid, Rooted, Rousing, Routine, Rugged, Run

Safe, Saleable, Salubrious, Salutary, Sanctioned, Sanguine, Satisfactory, Satisfying, Savvy, Scholarly, Scientific, Scrupulous, Seamless, Seasoned, Second-to-none, Secure, Secured, Sedulous, Select, Selected, Self-assertive, Self-assured, Self-confident, Self-disciplined, Self-made, Self-starting, Self-sufficient, Self-sustaining, Sellable, Sensible, Serendipitous, Serious, Service-minded, Service-oriented, Set, Set-up, Settled, Shared, Sharp, Sharp-eyed, Sharp-witted, Shining, Shipshape, Shrewd, Significant,

Skilled, Skillful, Smart, Smooth, Solid, Solid gold, Sought, Sought-after, Sound, Sparkling, Spectacular, Speedy, Spirited, Splendid, Sporting, Sportsmanlike, Spotless, Spot on, Square, Stable, Stabilized, Staid, Stainless, Stalwart, Standard, Standardized, Stand-up, Star, Stately, State-of-the-art, Stationed, Staunch, Steady, Steadfast, Stellar, Sterling, Stick-to-itive, Stipendiary, Straight, Straightforward, Strategic, Strengthening, Strenuous, Strong, Structural, Structured, Studious, Sturdy, Suasive, Suaviloquent, Subsidiary, Substant, Substantial, Substantiated, Substantive, Successful, Succinct, Sufficient, Suitable, Suited, Summary, Sunny, Superabundant, Superb, Superior, Superlative, Supersonic, Supple, Supportive, Sure, Sure-fire, Sure-footed, Sure-handed, Surpassing, Sustained, Sustentative, Swaying, Swift, Synergistic, Systematic, Systematized

Tactful, Tactical, Tailor-made, Take-charge, Talented, Tall, Tangible, Taught, Teachable, Temperate, Tenable, Tenacious, Thorough, Thoroughgoing, Thoughtful, Thriving, Tidy, Tight, Time-honoured, Timely, Timeous, Time-saving, Tip-top, Tireless, Titanic, Top, Top drawer, Top-notch, Tough, Trading, Trail-blazing, Trained, Transformative, Transparent, Transpicuous, Tremendous, Tried, Tried-and-true, Trim, True, Trusted, Trustworthy, Truthful, Twenty-first century, Twenty-four carat

Ultra-precise, Unabashed, Unadulterated, Unambiguous, Unarguable, Unbeatable, Unbeaten, Unbiased, Unblemished, Unbroken, Uncommon, Uncomplicated, Uncompromising, Unconditional, Uncontestable, Uncorrupted, Undamaged, Undauntable, Undaunted, Undefeated, Undeniable, Under control, Understandable, Understanding, Understood, Undiminished, Undisputed, Undivided, Undoubted, Unencumbered, Unequalled, Unequivocable, Unequivocal, Unerring, Unfailing, Unfaltering, Unfaultable, Unfeigned, Unfettered, Unflagging, Unflappable, Unhampered, Unhesitating, Unified, Unimpaired, Unimpeachable, Unimpeded, Unique, Unisonous, Unisonal, Unisonant, United, Unlimited, Unmistakable, Unmitigated, Unobjectionable, Unobstructed, Unobtrusive, Unopposed, Unparalleled, Unprejudiced, Unquestionable, Unrefuted, Unreserved, Unrivalled, Unruffled, Unselfish,

Unshakable, Unshaken, Unspoiled, Unspoilt, Unstoppable, Unsullied, Unsurpassed, Untarnished, Untiring, Untroubled, Unwavering, Unwithdrawing, Up-and-coming, Upbeat, Upbuilding, Upfront, Uppermost, Up-to-date, Upright, Upstanding, Up to par, Up to snuff, Up to speed, Up-to-the-minute, Upwardly, Usable, Useful, User-friendly, Utile, Utile dulci, Utilitarian, Utilizable

Valiant, Valid, Validated, Validating, Validatory, Valuable, Valued, Vehement, Velocious, Vendible, Venerated, Ventorious, Venturesome, Venturous, Veracious, Veridical, Verified, Verifiable, Versatile, Versed in, Vested, Viable, Vibrant, Vigilant, Vigorous, Virtuous, Visionary, Vivid, Vital, Volable

Wanted, Warranted, Weighty, Welcomed, Welcoming, Well-balanced, Well-built, Well-established, Well-disposed, Well-done, Well-founded, Well-informed, Well-kept, Well-known, Well-liked, Well-made, Well-ordered, Well-organized, Well-paying, Well-planned, Well-proportioned, Well-qualified, Well-received, Well-spent, Well-spoken, Well-suited, Well-taught, Well-timed, Well-regulated, Whiz-bang, Whole, Widely used, Winning, Without equal, Without limit, Wired, Wise, Wholesale, Workable, Working, World class, Worthwhile, Worthy

Yare

Zealous, Zestful

Advice to a businessman who was able and capable
of making and keeping friends in every land:

"Do not abuse that ability. Rather let it, the ability, be used as a servant and a service TO those whom the entity contacts, for the entity knows full well that, to self, a handclasp or a smile often changes the whole trend of a day, a week, a year - yea, a life."
(Edgar Cayce Reading 2917-1)

Chapter 4

NOUNS

POSITIVE PERSONAL NOUNS
Positive Nouns that Describe People

"Know the meaning of writing one word that would be helpful to anyone and it'll be helpful to self." (Edgar Cayce Reading 1731-3)

Nouns are often considered to be neutral inasmuch as any one of them could potentially be either good or bad. The nouns listed here have inherent 'normally good' qualities. They're good in absence of an external moral bias.

"I am a(n)... "

Academician, Acceptor, Ace, Ace-in-the-hole, Achiever, Adept, Adherent, Administrator, Admirer, Adorer, Adviser, Advisor, Advocate, Ae, Aelurophile, Aerophile, Aesthete, Aficionada, Aficionado, Affluential, Afrophile, Agent, Aid, Aide, Ailurophile, Alannah, Alleviator, Ally, Almsgiver, Almsperson, Alternate, Altruist, (noun)-aholic [e.g. workaholic], Ambassador, Americophile, Angel, Anglophile, Apostle, Appreciator, Apprentice, Arbiter, Arctophile, Archetype, Architect, Artisan, Artist, Artiste, Ascendant, Aspirant, Asset, Assignee, Assigner, Assistant, Associate, Astrophile, Athlete, Attendant, Audiophile, Author, Authority, Autodidact, Awardee

At the root of the word 'Amateur' is the Latin 'Amat' meaning that an amateur is someone who does something purely for the love of it.

Baby, Backbone, Backer, Backup, Ball of fire, Baron, Beata (female version of:), Beatus, Beau ideal, Beauty, Begetter, Being, Bel-esprit, Believer, Belle, Benchmark, Benefactor, Benefactress, Beneficiary,

Benefit, Bestower, Bibliophile, Big cheese, Big enchilada, Big fish Big gun, Big wheel, Bigwig, Biophile, Blessing, Bodyguard, Bon vivant, Boss, Booster, Brain, Brass, Brother, Bud, Buddy, Buff, Builder, Bundle of energy, Bundle of joy

Campaigner, Captain, Carer, Caretaker, Catalyst, Cause, Celebrant, Celebrator, Center of attention, CEO, CFO, Chair, Chairperson, Chamberlain, Champ, Champion, Chaperon, Charmer, Cherub, Cherisher, Chief, Chieftan, Child, Chum, Cinephile, Clerisy, Climber, Coadjutant, Coadjutor, Cognoscente, Cognoscenti, Cohort, Coiner, Collaborator, Colleague, Collector, Comforter, Commander, Companion, Compeller, Composer, Comrade, Concert pianist, Concierge, Conductor, Confederate, Conferrer, Confidant, Confrere, Connoisseur, Conservator, Consoler, Consul, Consultant, Contributor, Controller, Convive, Cooperator, Cornerstone, Cosmocrat, Cosmopolitan, Cosmopolite, Councilor, Counsel, Counselor, Counsellor, Count, Co-worker, Craftsperson, Creator, Credit, Crew, Cub, Curator, Custodian, Cynosure

Dad, Dancer, Darling, Daughter, Dean, Dear, Defender, Deipnosophist, Designer, Devisee, Devisor, Devotee, Digerati, Dilly, Director, Disciple, Discophile, Discoverer, Distributor, Doer, Doll, Donee, Donor, Doter (rare: Doater), Doozy, Doula, Doyen, Doyenne, Dreamboat, Duke, Dynamo

Eager beaver, Earl, Ecstatic, Einstein, Elder, Employer, Enchanter, Enchantress, Encourager, Endorser, Engineer, Enkindler, Enophile, Ensurer, Entertainer, Enthusiast, Entrepreneur, Epididact, Epicure, Epicurean, Epitome, Ergophile, Escort, Essence, Eudaimonist, Europhile, Example, Exec, Executive, Exemplar, Excellency, Experimenter, Expert, Exponent

Family, Fan, Fancier, Fascinator, Fashioner, Favourite, Fellow worker, Fiancé, Financier, Fireball, Fireman, First in command, Flame, Folks, Foodie, Foodophile, Force, Forebearer, Forefather, Foreman, Forerunner, Foreseer, Foundation, Founder, Fount, Fountain, Fountainhead, Francophile, Friend, Frontrunner

Gabriel, Galanthophile, Gallophile, Gastronome, Gastronomer, Gastronomist, Gem, Generator, Genius, Gentleman, Gentlewoman, Germanophile, Gift, Givee, Giver, Godparent, Godsend, Go-getter, Good egg, Good Samaritan, Good spirit, Good thing, Gourmet, Governor, Grandee, Grantee, Grantor, Grubstaker, Guarantor, Guardian, Guest, Guidance counsellor, Guide, Guru

Handler, Hard worker, Head, Head honcho, Head person, Heart, Heartthrob, Heavy hitter, Heavyweight, Height, Heir, Heiress, Heliophile, Hellenophile, Help, Helper, Helpmate, Heritor (Middle English), Heritress (Middle English), Heritrix (Middle English), Hero, Heroine, Highflier, High-flier, Hippophile, Hispanophile, Hit, Homemaker, Hopeful, Host, Hotshot, House-sitter, Human being, Humanitarian, Humdinger, Husband

Icon, Ideal, Idol, Idolizer, Illuminator, Impetrator, Improvement, Improver, Inamorata, Inamorato, Individual, Indophile, Industrialist, Infant, Influence, Influencer, Influential, Inheritor, Initiator, Innocent, Innovator, Inspiration, Inspirer, Inspiriter, Institutor, Intellect, Intellectual, Intelligentsia, Intimate, Introducer, Inventor, Invitee, Inviter, Iranophile

Japanophile, Jazzophile, Jewel

Keeper, Key, Kingpin, Knight, Knock out

Ladies' man, Lady, Lamb, Latitudinarian, Laureate, Lead, Leader, Leading figure, Leading light, Legatee, Legator, Legend, Legislator, Liberal, Libertarian, Lieutenant, Life-of-the-party, Lightworker, Linguaphile, Little one, Livewire, Live one, Logophile, Lord, Lover, Lulu, Luminary

Maestro, Magician, Magistrate, Majordomo/Major-domo, Maker, Manager, Marquess, Marquis, Marvel, Master, Mastermind, Mate, Materfamilias, Matriarch, Maven, Mediator, Meditator, Meliorist, Memory-maker, Mentor, Metropolitan, Minder, Miracle, Miracle worker, Mitigator, Model, Mom, Monitor, Moppet, Mother, Motivator, Motor, Mover, Mover and shaker, Musicophile, Mycophile

Nabob, Neighbour, Nemophilist, Neophile, Neonate, Neoteric, Nestling, Newborn, Nipper, Nobleman, Nonesuch, No slouch, Notable, Number one, Numero uno, Nurse, Nursling, Nurturer

Object of affection, Oenophile, Officer, Official, Offspring, Omnist, One and only, Operator, Optimist, Orchestrator, Orchidophile, Organizer, Original, Originator, Ornithophile, Overseer, Owner

Pacifier, Pal, Paladin, Pangloss, Pansophist, Paradigm, Paragon, Paramount, Pard, Parent, Participant, Partisan, Partner, Paterfamilias, Pathfinder, Patriarch, Patron, Peach, Peacekeeper, Peacemaker, Pearl, Peer, Percipient, Perfectibilian, Perfectibilist, Perfectionist, Performer, Personality, Pet, Phenom, Phenomenon, Philalethist, Philanthropist, Philogynist, Philomath, Philonoist, Philosopher, Pigsney, Pilot, Pinnacle, Pinup, Pin-up, Pioneer, Pip, Pippin, Pistol, Planner, Player, Playmate, Plum, Pluviophile, Poet, Pogonophile, Policy maker, Polymath, Possessor, Postulant, Potentate, Power broker, Powerhouse, Preceptor, Premier, Presence, Presenter, President, Prevailer, Prime mover, Primogenitor, Prince, Princess, Principal, Pro, Problem-solver, Proconsul, Procreator, Proctor, Prodigy, Producer, Professional, Professor, Progenitor, Progeny, Promoter, Promulgator, Prophet, Propitiator, Proponent, Proposer, Proprietor, Protagonist, Protector, Protégé, Protégée, Provider, Publisher, Purist, Purveyor

Qualtagh

Raconteur, Raconteuse, Rain-maker, Reacher, Receiver, Recipient, Regulator, Rejoicer, Reliever, Representative, Researcher, Resolver, Resource, Retrophile, Rewarder, Right-hand person, Ripsnorter, Role model, Romantic, Romeo, Rooter, Ruler, Runner, Russophile

Sage, Saint, Salt of the earth, Sanctifier, Santa Claus, Savant, Saver, Saviour, Schatzi, Scholar, Scholarch, Scion, Scripter, Sculptor, Secret weapon, Seeker, Self-Starter, Sentinel, Servant, Server, Sharpy, Shaver, Significant other, Sinophile, Sire, Sister, Skipper, Slavophile, Smoothie, Socializer, Socius, Sockdologer, Solon, Something, Something else, Soul, Soul mate,

Sovereign, Spark plug, Specialist, Sponsor, Sprite, Sprout, Squire, Standard, Star, Stipendiary, Straight shooter, Stabilizer, Staker, Steward, Strategist, Striver, Student, Stylist, Success, Successor, Suitor, Superintendent, Superior, Superman, Superstar, Superwoman, Supervisor, Supplier, Support, Supporter, Surety, Survivor, Swain, Swedophile, Sweetheart

Tadpole, Teacher, Teammate, Technophile, a Ten, Testator, Thalassophile, Thaumatologist, Theodidact, Theophilanthropist, Theotokos, Thinker, Titleholder, Tootsie, Top dog, Tot, Trailblazer, Trainer, Treasure, Trier, True love, Trustee, Turophile, Tutor, Tycoon, Typhlophile

Underwriter, Up-and-comer, Upbuilder, Upholder, Urchin

Validator, Valedictorian, Vaulter, Victor, Victress, Victrix, Videophile, Viscount, VIP, Visitor, Visionary, Virtuoso, Volunteer, Votary

Warantor, Warden, Wellspring, Well-wisher, Wheeler and dealer, Whip, Whippersnapper, Whiz, Whiz kid, Whizz, Wife, Winner, Wizard, Wonder, Wooer, Wordsmith, Workhorse, Workmate, Worshiper, Writer, Wunderkind

Youngster, Younker, Youth

Xenophile

Brilliant Things

POSITIVE ABSTRACT NOUNS

"That as the mind dwells upon is builded."
(Edgar Cayce Reading 257-53)

This category has many of the best words. It has wonderfulness.

"I have/am..."

Abidingness, Ability, Absoluteness, Absolution, Abundance, Acceleration, Acceptability, Acceptance, Accessibility, Accession, Acclaim, Acclamation, Accolade, Accommodation, Accomplishment, Accord, Accountability, Accreditation, Accumulation, Accuracy, Ace-in-the-hole, Aceology, Ace up one's sleeve, Achievement, Acknowledgment, Acme, Acquisition, Actability, Action, Activation, Activity, Actuality, Actualization, Acuity, Acumen, Acuteness, Adaptability, Adeptness, Addition, Administration, Admirability, Admirableness, Admiration, Adoration, Adroitness, Adulation, Advancement, Advantage, Adventure, Advice, Advocacy, Aegis, Aesthetic, Affiliation, Afflation, Afflatus, Affability, Affection, Affinity, Affirmation, Affluence, Afterglow, Agape, Agapism, Agelessness, Agency, Agility, Agreeableness, Agreeability, Agreement, (noun)-aholism [ex. workaholism], Aid, Aim, Alacrity, Alertness, Aliveness, Allegiance, Alleviation, Alliance, Allure, Allurement, Alpenglow, Alternative, Altruism, Amalgamation, Amazedness, Amazement, Ambition, Amelioration, Amen, Amenity, Amiability, Amiableness, Amicability, Amity, Amore, Amour-propre, Amusement, Angelocracy, Angelology, Angelus, Animatedness, Animation, Anticipation, Apex, Aplomb, Apogee, Apotheosis, Appeal, Apperception, Appetence, Applause, Appropriateness, Applicability, Application, Appositeness, Appraisal, Appreciation, Appreciativeness, Approbation, Approval, Aptitude, Aptness, Arrangement, Ardency, Ardour, Aristocracy, Armistice, Aroha, Arousal, Arrival, Artfulness, Articulacy, Artistry, Ascension, Ascendancy, Aspiration, Assertiveness, Asset, Assimilation, Assist, Assistance, Association, Assurance, Assuredness, Astonishment, Astrophilia, Astuteness, Ataraxia, Ataraxis, Ataraxy, Atonement,

At-oneness, Attendance, Attention, Attentiveness, Atticism, Attraction, Attractiveness, Aubade, Audiophilia, Augmentation, Augustness, Aureole, Auspiciousness, Augustness, Authentication, Authenticity, Authoritativeness, Authority, Authorization, Autonomy, Avail, Availability, Avidity, Avidness, Awakening, Award, Awareness, Awe, Awesomeness

Backbone, Backing, Badinage, Balance, Bargain, Basiation, Basorexia, Beatitude, Beauty, Beckon, Bedazzlement, Bed of roses, Behoof, Belief, Belonging, Benedicite, Benediction, Benefaction, Beneficence, Benefit, Benevolence, Benevolentness, Benison, Bestowal, Bestowment, Betterment, Bibelot, Bibliophilia, Bibliotherapy, Big deal, Bigheartedness, Bigness, Billet-doux, Biophilia, Blast, Blessing, Blessedness, Bliss, Blissfulness, Blitheness, Blithesomeness, Blossom, Boisterousness, Boldness, Bonanza, Bonhomie, Bonniness, Bon ton, Bonus, Boomlet, Boom, Boon, Boost, Bounce, Bounteousness, Bountifulness, Bounty, Brainchild, Brains, Brass, Braveness, Bravery, Bravura, Break, Breakthrough, Breeze, Breeziness, Breviloquence, Brightness, Bright side, Brilliance, Brio, Briskness, Broadmindedness, Brotherhood, Brotherliness, Bundle, Bullishness, Buoyancy, Buss, Busyness

Cachet, Caliber, Call forth, Calling, Calm, Calmness, Camaraderie, Camelot, Candor, Candour, Canniness, Canorousness, Capability, Capacity, Capital, Captivation, Card up one's sleeve, Care, Carefreeness, Carefulness, Caritas, Carnival, Carrot, Casualness, Catalyst, Causality, Celebration, Celerity, Cerebration, Ceremony, Certainty, Certification, Certitude, Challenge, Championing, Championship, Character, Charisma, Charge, Charitableness, Charity, Charm, Cheer, Cheerfulness, Cheeriness, Chemistry, Chill, Chivalry, Choice, Christmas, Christmastide, Cinch, Cinephilia, Civic-mindedness, Civility, Civilization, Clairvoyance, Clarity, Class, Classic, Classiness, Cleanliness, Clearness, Clemency, Cleverness, Climax, Climb, Closeness, Cloud nine, Clout, Coadjuvancy, Cockaigne, Coequality, Cogence, Cogency, Cognition, Cognizance, Coherence, Collaboration, Collation, Collectedness, Collectivism, Collegiality, Colourfulness, Comedy, Comeliness, Comfort, Comity, Command, Commencement, Commendation,

Commiseration, Commission, Commitment, Communication, Communion, Community, Community-mindedness, Commutuality, Companionship, Compassion, Compassionateness, Compatibility, Compatibleness, Compendiousness, Compensation, Competence, Competency, Complement, Completion, Completeness, Compliment, Composedness, Composition, Composure, Comprehension, Conceivability, Concent, Concentration, Conception, Concertedness, Conciseness, Concision, Concord, Concordance, Concurrence, Conduct, Confelicity, Conferment, Confidence, Confirmation, Congeniality, Congenialness, Congratulation, Congratulations, Congruence, Congruity, Congruousness, Conjunction, Connectedness, Connection, Consanguinity, Conscience, Conscientiousness, Consciousness, Consecration, Consensus, Consent, Consentaneity, Consentience, Consideration, Consistency, Consonance, Constancy, Constructiveness, Consulship, Contemporariness, Contentedness, Contentment, Continuity, Contribution, Control, Convenience, Conversance, Conviction, Convincingness, Conviviality, Coolheadedness, Coolness, Cooperation, Cooperative, Coordination, Copiousness, Cordiality, Cordialness, Cornerstone, Correctness, Corroboration, Cosiness, Cosmolatry, Cosmotheism, Cost-effectiveness, Courage, Courageousness, Courteousness, Courtesy, Courtliness, Cream, Creaminess, Cream of the crop, Creation, Creativeness, Creativity, Cred, Credence, Credentials, Credibility, Credit, Creditableness, Creditability, Crest, Crown, Cuddle, Cuddliness, Culmen, Culmination, Cultivation, Culture, Cure, Cure-all, Curio, Curiosity, Cuteness

Dapperness, Daring, Darling, Dash, Dauntlessness, Dawning, Dazzle, Dazzlement, Debonairness, Dear, Dearness, Decency, Decisiveness, Decorum, Dedication, Deduction, Deepness, Deference, Definiteness, Definitiveness, Deftness, Deity, Deification, Delectableness, Delectation, Delicacies, Delicacy, Deliciousness, Delight, Delightedness, Delightfulness, Deliverance, Demand, Democracy, Dependableness, Dependability, Dessert, Deservedness, Deservingness, Desiderata, Desideratum, Desirability, Desirableness, Detachment, Determination, Determinant, Determinedness, Development, Devotedness, Devotee, Devotion, Devoutness, Dexterity, Dexterousness, Diagnosis, Diagnostics, Dignity, Diligence,

Diplomacy, Direction, Directness, Discernment, Discipline, Discovery, Discreteness, Discretion, Dispassion, Distinction, Distinguishability, Distinguishableness, Distinguishment, Discipline, Dithyramb, Diversity, Dividend, Divinity, Dough, Doughtiness, Doxology, Draw, Dream, Dreaminess, Drive, Drollness, Durability, Duty, Dynamism

Eagerness, Earnestness, Earthiness, Earthliness, Ease, Easiness, Easygoingness, Ebullience, Economy, Ecstasy, Ectropy, Edge, Edification, Education, Effectiveness, Effect, Effectuality, Effectualness, Effervescence, Efficaciousness, Efficacy, Efficiency, Effortlessness, Effulgence, Eirenicon, Élan, Elation, Electuary, Elegance, Elevation, Eligibility, Elite, Eloquence, Elysium, Embrace, Emergence, Eminence, Empathy, Emphasis, Employability, Employment, Empowerment, Empyrean, Emulation, Enablement, Enamouredness, Enchantingness, Enchantment, Encomium, Encouragement, Endearment, Endeavour, Endorsement, Endowment, Endurance, Energization, Energy, Engagement, Engagingness, Engrossingness, Engrossment, Enhancement, Enjoyableness, Enjoyment, Enkindlement, Enlightenment, Enlivenment, Ennoblement, Enophilia, Enough, Enrapturement, Enrichment, Entaxy, Enterprise, Entertainment, Enthrallment, Enthusiasm, Enticement, Entirety, Entrancement, Entrepreneurialism, Entrepreneurship, Entrustment, Environment, Environmentalism, Epicureanism, Epimyth, Epinicion, Epithalamion, Equability, Equality, Equalization, Equanimity, Equilibrium, Equiparation, Equipoise, Equipollence, Equiponderance, Equity, Equivalence, Erudition, Esprit, Esse, Essence, Essentiality, Estate, Esteem, Eternity, Ethicality, Ethicalness, Ethics, Ethography, Etiquette, Eudaimonia, Eudaimonism, Eunoia, Eupathy, Euphony, Euphoria, Eutaxy, Euthenics, Eutrapely, Even-handedness, Evenness, Evocativeness, Evolution, Evolvement, Exactitude, Exactness, Exaltation, Excellence, Excellency, Exceptionality, Exceptionalness, Excitation, Excitement, Exemplariness, Exercise, Exhilaration, Existence, Expansiveness, Expectancy, Expediency, Expedience, Expedition, Expeditiousness, Expergefaction, Experience, Expertise, Expertness, Exploration, Expressiveness, Exquisiteness, Extraordinariness, Extropy, Exuberance, Exuberancy, Exultance, Exultation

Fabulousness, Facilitation, Facility, Fact, Factuality, Factualness, Facundity, Faculty, Fairness, Faith, Faithfulness, Fame, Family, Fancy, Fantasy, Farsightedness, Fascination, Fastness, Favour, Favourability, Favourite, Fearlessness, Feasibility, Feat, Fecundity, Feeling, Felicity, Fellowship, Feminacy, Fertility, Fervour, Festival, Festiveness, Festivity, Fete, Fettle, Fidelity, Finances, Fineness, Finesse, Fire, Fitness, Flair, Flamboyance, Flavour, Flawlessness, Fleetness, Flexibility, Firmness, Fittingness, Flourish, Flow, Fluency, Focus, Foison, Fondness, Forbearance, Foresight, Foreseeability, Foresightedness, Forgiveness, Forthcomingness, Forthrightness, Fortitude, Fortuity, Fortunateness, Fortune, Foundation, Fount, Francophilia, Frankness, Fraternity, Freedom, Freshness, Friendliness, Friendship, Friskiness, Frivolity, Frolic, Frolicsomeness, Fruitfulness, Fruition, Fulfillment, Fullness, Fulgor, Fun, Functionality, Fundament, Funds, Funniness, Furbelow, Furtherance

Gaiety, Gain, Gainfulness, Gallantry, Gallophilia, Galvaniza-tion, Gamesomeness, Gas, Gayness, Gelasin, Gem, Generation, Generativity, Generator, Generosity, Geniality, Genialness, Genius, Gentleness, Genuineness, Germanophilia, Get-up-and-go, Gift, Giftedness, Givingness, Gladness, Gladsomeness, Glamour, Glee, Gleefulness, Glorification, Glory, Glow, Gnosis, Go, Go-ahead, Goal, God, Goddess, Godliness, Good, Good fortune, Good looks, Good nature, Goodness, Good spirit(s), Good thing, Goodwill, Good wishes, Gorgeousness, Government, Grab, Grace, Gracefulness, Graciousness, Gramercy, Grandeur, Grant, Grasp, Gratefulness, Gratification, Gratitude, Gratulation, Gravitas, Gravy, Greatness, Great respect, Green light, Greenness, Greeting, Grin, Grooviness, Growth, Guarantee, Guaranty, Guidance, Gumption, Gusto, Guts, Gutsiness

Habilitation, Haleness, Halo, Hailing, Handiness, Handsomeness, Halcyon, Hallmark, Happiness, Hardihood, Hardiness, Harmlessness, Harmoniousness, Harmony, Headway, Health, Healthiness, Heart, Heartiness, Heartsease, Heartsomeness, Heaven, Heavenliness, Heed, Height, Heliophilia, Hellenophilia, Help, Helpfulness, Henosis, Heroism, Heuristic(s), Hey-day, High, High-mindedness,

High point, High-spiritedness, Hilariousness, Hilarity, Hipness, Hippophilia, Hold, Holdings, Holiness, Homage, Honesty, Honorificabilitudinitatibus, Honorificabilitudinity, Honour, Honouring, Hook, Hoot, Hope, Hopefulness, Hospitableness, Hospitality, Hotness, Hugeness, Humaneness, Humanism, Humanity, Humanitarianism, Humdinger, Humility, Humour, Humourousness, Hurrah, Hygiastics, Hygiene, Hygienics, Hygiology

Iamatology, Icon, Idea, Ideal, Idealism, Idealization, Ideals, Identity, Idol, Idolization, Idoneity, Idoneousness, Illuminati, Illumination, Illustriousness, Imagination, Imitability, Immaculateness, Immanentism, Immediacy, Immensity, Immunity, Impartiality, Impassionedness, Impeccability, Impeccancy, Imperative, Imperturbability, Imperturbation, Impetration, Impishness, Implementation, Import, Importance, Impressiveness, Improvement, Incentive, Inception, Incisiveness, Inclusion, Inclusiveness, Income, Incomparability, Incontestability, Incontrovertibility, Incorruptibility, Incorruption, Increase, Indefatigability, Independence, Indestructability, Indifferentism, Indispensability, Indisputability, Indisturbance, Individuality, Indomitability, Indophilia, Indubitability, Indubitableness, Inducement, Industriousness, Industry, Inerrancy, Inexcitability, Infallibility, Infatuation, Infiniteness, Infinity, Influence, Information, Informativeness, Ingeniousness, Ingenuity, Inheritance, Initiative, Inimitability, Inimitableness, Inner peace, Inner voice, Innocence, Innovation, Innovativeness, Input, Inquisitiveness, Insight, Insightfulness, Inspiration, Inspiritment, Instauration, Instinct, Instruction, Integration, Integrity, Intellect, Intelligence, Intelligentsia, Intensity, Intent, Intentness, Interaction, Interconnectedness, Interconnection, Interdependence, Interest, Interestingness, Intertwinement, Intimacy, Intrepidness, Intrigue, Intuition, Inventiveness, Invigoration, Invincibility, Inviolability, Invitation, Invitingness, Iranophilia, Irenology, Irrefragability, Irrefragableness, Irrefutability, Irreplaceability, Irrepressibility, Irreproachability, Irreproachableness, Irresistibility, Isness, Isonomy, Isopolity, Izzat

Jauntiness, Jazziness, Jest, Jewel, Jnana, Jocosity, Jocularity, Jocundity, Joie de vivre, Joke, Jollies, Jollification, Jolliness, Jollity,

Joviality, Joy, Joyance, Joyfulness, Joyousness, Joy to the world, Jubilance, Jubilation, Jubilee, Judgement, Judiciousness, Juice, Juiciness, Jumboism, Jump, Junction, Jurisdiction, Jurisprudence, Juste-milieu, Justice, Justifiability, Justness

Kairos, Kalon, Keenness, Ken, Key, Key resource, Kick, Kindheartedness, Kindliness, Kindness, Kinship, Kiss, Knack, Knightliness, Know-how, Knowledge, Kudos

Lagniappe, Largeheartedness, Largesse, Lark, Latria, Laudability, Laudation, Laugh, Laughter, Laurels, Lavishness, Law, Lawfulness, Law & order, Lead, Leadership, Learned optimism, Learning, Leave, Leading edge, Leeway, Legality, Legitimacy, Legend, Legerity, Leg-up, Leisure, Lenience, Leniency, Lenity, Lepidity, Level, Levelheadedness, Leverage, Levity, Lexicology, Lexicography, Liberation, Liberty, License, Life, Lifesaver, Lift, Light-heartedness, Lightness, Likeableness, Like-mindedness, Liking, Limberness, Lionheartedness, Literacy, Literati, Litmus test, Liveliness, Living, Lodestone, Logic, Logos, Lollapalooza, Longanimity, Longevity, Lordliness, Lovability, Love, Loveableness, Loveliness, Loving, Loving-kindness, Lovingness, Loyalty, Lucidity, Luck, Lucubration, Lucrativeness, Luminosity, Lusciousness, Lushness, Lustre, Luxury, Luxuriousness

Macarism, Magic, Magistracy, Magistrature, Magnanimity, Magnetics, Magnification, Magnificence, Magnitude, Majesty, Majority, Malleableness, Malleability, Manageability, Manageableness, Management, Mankind, Manifestation, Manliness, Manners, Mansuetude, Manuduction, Manumission,   Marmoreal repose, Marvel, Masterdom, Masterfulness, Materiality, Mastermind, Masterpiece, Mastership, Mastery, Maternity, Maturity, Maximization, Maximum, Meaningfulness, Meditation, Meliorism, Mellifluousness, Mellowness, Mercy, Merit, Merriment, Merriness, Merrymaking, Mesmerism, Metaphysics, Meteor, Method, Methodicalness, Meticulousness, Mettle, Mettlesomeness, Middle way, Might, Mildness, Mind, Mindfulness, Ministration, Ministry, Mint, Mirabilia, Miracle, Mirth, Mirthfulness, Mischief, Mischievousness, Moderateness, Model, Money, Money-maker

Naissance, Name, Nascence/Nascency, Naturalness, Nature, Neatness, Negentropy, Neighbourlikeness, Neighbourliness, Nepenthe, Ne plus ultra, Nest egg, Neutrality, Newness, Niceness, Nicety, Niftiness, Nimbleness, Nirvana, Nisus, Nitency, Nobility, Nobleness, Nocturne, Nod, Noegenesis, Noiselessness, Nonaggression, Nonchalance, Nonviolence, Normalism, Notability, Note, Noteworthiness, Notice, Nothing in excess, Nourishment, Novelty, Novity, Nurture, Nutrication, Nutrition, Nyctophilia

Obeisance, Objectiveness, Objectives, Oblectation, Obligingness, Observation, Oenomel, Oenophilia, Om, Omnism, Oneness, Oneirocriticism, Ongoingness, Oomph, Openness, Open-handedness, Open-heartedness, Opening, Open-mindedness, Ophelimity, Opportunity, Optimism, Optimization, Optimum, Option, Opulence, Order, Orderliness, Origin, Originality, Origination, Orison, Outgoingness, Outspokenness, Outstandingness, Ovation

Pabulum, Pacification, Pacifism, Paean, Painlessness, Panacea, Panache, Panaesthesia, Panaesthetism, Panegyric, Pansophism, Pansophy, Pantheism, Pantisocracy, Paraclete, Paradigm, Paradise, Parage, Paragon, Pardon, Parousia, Partiality, Participation, Pash, Passion, Passiveness, Passivity, Patefaction, Paternity, Pathopoeia, Patience, Patronage, Pay, Payment, Payout, Peace, Peace and quiet, Peaceableness, Peacefulness, Peace of mind, Peach, Peak, Pedagogics, Peerage, Peerlessness, Penchant, Pep, Pepper-upper, Peppiness, Perception, Perceptiveness, Percipience, Perfectibilism, Perfectibility, Perfection, Perfectionism, Performance, Perk, Perkiness, Permission, Perseverance, Persistence, Personableness, Personage, Personality, Persophilia, Perspicacity, Perspicuity, Persuasiveness, Pertinence, Pertness, Phenomena, Phenomenon, Philalethia, Philanthropism, Philanthropy, Philocaly, Philogyny, Philology, Philomathy, Philonoism, Philosophicalness, Philosophy, Philoxenia, Phlegmaticalness, Phlegmaticness, Pick-me-up, Pietism, Piety, Pinnacle, Piousness, Piquancy, Pivot, Pizzazz, Placidity, Placidness, Plan, Plaudit, Play, Playfulness, Pleasantness, Pleasantry, Pleasure, Plenitude, Plenteousness, Plentifulness, Plenty, Pluck, Pluckiness, Plus, Plushness, Pluviophilia, Poignancy, Poiesis, Poise, Polish, Politeness, Polymathy, Popularity, Position, Positive,

Positiveness, Positivity, Possibility, Potency, Potential, Power, Powerfulness, Powerhouse, Practicality, Practice, Praise, Praiseworthiness, Prayer, Prayerfulness, Precedence, Preciousness, Preciseness, Precision, Precosity, Predilection, Predisposition, Predominance, Pre-eminence, Preferability, Preferableness, Preference, Prefulgence, Premium, Premiership, Preparedness, Prepollence, Preponderance, Presence, Presence of mind, Present, Preservation, Presidency, Presidentship (British), Prestige, Prettiness, Prevalence, Prevailing, Prevailingness, Prevision, Prevoyance, Pride, Primitivism, Principle, Principles, Priority, Privacy, Privilege, Prize, Proactiveness, Proactivity, Probity, Procinct, Proclivity, Procurability, Productiveness, Professionalism, Proficiency, Profit, Profitability, Profundity, Profoundness, Properness, Progress, Progression, Prolificacy, Prolificity, Prolific-ness, Prominence, Promise, Promotion, Promptness, Promulgation, Pronoia, Proof, Propensity, Property, Propinquity, Propitiation, Propitiousness, Propriety, Prospects, Prosperity, Prosperousness, Protection, Protectiveness, Protectorate, Protectorship, Prototype, Proudness, Provenance, Provenience, Providence, Provision, Prowess, Proxy, Prudence, Prudency, Public-spiritedness, Pudicity, Punctuality, Pundonor, Pulchritude, Pull, Punch, Punctuality, Purification, Purity, Purpose, Purposefulness

Quaintness, Qualification, Qualifiedness, Quality, Quantity, Quickening, Quickness, Quiescence, Quiescency, Quiet, Quietism, Quietness, Quietude, Quiety, Quintessence, Quixotism

Radiance, Raillery, Raise, Rapidity, Rapport, Rapprochement, Rapture, Rara avis, Rarity, Ratification, Ratiocination, Rationality, Rave, Ravishment, Reach, Reaction, Readiness, Reaffirmation, Realism, Reality, Realization, Realm, Realness, Reason, Reasonability, Reasonableness, Reasoning, Reassurance, Reception, Receptiveness, Recipience, Reciprocity, Recognition, Recommen-dation, Reconciliation, Recovery, Rectification, Rectitude, Rede, Redemption, Refinement, Reflation, Reform, Refresher, Refresh-ment, Refund, Regalement, Regality, Regard, Regardfulness,

Reguerdon, Regularity, Reinforcement, Rejoicing, Rejuvenation, Relaxation, Relaxedness, Release, Relevance, Relevancy, Reliability, Relief, Relish, Remarkableness, Remedy, Remission, Remuneration, Renaissance, Renewal, Renown, Repletion, Republic, Reputability, Reputation, Repute, Requiescence, Rescue, Reserve, Reserves, Resilience, Resolution, Resource, Resources, Resourcefulness, Respect, Respectability, Respectfulness, Respite, Responsibility, Responsiveness, Rest, Restfulness, Restoration, Retention, Retentiveness, Retrocognition, Retrophilia, Return, Revelation, Revelry, Revenue, Reverence, Reverential regard, Reverential wonder, Revival, Revivescence, Revivescency, Reward, Rhapsody, Riches, Richness, Right, Rights, Righteousness, Rightfulness, Right-mindedness, Rightness, Rigorousness, Rise, Risibility, Robustness, Rock solidness, Rollick, Romance, Romanticism, Romp, Rosiness, Royalty, Ruggedness, Rule, Russophilia

Sacredness, Safeness, Safety, Sagaciousness, Sagacity, Sageship, Saintliness, Salad days, Salience, Salubriousness, Salubrity, Salutation, Salutariness, Salvation, Sanctanimity, Sanctification, Sanction, Sanctum, Sangfroid, Sanguineness, Sanguinity, Sapidity, Sapience, Satiation, Satiety, Satisfaction, Satori, Sauciness, Savings, Savoir faire, Savouriness, Savvy, Scholarliness, Scholarship, Science, Scintillation, Scrumptiousness, Scrupulousness, Seamlessness, Seasoning, Security, Securities, Securement, Sedateness, Sedulousness, Seemliness, Selection, Self-acceptance, Self-assertion, Self-assertiveness, Self-assurance, Self-assuredness, Self-composedness, Self-composure, Self-confidence, Self-control, Self-determination, Self-discipline, Self-esteem, Self-expression, Self-forgiveness, Self-help, Selflessness, Self-love, Self-possession, Self-regard, Self-reliance, Self-respect, Self-restraint, Self-satisfaction, Self-sufficiency, Self-sustenance, Self-trust, Self-worth, Sense, Sensation, Sensibility, Sensitivity, Sentiment, Sentimentality, Serendipity, Sereneness, Serenity, Service, Service-mindedness, Seva, Seventh heaven, Shapeliness, Sharing, Sharpness, Sharp-wittedness, Sheltering, Shielding, Shine, Shot in the arm, Shrewdness, Significance, Silence,

Simplicity, Simplification, Sincerity, Sinophilia, Sisterhood, Skill, Skillfulness, Slavophilia, Sleep, Smartness, Smarts, Smile, Smiling, Smoothness, Snazziness, Snuggle, Snuggling, Snugness, Sobriety, Sociability, Social grace, Sociality, Sodality, Softheartedness, Solace, Solidarity, Solid gold, Solidity, Solidness, Sooth, Soothingness, Sophistication, Soul, Soulfulness, Soundlessness, Soundness, Source, Sovereignty, Space, Spark, Sparkle, Sparkles, Specialness, Spectacularism, Spectacularity, Speed, Spice, Spiciness, Spirit, Spiritedness, Spirituality, Splendidness, Splendour, Spontaneity, Sportiveness, Sportsmanship, Spotlessness, Spree, Sprightliness, Spring, Spunk, Stability, Staidness, Stainlessness, Stake, Stalwartness, Standard, Standards, Standing, Start, Starting point, Stateliness, Stature, Status, Staunchness, Steadfastness, Steadiness, Steam, Stick-to-itiveness, Stillness, Stimulant, Stimulation, Stimulus, Stipend, Straightforwardness, Straightness, Strategy, Strength, Strenuousness, Stroke of luck, Studiousness, Stuff, Sturdiness, Style, Stylishness, Suasion, Suavity, Sublimity, Subsidiary, Substance, Substantiality, Substantiation, Subtleness, Success, Successfulness, Succinctness, Succor, Suffisance, Sufficiency, Suitability, Suitableness, Summit, Sumptuousness, Sunniness, Sunshine, Superabilty, Superabundance, Superbness, Superiority, Supplement, Support, Supremacy, Sure-footedness, Sure-handedness, Sureness, Surety, Surprise, Survival, Sustainability, Sustainment, Sustenance, Sustentation, Swankiness, Sway, Sweetener, Sweetening, Sweetheart, Sweetness, Sweven, Swiftness, Sylph, Symbol, Symmetry, Sympathy, Synergy, Syngenesis, Syntropy, Systematization

Speed (aka. Spede) originally meant 'prosperity and/or success and/or rapidity'

Tact, Talent, Tang, Tantalization, Taste, Teamwork, Technophilia, Telegnosis, Telergy, Temper (not "a" temper), Temperance, Temperateness, Tenaciousness, Tenacity, Tenderheartedness, Tenderness, Testamur, Thankfulness, Thanks, Thanksgiving, Thaumatogeny, Thaumatography, Thaumatology, Thaumaturgy, Theanthropism, Theanthroposophy, Theocentrism, Theological virtue, Theopanism, Theopathy, Theophilanthropism, Theopsychism,

Theosophy, Theotherapy, Therapy, Theurgy, Thinkableness, Think tank, Thoroughness, Thoughtfulness, Threpsology, Thrift, Thrill, Thriving, Thumbs-up, Tickle, Tidiness, Timelessness, Timeliness, Tiptop, Tirelessness, Titillation, Togetherness, Tolerance, Top, Touch, Toughness, Traction, Trade, Training, Tranquility, Tranquilness, Transcendence, Transcendentalism, Transfixion, Transformation, Transparency, Transport, Transvolation, Treasure, Treat, Tribute, Triumph, Trophism, Trophy, Trophology, Trouvaille, True love, Trueness, Trump card, Trust, Trustworthiness, Truth, Truthfulness, Tucket, Turn on, Turophilia, Tutelage

Uberty, Ubiquitousness, Ubiquity, Ubuntu, Unaffectedness, Understandability, Understanding, Unexcitability, Unfailingness, Unflappability, Unicity, Unification, Uniqueness, Union, Unison, Unity, Universalism, Unreservedness, Unruffledness, Unselfishness, Untroubledness, Upgrade, Uplift, Upper hand, Uprightness, Upside, Upstandingness, Upwardness, Usability, Use, Usefulness, Utility, Utilization, Utopia

Valiance, Validity, Validation, Valour, Valuation, Value, Values, Variety, Vehemence, Velocity, Veneration, Venture, Venturesomeness, Venturousness, Veracity, Veraciousness, Verdancy, Veridicality, Verification, Verity, Vernality, Versatility, Vertex, Verve, Viability, Vibrancy, Victoria, Victory, Vigilance, Vigorousness, Vigour, Vim, Virtu, Virtue, Virtuousness, Virtuosity, Vision, Vitalism, Vitality, Vitalization, Vivaciousness, Vivacity, Vivat, Vivency, Vividness, Vivification, Volition, Voluptuousness, Volupty, Vow, Vraisemblance

Walk, Warmheartedness, Warmth, Warrant, Warranty, Ways, Ways and means, Weal, Wealth, Weight, Weightiness, Welcome, Welcomeness, Welfare, Wellbeing, Wellness, What it takes, Wherewithal, Whimsy, Wholeness, Wholeheartedness, Wholesomeness, Whole-spiritedness, Will, Willingness, Win, Windfall, Winningness, Winning(s), Winsomeness, Wish, Wisdom, Wit, Witticism, Wittiness, Womanliness, Wonder, Wonderfulness, Wonderment, Wonderwork, Wondrousness, Woodnote, Word, Worldliness, Work, Workability, Working, Worship, Worth, Worthiness, Wow

Xenophilia, Xenophily

Yen, Youthquake

Zaniness, Zap, Zeal, Zealousness, Zenith, Zest, Zestfulness, Zestiness, Zing, Zip, Zoomagnetism

Natural Depression Therapies
Including all of Edgar Cayce's

POSITIVE NOUNS THAT DESCRIBE MOM
All the jobs that mothers perform

"Know that the purpose for which each soul enters a material experience is that it may be as a light unto others..."
(Edgar Cayce Reading 641-6)

Acceptor, Ace-in-the-hole, Achiever, Adherent, Administrator, Admirer, Adorer, Adviser, Advisor, Advocate, Agent, (noun)-aholic [e.g. workaholic], Aide, Alleviator, Ally, Altruist, Appreciator, Arbiter, Archetype, Asset, Assistant, Attendant, Authority

Baby sitter, Backer, Backup, Begetter, Being, Believer, Benchmark, Benefactor, Benefactress, Benefit, Bestower, Big wheel, Blessing, Bodyguard, Booster, Boss, Bundle of energy, Builder

Caretaker, Carrier, Catalyst, Cause, Chambermaid, Chaperon, Chauffer, Cheer leader, Chef, Cleaning lady, Coadjutant, Collaborator, Comforter, Commander, Companion, Confidant, Conservator, Consoler, Consultant, Contributor, Controller, Cook, Cooperator, Cornerstone, Counsel, Counsellor, Counselor, Creator, Custodian

Dear, Defender, Deipnosophist, Devotee, Director, Doer, Domestic, Donor, Driver, Dynamo

Economist, Elder, Encourager, Endorser, Enthusiast, Escort, Eudaimonist, Example, Exemplar, Experimenter, Expert, Exponent

Family, Financier, Fireball, First in command, Force, Forebearer, Forerunner, Foundation, Fount, Fountain, Fountainhead, Friend

Gem, Generator, Gentlewoman, Gift, Gift-Giver, Giver, Godsend, Go-getter, Good egg, Good Samaritan, Good spirit, Good thing, Grantor, Grubstaker, Guarantor, Guardian, Guidance counsellor, Guide, Guru

Handler, Hard worker, Head, Heart, Help, Helper, Heroine, Homemaker, Host, House keeper, Housewife, Human being, Humanitarian

Icon, Ideal, Individual, Influence, Initiator, Innovator, Inspiration, Institutor, Introducer, Inviter

Jewel

Lady, Leader, Leading light, Liberal, Lightworker, Lover, Luminary

Ma, Ma-ma, Maid, Maker, Manager, Marvel, Mater familias, Matriarch, Mediator, Meliorist, Memory-maker, Mentor, Minder, Miracle, Miracle worker, Mom, Mommy, Monitor, Mother, Motor, Motivator, Mover, Mum, Mummy

Nonesuch, No slouch, Number one, Numero uno, Nurse, Nursemaid

Object of affection, Oenophile, One and only, Operator, Optimist, Orchestrator, Organizer, Original, Originator, Overseer

Pacifier, Paradigm, Paragon, Parent, Participant, Pathfinder, Patron, Peacekeeper, Peacemaker, Pearl, Perfectibilian, Perfectibilist, Perfectionist, Personality, Phenom, Phenomenon, Philalethist, Planner, Playmate, Policy maker, Predecessor, Presence, Presenter, Prime mover, Primogenitor, Problem-solver, Producer, Progenitor, Promoter, Promulgator, Proponent, Proposer, Proprietor, Protagonist, Protector, Provider, Purist, Purveyor

Reader, Referee, Regulator, Reliever, Resource, Right-hand person, Role model, Rooter, Runner

Saint, Salt of the earth, Saver, Saviour, Scripter, Sculptor, Self-starter, Sentinel, Servant, Server, Something, Something else, Soul, Sponsor, Stabilizer, Standard, Star, Straight shooter, Stipendiary, Strategist, Staker, Stylist, Superstar, Supervisor, Superwoman, Supplier, Support, Supporter

Teacher, Testator, Thinker, Transporter, Trainer, Treasure, Tutor

Underwriter, Upbuilder, Upholder

Validator, VIP, Visionary, Volunteer

Wellspring, Well-wisher, Wife, Winner, Wizard,
Woman, Wonder, Workhorse

ROMANTIC NOUNS

Abidingness, Acceptance, Accord, Acknowledgement, Admiration, Admirer, Adoration, Adulation, Advantage, Affability, Affection, Affinity, Agreeability, Agreeableness, Allegiance, Alleviation, Alliance, Allure, Allurement, Amiability, Amiableness, Amicability, Amicableness, Amore, Amour-propre, Aperitive, Appeal, Appetence, Appositeness, Appreciation, Appreciativeness, Aroha, Assistance, Assisting, Attachment, Attentiveness, Attraction, At-oneness, Avidity, Avidness

Balloons, Beau, Beau ideal, Beauty, Beckoning, Bee's knees, Beguin, Belle, Belonging, Benefit, Betrothal, Bigheartedness, Billet-doux, Blast, Bliss, Blissfulness, Blitheness, Blithesomeness, Bonniness, Boost, Bouquet, Boyfriend, Brightness, Bright side, Buoyancy

Candles, Candlelight, Candy, Captivation, Care, Caress, Caressing, Cavalier, Celebration, Cheer, Cheerfulness, Cheeriness, Chemistry, Chocolate(s), Choice, Cloud Nine, Cognizance, Comfort, Commiseration, Commitment, Communion, Companionship, Compassion, Compassionateness, Compatibility, Completion, Condolence, Connection, Consideration, Consonance, Contentedness, Contentment, Conviviality, Cooperation, Courtship, Corsage, Crush, Cuddle, Cuddling

Date, Deference, Delight, Delightedness, Delightfulness, Desiderata, Desirableness, Devotedness, Devotion, Diversion, Draw

Eagerness, Ebullience, Effervescence, Elan, Elation, Elevation, Embrace, Embracing, Emotion, Empathy, Enamouredness, Enchantment, Endearment, Engagingness, Enjoyableness, Enjoyment, Enlivenment, Enthrallment, Enthusiasm, Euphoria, Exaltation, Excitation, Exhilaration, Exuberance, Exultance, Exultation

Faithfulness, Fancy, Favour, Favourite, Feeling, Felicity, Fiancé, Fidelity, Flame, Flight, Flirtation, Flirting, Flowers, Fondness, Forbearance, Forget-me-not, Forgiveness, Fortunateness, Friendliness, Friendship, Frivolity, Frolic, Fulfillment, Fun

Gaiety, Gayness, Generosity, Geniality, Gentleness, Gifting, Gift basket, Gifts, Girlfriend, Giving, Gladness, Gladsomeness, Glee, Gleefulness, Glow, Good, Good fortune, Good spirits, Good wishes, Goodness, Goodwill, Graciousness, Gratification, Gusto

Happiness, Harmony, Heart, Heaven, Helpfulness, Helping, High, Hold, Honour, Hoot, Hug, Hugging, Humour

Ideal, Impassionedness, Impulse, Increase, Infatuation, Insouciance, Inspiration, Inspiriter, Inspiritment, Interest, Intoxication, Intrigue, Invitation, Invitingness, Involvement,

Jewellery, Jocosity, Jocularity, Jocundity, Joie de Vivre, Jollification, Jolliness, Jollity, Joviality, Joy, Joyance, Joyfulness, Joyousness, Jubilance, Jubilation

Kairos, Keenness, Kindheartedness, Kindness, Kinship, Kiss, Kissing

Largeheartedness, Largesse, Laughs, Laughter, Lenience, Leniency, Lenity, Levity, Liaison, Lift, Lightheartedness, Like, Like-mindedness, Liking, Liveliness, Lollapalooza, Love, Loveableness, Lover, Loving, Love story

Magnanimity, Magnetization, Merriment, Merriness, Merrymaking, Mirth, Mirthfulness, Mindset, Mood, Motivation, Mutuality

Nestle, Nestler, Nourishment, Nurture, Nurturing, Nuzzle, Nuzzler,

Oneness, Optimism

Paradise, Partiality, Pash, Penchant, Pep, Peppiness, Perkiness, Philogyny, Pigsney, Play, Playfulness, Pleasantness, Poem, Poetry, Preciousness, Predilection, Predisposition, Preference, Preoccupation, Priority, Propensity, Pursuance, Pursuit

Quality, Quintessence

Rapport, Reaction, Real deal, Reciprocity, Recognition, Regard, Regardfulness, Relation, Relationship, Relish, Relishing, Rendezvous, Rendezvousing, Repletion, Respect, Responsiveness, Revellings, Revelry, Reverence, Rhapsody, Rollick, Rollicking, Romance, Romanticism, Roses, Rosiness

Sanction, Satiety, Satisfaction, Schatzi, Selection, Sensation, Sensing, Sentiment, Sentimentality, Service, Seventh heaven, Sharing, Sheltering, Shielding, Sincerity, Singing telegram, Snuggle, Snuggling, Softheartedness, Soft spot, Solicitude, Solidarity, Spa day gift, Spark, Sparkle, Spice, Spiciness, Spirit, Spiritedness, Sprightliness, Steadfastness, Suitor, Sunshine, Support, Sweetener, Sweetening, Sweetness, Sympathizing, Sympathy

Tang, Tenderheartedness, Tenderness, Thoughtfulness, Thrill, Tickle, Togetherness, Tolerance, Transport, Treasure, Treat, Trust, Truth, Twitterpation

Understanding, Unfailingness, Union, Unison, Unity, Uplift, Utopia

Valentine, Valuation, Value, Vehemence, Verve, Vigour, Vim, Vitality, Vitalization, Vivaciousness, Vivacity, Vivification

Warmheartedness, Warmth, Welcome, Well-being, Whimsy, Wholeheartedness

Yearning, Yen

Zeal, Zest, Zestfulness, Zing, Zip

PET NAMES

Angel, Angle eyes, Angelface

Baboo, Babycakes, Baby doll, Bambi, Blossom, Boo-boo bear, Bright (or eye colour) eyes, Bunny, Buttercup, Butterfly

Care bear, Chickadee, Chipmunk, Chocolate drop, Cookie, Cuddle bear, Cuddle bunny, Cuddles, Cuddly-wuddly, Cupcake, Cutie-patootie, Cutiepie, Cuteness, Crumpet

Darling, Dew drop, Dimples, Doodlebug, Duckling, Dumpling

Firecracker

Glitter bug, Googly bear, Gum drop, Gummy bear

Honey, Honey bear, Honey bunch, Honey-bunny, Honey buns, Honey lips, Honey muffin, Honey pie, Honey plum

Kissyface, Kitten, Kitty-cat

Lamb chop, Lambkin, Lemon drop, Little strudel, Lollipop, Love bird, Love bug, Love muffin, Love nugget, Lovey dove

Muffin, Munchkin

Peaches, Pookie, Poopsy, Precious, Princess, Pudin', Punkin', Pussycat

Schatzi, Shmoopsiepoo, Smoochy-poo, Snickerdoodle, Snookums, Snugglebunny, Sparkles, Squishybaby, Sugar cookie, Sugarlips, Sugarplum, Sun beam, Sunshine, Sweetheart, Sweet cheeks, Sweetyface, Sweetypie

Tater tot, Teddybear, Toots, Tootsie, Turtledove, Twinkles, Treasure

Wiggles

POSITIVE BUSINESS NOUNS

Personal & Abstract

Personal Nouns

Academician, Ace, Ace-in-the-hole, Achiever, Adept, Adherent, Administrator, Advantage, Adviser, Advisor, Advocate, Aficionada, Aficionado, Affluential, (noun)-aholic [ex. workaholic], Aid, Aide, Alleviator, Ally, Ambassador, Appreciator, Apprentice, Arbiter, Artisan, Artist, Ascendant, Aspirant, Asset, Assignee, Assigner, Assistant, Associate, Author, Authority, Autodidact, Awardee

Backbone, Backer, Backup, Ball of fire, Begetter, Bel-esprit, Benefactor, Benefactress, Beneficiary, Benefit, Bestower, Big cheese, Big enchilada, Big fish, Big gun, Big wheel, Bigwig, Boss, Booster, Brain(s), Brass, Builder, Bundle of energy

Campaigner, Captain, Carer, Caretaker, Catalyst, CEO, CFO, Chair, Chairperson, Champ, Champion, Chaperon, Charmer, Chief, Chieftan, Climber, Coadjutant, Cognoscente, Cognoscenti, Collaborator, Colleague, Commander, Companion, Compeller, Complement, Composer, Comrade, Conductor, Confederate, Conferrer, Confidant, Confrere, Connoisseur, Conservator, Consul, Consultant, Contributor, Controller, Cooperator, Cornerstone, Cosmopolitan/Cosmopolite, Councillor, Counsel, Counsellor, Counselor, Co-worker, Craftsperson, Creator, Credit, Crew, Curator, Custodian, Cynosure

Defender, Designer, Devisee, Devisor, Devotee, Digerati, Director, Discoverer, Distributor, Doer, Donee, Donor, Doyen/Doyenne, Dynamo, Dynamite

Eager beaver, Elder, Employer, Encourager, Endorser, Engineer, Entrepreneur, Ensurer, Epididact, Epitome, Ergophile, Essence, Example, Exec, Executive, Exemplar, Experimenter, Expert, Exponent

Fashioner, Favourite, Fellow worker, Financier, Fireball, First in command, Force, Forebearer, Forefather, Foreman, Forerunner, Foreseer, Foundation, Founder, Fount, Fountain, Fountainhead

Generator, Gem, Genius, Gentleman, Gentlewoman, Gift, Giver, Godsend, Go-getter, Good egg, Governor, Grantee, Grantor, Grubstaker, Guarantor, Guardian, Guest, Guide

Handler, Hard worker, Head, Head honcho, Head person, Heart, Heavy hitter, Heavyweight, Height, Heir, Heiress, Help, Helper, Helpmate, Heritor (Middle English), Heritress (Middle English), Heritrix (Middle English), Hero, Heroine, Highflier, High-flier, Hit, Host, Hotshot, Humanitarian, Hustler

Icon, Ideal, Illuminator, Improvement, Individual, Industrialist, Influence, Influential, Inheritor, Initiator, Innovator, Inspiration, Inspirer, Inspiriter, Institutor, Intellect, Intellectual, Intelligentsia, Introducer, Inventor, Invitee, Inviter

Keeper, Key, Kingpin

Lead, Leader, Leading figure, Leading light, Legatee, Legator, Legend, Legislator, Liberal, Libertarian, Lieutenant, Luminary

Maestro, Magician, Majordomo/Major-domo, Maker, Manager, Marvel, Master, Mastermind, Maven, Mediator, Meliorist, Mentor, Metropolitan, Minder, Mitigator, Model, Monitor, Motor, Mover, Mover and shaker, Motivator

Neoteric, Notable, No slouch, Number one, Numero uno, Nurturer

Officer, Official, One and only, Operator, Optimist, Orchestrator, Organizer, Original, Originator, Overseer, Owner

Pacifier, Paradigm, Paragon, Paramount, Participant, Partisan, Partner, Pathfinder, Patriarch, Patron, Peacekeeper, Peacemaker, Peer, Perfectibilian, Perfectibilist, Perfectionist, Performer, Personality, Phenom, Phenomenon, Philanthropist, Pilot, Pioneer, Player,

Pistol, Planner, Plum, Poet, Policy maker, Possessor, Postulant, Potentate, Power broker, Powerhouse, Premier, Presence, Presenter, President, Prevailer, Prime mover, Principal, Pro, Problem-solver, Proconsul, Proctor, Prodigy, Producer, Professional, Promoter, Promulgator, Proponent, Proposer, Proprietor, Protagonist, Protean, Protector, Protégé, Protégée, Provider, Publisher, Purist, Purveyor.

Rain-maker, Reacher, Receiver, Recipient, Regulator, Reliever, Representative, Researcher, Resolver, Resource, Rewarder, Right-hand person, Role model, Rooter

Sage, Salt of the earth, Saver, Saviour, Savant, Scholar, Scripter, Secret weapon, Self-starter, Sentinel, Servant, Server, Solon, Specialist, Sponsor, Stabilizer, Staker, Standard, Star, Steward, Stipendiary, Straight shooter, Strategist, Striver, Student, Success, Successor, Superintendent, Superior, Superman, Superstar, Superwoman, Supervisor, Supplier, Support, Supporter, Surety, Survivor

Teacher, Teammate, a 10, Thinker, Think, Titleholder, Top dog, Trailblazer, Trainer, Trustee, Tutor, Tycoon

Underwriter, Up-and-comer, Upbuilder, Upholder

Validator, Vaulter, Vice president, Victor, Victress, Victrix, VIP, Virtuoso, Visitor, Visionary, Volunteer

Warantor, Wellspring, Well-wisher, Wheeler and dealer, Whip, Whiz, Whiz kid, Whizz, Winner, Wizard, Wonder, Wordsmith, Workhorse, Workmate, Writer, Wunderkind.

Abstract Nouns

Ability, Abundance, Acceleration, Acceptability, Acceptance, Accessibility, Accommodation, Accomplishment, Accord, Accountability, Accreditation, Accumulation, Accuracy, Achievement, Acknowledgement, Acme, Acquisition, Actability, Activity, Actuality, Actualization, Acuity, Acumen, Adaptability, Addition, Adeptness, Administration, Admirability, Admirableness, Admiration,

Advancement, Advantage, Aegis, Affiliation, Afflation, Agency, Agility, Agreement, (noun)-aholism [e.g. workaholism], Amalgamation, Aplomb, Apogee, Apotheosis, Appraisal, Appreciation, Approachability, Approbation, Appropriateness, Approval, Aptness, Ardency, Arrangement, Arrival, Artfulness, Articulacy, Ascendancy, Aspiration, Assertiveness, Assets, Assiduousness, Assistance, Association, Assurance, Assurgency, Astuteness, Ataraxia, Ataraxis, Ataraxy, Attentiveness, Augustness, Authentication, Authenticity, Authority, Authorization, Avidness, Awareness

Backbone, Backing, Balance, Ball of fire, Benchmark, Beneficence, Benefit, Betterment, Bigness, Blockbuster, Blue Ribbon, Boldness, Bonanza, Bonus, Boom, Boomlet, Boon, Bounty, Business, Busyness, Brainchild, Brains, Brass, Braveness, Brightness, Brilliance, Bullishness, Bundle, Buoyancy, Bustle

Cachet, Caliber, Calm, Calmness, Canniness, Capability, Capacity, Capital, Care, Carefulness, Carrot, Celerity, Center, Centrality, Certainty, Certification, Certitude, Championing, Championship, Charisma, Civic-mindedness, Civility, Civilization, Clarity, Class, Clear-headedness, Clemency, Cleverness, Climb, Coadjuvancy, Coequality, Cogence, Cognizance, Coherence, Collaboration, Collation, Collection, Collegiality, Comity, Command, Commendation, Commerce, Commerciality, Commercialization, Commitment, Communication, Community-mindedness, Commutuality, Compatibility, Compatibleness, Compendiousness, Compensation, Competence, Competency, Complement, Composure, Comprehension, Concertedness, Conscientiousness, Conciseness, Concord, Concordance, Conduciveness, Conferment, Conferral, Confidence, Confirmation, Congeniality, Congruousness, Conjunction, Connection, Conscientiousness, Consentaneity, Consentience, Consideration, Consistency, Consolidation, Consonance, Constancy, Construction, Constructiveness, Consumption, Contemporariness, Continuity, Contribution, Control, Conversance, Conversation, Conviction, Convincingness, Cooperation, Coordination, Copiousness, Corporation, Correctness, Corroboration, Cost-effectiveness, Courage, Courageousness, Courtesy, Creation, Creativity, Credence,

Credentials, Credibility, Credit, Cultivation, Culture, Cumulation, Currency, Cycle

Dauntlessness, Decency, Decisiveness, Dedication, Deduction, Definiteness, Definitiveness, Deftness, Demand, Department, Dependability, Dependableness, Design, Desirability, Destiny, Determination, Development, Devotion, Dexterity, Diagnosis, Diagnostics, Dignity, Diligence, Diplomacy, Direction, Directness, Discernment, Discipline, Discreteness, Discretion, Discrimination, Dispassion, Distinction, Distinguishability, Distinguishableness, Distinguishment, Distinguisher, Distinguishment. Discipline, Diversity, Dividend, Doughtiness, Drive, Durability, Duty, Dynamics, Dynamite

Eagerness, Earnestness, Eco-friendliness, Economics, Economy, Edification, Education, Effectiveness, Effectuality, Efficaciousness, Efficiency, Electricity, Electrification, Eloquence, Emergence, Eminence, Empirical, Employability, Employment, Enactment, Encouragement, Endorsement, Endurance, Energy, Energization, Engagement, Engagingness, Enkindlement, Enlightenment, Enrichment, Enterprise, Enthusiasm, Entrepreneurship, Entrustment, Environment, Environmentalism, Equableness, Equality, Equalization, Equanimity, Equanimousness, Equitableness, Erudition, Essentiality, Establishment, Esteem, Estimableness, Ethics, Eutaxy, Evenhandedness, Exactitude, Excellence, Exceptionality, Exemplariness, Expedience, Expeditiousness, Experience, Expertise, Expertness, Extraordinariness, Exuberance

Facilitation, Fact, Fairness, Faithfulness, Farsightedness, Fastness, Favour, Favourability, Fearlessness, Feasibility, Fecundity, Fertility, Finance, Firm, Firmness, Fittingness, Flawlessness, Flourish, Fluency, Focus, Forbearance, Foresightedness, Formality, Formidableness, Forthcomingness, Forthrightness, Fortification, Fortitude, Fortuity, Fortune, Foundation, Frankness, Freshness, Friendliness, Fruitfulness, Functionality, Fundament

Gain, Gainfulness, Galvanization, Generation, Generativity, Genuineness, Get-up-and-go, Gift, Go, Go-ahead, Goal, Gold,

Good, Goodness, Gravitas, Greenness, Growth, Guaranty, Guide, Guidance, Gumption, Gutsiness

Handiness, Hardiness, Harmony, Harmoniousness, Heartiness, Health, Heed, Helpfulness, Henosis, Heuristic, Honesty, Honour, Hugeness, Humanitarianism

Idoneity, Idoneousness, Imagination, Imitability, Imitableness, Immaculateness, Immediacy, Immensity, Impartiality, Impeccability, Impeccancy, Imperative, Imperturbability, Importance, Impressiveness, Improvement, Incisiveness, Inclusion, Income, Incomparability, Incontestability, Incontrovertibility, Incorporation, Incorruptibility, Incorruption, Increase, Indefatigability, Independence, Indispensability, Indisputability, Indomitability, Indubitability, Indubitableness, Inducement, Industriousness, Industry, Inerrancy, Inexhaustibility, Information, Informativeness, Influence, Ingeniousness, Inimitability, Initiative, Innovation, Innovativeness, Inquisitiveness, Insightfulness, Inspiration, Inspiritment, Institution, Instruction, Instrumentality, Insurance, Integrality, Integration, Integrity, Intellect, Intellectuality, Intelligence, Intensity, Intensification, Intent, Interconnectedness, Interconnection, Interdependence, Intrepidness, Intrigue, Inventiveness, Investigation, Investment, Invigoration, Irrefragability, Irrefragableness, Irrefutability, Irrepressibility, Irreproachability, Irreproachableness

Joint venture, Judiciousness, Junction, Justice, Justness, Justifiability

Keenness, Key, Kinetics, Know-how, Knowledge

Laudation, Lawfulness, Lead, Leading edge, Learning, League, Legality, Level, Likableness, Like-mindedness, Location, Logic, Longanimity, Lucrativeness

Magnetics, Majority, Major league, Malleability, Malleableness, Manageability, Manageableness, Management, Manifestation, Marketability, Mastery, Materiality, Maximization, Maximum, Meaning, Meaningfulness, Measure, Merchandising, Merit,

Meteor, Method, Methodicalness, Meticulousness, Mettle, Mettle-someness, Mindfulness, Mitigation, Model, Modernity, Money, Money-maker, Morale, Morality, Morals, Motivation, Mutuality

Neatness, Need, Ne plus ultra, Nimbleness, Nobility, Nobleness, Notability, Noteworthiness, Novelty

Objectives, Objectivity, Obligingness, Observation, Office, Ongoingness, Open-mindedness, Openness, Operation, Opportunity, Optimism, Optimization, Optimum, Order, Organization, Originality, Origination, Outspokenness, Outstandingness

Painstakingness, Paradigm, Paragon, Paramountcy, Pardon, Participation, Particularity, Patience, Peak, Peerlessness, Penetration, Perception, Percipience, Performance, Perseverance, Persistence, Personableness, Perspicacity, Perspicuousness, Persuasion, Persuasiveness, Pertinence, Philanthropy, Phlegmaticalness, Phlegmaticness, Pivot, Plan, Pleasantness, Plenaries, Plenitude, Plenteousness, Plentifulness, Plenty, Pluck, Pluckiness, Plus, Poise, Polish, Politeness, Popularity, Positiveness, Possibility, Potency, Potential, Power, Practicability, Practicality, Practice, Pragmatism, Praise, Praiseworthiness, Precision, Predominance, Pre-eminence, Preferability, Preferableness, Premiership, Premium, Preparedness, Preponderance, Presence, Presidency, Prevailingness, Prevalence, Pride, Principal, Priority, Proactiveness, Proactivity, Probability, Probity, Procurability, Prodigiousness, Productiveness, Professionalism, Proficiency, Profit, Profitability, Progress, Progression, Prolificacy, Prolificity, Prolific-ness, Promise, Promotion, Promptness, Proof, Properness, Property, Propitiousness, Propriety, Propulsion, Prospects, Prosperity, Prosperousness, Protectiveness, Provision, Prudence, Prudency, Public-spiritedness, Punch, Punchiness, Punctuality, Punctilious-ness, Purity, Purification, Purpose, Purposefulness

Quantity, Qualification, Quality, Quickness

Rapidity, Rapport, Rapprochement, Ratheness, Ratification, Ratio-cination, Rationality, Razor-sharpness, Reach, Readiness, Realism,

Realization, Reason, Reasonableness, Reasonability, Reasoning, Reassurance, Receptiveness, Recipience, Reciprocity, Recognition, Recommendation, Refinement, Regularity, Regulation, Relevance, Reliability, Remarkableness, Remuneration, Repletion, Reputation, Resilience, Resolution, Resourcefulness, Resources, Respect, Respectability, Respectfulness, Responsibility, Responsiveness, Retail, Retention, Reward, Rewardableness, Revenue, Riches, Righteousness, Rightfulness, Right-mindedness, Rigorousness, Robustness, Rock solidness, Rootedness, Ruggedness

Safety, Saleability, Salubriousness, Salubrity, Salutariness, Sanction, Sangfroid, Sanguineness, Sanguinity, Satisfaction, Savvy, Scholarliness, Science, Scrupulousness, Seamlessness, Seasoning, Securement, Security, Sedulousness, Selection, Self-assertiveness, Self-assuredness, Self-confidence, Self-discipline, Self-sufficiency, Self-sustenance, Sensibility, Service, Service-mindedness, Share, Sharpness, Sharp-wittedness, Shine, Shrewdness, Significance, Skill, Skillfulness, Smartness, Smoothness, Solidness, Solid gold, Soundness, Sparkle, Speed, Spirit, Sportsmanship, Spotlessness, Stability, Staidness, Stainlessness, Stalwartness, Standard, Standardization, Standing, Stateliness, Station, Staunchness, Steadiness, Steadfastness, Stick-to-itiveness, Stipend, Straightforwardness, Straightness, Strategy, Strength, Strenuousness, Structure, Studiousness, (right) Stuff, Sturdiness, Suasion, Subsidiary, Substance, Substantiality, Substantiation, Success, Successfulness, Succinctness, Sufficiency, Suitability, Suitableness, Sum, Superabundance, Superbness, Superiority, Superlative, Suppleness, Support, Sureness, Surety, Sure-footedness, Sure-handedness, Sustainment, Sustenance, Sustentation, Sway, Swiftness, Synergy, Systematization

Tact, Tactic, Talent, Tangibility, Teaching, Teamwork, Temper (not "a" temper), Temperateness, Tenability, Tenaciousness, Tenacity, Think tank, Thoroughness, Thoughtfulness, Thriving, Tidiness, Tightness, Timeliness, Tirelessness, Top, Toughness, Trade, Training, Transformation, Transparency, Transport, Tremendousness, Trimness, Trust, Trustworthiness, Truth, Truthfulness, Trying, Tour de force, Tutelage

Understandability, Understanding, Uniqueness, Unison, Unity, Uprightness, Upstandingness, Usability, Usefulness, User-friendliness, Utilitarianism, Utility, Utilization

Valiance, Validity, Validation, Valuation, Value, Values, Vehemence, Velocity, Vendibles, Venture, Venturesomeness, Venturousness, Veraciousness, Veracity, Veridicality, Verification, Versatility, Vertex, Verve, Viability, Vibrancy, Vigilance, Vigorousness, Virtuosity, Vision, Vitality, Vivency, Vividness

Warranty, Ways and means, Wealth, Weight, Welcome, What it takes, Wherewithal, Wholeness, Wholesale, Windfall, Winningness, Winning(s), Wisdom, Work, Workability, Worthiness

Xenophilia, Xenophily

Zeal, Zest

Edgar Cayce's Association
This book has no direct affiliation.

Chapter 5

POSITIVE RESUME' VERBS

Among a person's many skills and abilities from previous jobs, or transferable from life, can be found vibrant self-motivated action words; a human resource that can make a job resume more attractive. Starting each sentence of a resume's *Experience* section with these eye-catching positive past tense verbs can make statements resonate better as employer touchstones.

"Let thy light so shine that others seeing thy good work may take hope again."
(Edgar Cayce Reading 254-101)

"I..."

Absorbed, Accelerated, Accepted, Accessed, Acclimated, Accommodated, Accomplished, Accorded, Accrued, Acculturated, Accumulated, Accustomed, Achieved, Acquainted, Acquired, Acted, Activated, Actualized, Actuated, Adapted, Added, Added to, Addressed, Adjusted, Administered, Administrated, Admired, Adopted, Advanced, Advantaged, Advertised, Advised, Affiliated, Affirmed, Agglomerated, Aggregated, Agreed, Aided, Alerted, Alleviated, Allotted, Allowed, Altered, Amalgamated, Amassed, Amazed, Ameliorated, Amplified, Analyzed, Animated, Announced, Anticipated, Applied, Appointed, Appraised, Appreciated, Apprised, Approbated, Approached, Approved, Arbitrated, Aroused, Arranged, Arrested, Arrived, Ascertained, Assented, Assembled, Assessed, Assigned, Assisted, Assuaged, Assumed, Assured, Astounded, (Ate, slept, and breathed), Attacked, Attained, Attended, Attended to, Attracted, Attuned, Audited, Augmented, Awakened

Backed, Balanced, Beatified, Became, Beefed up, Began, Belonged, Benefited, Bid, Billed, Blended in, Bloomed, Blossomed, Blueprinted, Bolstered, Boosted, Bound, Bounded, Bought, Bore,

Briefed, Broadcasted, Broke ground, Brought, Brought about, Brought in, Brought into play, Brought off, Brought to bear, Brought together, Brought to fruition, Brought to pass, Budgeted, Built, Built up

Cached, Calculated, Calibrated, Called, Cancelled, Capped, Captivated, Carried, Carried on, Carried out, Cast, Catalogued, Caught, Caused, Celebrated, Challenged, Championed, Changed, Chaperoned, Characterized, Charted, Checked, Cheered, Chose, Circulated, Clarified, Classified, Cleaned, Cleaned up, Cleansed, Cleared, Closed, Coached, Coalesced, Coaxed, Collated, Collected, Collocated, Combined, Commanded, Commenced, Commended, Communicated, Compared, Compelled, Compensated, Competed, Compiled, Completed, Complied, Comported, Composed, Computed, Conceived, Concentrated, Concentrated on, Conceptualized, Concluded, Concurred, Conducted, Confirmed, Conformed, Confronted, Conjoined, Connected, Conquered, Conserved, Consigned, Consolidated, Constructed, Consulted, Consummated, Contained, Continued, Contracted, Controlled, Converted, Cooked, Cooperated, Coordinated, Corralled, Corrected, Correlated, Corresponded, Counselled, Counted, Counteracted, Counterbalanced, Covered, Cracked, Created, Critiqued, Cuddled, Cultivated, Cumulated, Curbed

Dazzled, Dealt, Débuted, Decided, Deepened, Defeated, Defended, Defined, Delegated, Delighted, Delivered, Delivered speech, Demonstrated, Designed, Detailed, Detected, Determined, Developed, Devised, Devoted oneself to, Diagnosed, Dialed back, Did justice, Did proud, Did the trick, Directed, Disambiguated, Discovered, Discussed, Dismissed, Dispensed, Dispersed, Dispatched, Displayed, Disposed, Disproved, Dissected, Distributed, Diverted, Diversified, Divided, Dovetailed, Drafted, Dramatized, Drew, Drew together, Drew up, Drove, Dug up, Dwelt

Earned, Eased, Edified, Edited, Educated, Effected, Effectuated, Electrified, Elevated, Elicited, Eliminated, Elucidated, Embarked on, Embodied, Embraced, Empathized, Employed, Empowered, Emulated, Enabled, Enacted, Encouraged, Ended, Endorsed,

Energized, Enforced, Engaged, Engaged in, Engineered, Engrossed, Enhanced, Enjoyed, Enlarged, Enlisted, Enlivened, Ensured, Entertained, Enthralled, Enticed, Enumerated, Epitomized, Equalized, Equaled, Espoused, Established, Estimated, Evaluated, Evened, Eventuated, Evinced, Evoked, Examined, Exceeded, Excited, Executed, Exercised, Exerted, Exerted influence, Exhibited, Expanded, Expedited, Experimented, Explained, Explicated, Exploited, Expressed, Extended, Extracted

Faced, Facilitated, Familiarized, Fascinated, Fastened, Fast tracked, Fed, Felicitated, Filed, Filled, Filmed, Finalized, Financed, Finessed, Fine-tuned, Finished, Fired up, Fit, Fixed, Fixed up, Fleshed out, Flew, Forecast, Foresaw, Foretold, Forewent, Formed, Formulated, Forwarded, Forewarned, Found, Framed, Freed, Fulfilled, Furnished, Furthered, Fused

Gained, Galvanized, Gathered, Gathered momentum, Gave, Gave a leg up, Gave a lift, Gave rise to, Gave rundown, Generated, Got, Got going, Got hold of, Got in there, Got into, Got ready, Got someplace, Got there, Got together, Governed, Graded, Graduated, Greased the wheels, Greeted, Grew, Guaranteed, Guarded, Guided, Gunned

Hammered out, Habituated, Handled, Handwrote, Harmonized, Hastened, Headed, Headed up, Heightened, Held, Held the reins on, Held office, Held with, Helped, Heralded, Hiked up, Hit, Honoured, Hustled, Hyped

Identified, Illustrated, Impelled, Implemented, Impressed, Improved, Improvised, Inaugurated, Incentivized, Included, Incorporated, Increased, Induced, Influenced, Informed, Initiated, Injected, Inlayed, Innovated, Input, Inspected, Inspired, Inspirited, Installed, Instituted, Instructed, Insured, Integrated, Intensified, Interacted, Interceded, Interconnected, Interested, Interfaced, Interfered, Interlaced, Interlaid, Interplayed, Interpreted, Interviewed, Intrigued, Introduced, Intuited, Invented, Inventoried, Investigated, Invigorated, Invited, Involved, Ironed out

Jacked up, Joined, Juggled, Justified

Kept, Kindled, Knew, Knit together, Knocked off, was Known, Knuckled down to

Labelled, Laboured, Laid foundation for, Laid out, Landed, Launched, Leaned in, Leant, Learned, Lectured, Led, Led to, Lengthened, Liberated, Licensed, Lifted, Lightened, Lined up, Linked, Listed, Listened, Livened, Loaded up, Loaned, Located, Locked, Locked up, Lured

Maintained, Made, Made a bundle, Made a hit with, Made hay, Made it, Made known, Made progress, Made rain, Made ready, Magnified, Managed, Manned, Manoeuvred, Manufactured, Mapped, Mapped out, Marketed, Massed, Matched, Mated, Mattered, Measured, Mediated, Melded, Memorialized, Memorized, Mended, Mentored, Meshed, Met, Meted, Mitigated, Mobilized, Modeled, Moderated, Modified, Monitored, Motivated, Mounted, Moved, Multiplied, Munified

Nailed, Nailed it, Named, Navigated, Negotiated, Nominated, Normalized, Noted, Notified, Nourished, Nurtured

Obliged, Observed, Obtained, Occupied, Occurred, Offered, Officiated, Offset, Opened, Opened the throttle, Operated, Orchestrated, Ordered, Organized, Oriented, Originated, Outgunned, Overcame, Oversaw, Owned

Packed, Paid, Painted, Paralleled, Parcelled, Participated, Partitioned, Patronized, Penetrated, Perceived, Percolated, Perfected, Performed, Permitted, Persevered, Persisted, Personified, Persuaded, Phoned, Photographed, Picked up, Piled up, Piloted, Pinpointed, Pioneered, Pitched, Placed, Planned, Planted, Planted seeds, Played, Played the game, Pleased, Plunged into, Polished, Portrayed, Possessed, Posted, Practiced, Predicted, Premiated, Prepared, Prescribed, Presented, Preserved, Presided, Pressed, Prevailed, Prevented, Primed, Printed, Processed, Procured, Produced, Proffered, Profited, Programmed, Progressed, Projected, Promoted, Prompted,

Promulgated, Proofread, Propelled, Proportioned, Proposed, Propitiated, Prorated, Prospered, Protected, Proved, Provided, Publicized, Pulled in, Pulled things together, Purchased, Purified, Pursued, Pushed, Put forward, Put on the map

Quadrated, Qualified, Quantified, Quarterbacked, Quelled, Quenched, Quickened, Quieted

Racked up, Raised, Rallied, Ran, Ran interference, Ran the show, Ran with the ball, Ranked, Rated, Ratified, Reached, Reacted, Read, Readjusted, Realigned, Realized, Reassured, Recalibrated, Recast, Received, Reciprocated, Recognized, Recommended, Reconciled, Reconstructed, Recorded, Recruited, Rectified, Redintegrated, Redressed, Reduced, Re-established, Refashioned, Referred, Reflected, Reformed, Refreshed, Regarded, Regimented, Regulated, Rehabilitated, Reinforced, Reinfunded, Reintegrated, Rejuvenated, Related, Relaxed, Released, Relied, Relieved, Reminded, Remitted, Remodeled, Removed, Rendered, Renovated, Reorganized, Repaired, Replaced, Reported, Represented, Reproduced, Requested, Requisitioned, Rescued, Researched, Reshaped, Resolved, Respected, Responded, Restored, Restructured, Retired, Retrieved, Returned, Revamped, Revealed, Reviewed, Revised, Revived, Revivified, Revved, Revved up, Rid, Riveted, Rode shotgun, Rolled up, Rolled with the punches, Rose, Rounded up, Roused, Routed

Satisfied, Saved, Savoured, Saw, Scared up, Scheduled, Scored, Sealed, Searched, Secured, was Seen, Seized, Selected, Sent, Separated, Served, Serviced, Set, Set in motion, Set in place, Set up, Settled, Sewed up, Shaped, Shaped up, Shared, Shipped´, Shone, Showed, Sided, Simplified, Smiled, Smoothed, Sold, Solicited, Solved, Sorted, Sought, Souped up, Sparked, Spellbound, Spoke, Spoke for, Specified, Sped (up), Spotted, Sponsored, Spread, Sprinted, Spruced up, Spurred, Squared, Squared away, Stabilized, Standardized, Started, Stayed, Steered, Stimulated, Stirred, Stockpiled, Stood by, Stopped, Stored, Straightened up, Streamlined, Strengthened, Stretched, Strove, Struck, Struck deals, Struck gold, Struck the market, Strove, Submitted, Succeeded, Suggested, Suited,

Summarized, Summated, Summed, Superintended, Supervised, Supplemented, Supplied, Supported, Surprised, Surveyed, Sustained, Swayed, Sweetened, Switched, Switchedon, Sympathized, Synchronized, Synthesized, Systemized

Tabulated, Tailored, Tailor-made, Tallied, Talked, Tamed, Targeted, Taught, Tempered, Tested, Thanked, Thrived, Thrust, Tied, Titivated, Toned, Took care of, Took control of, Took charge, Took part, Took possession of, Took on, Took over, Took steps, Took the floor, Took up, Took under one's wing, Took wing, Topped, Totaled, Toted up, Touted, Traced, Traded, Trained, Transacted, Transcribed, Transferred, Transformed, Translated, Transmitted, Transported, Travelled, Triumphed, Troubleshot, Tuned, Turned, Turned on afterburners, Tutored, Tweaked, Typed

Uncovered, Understood, Undertook, Underwent, Unified, United, Upbuilt, Updated, Upgraded, Upheld, Uplifted, Upraised, Upskilled, Upstayed, Urged, Used, Utilized

Vaulted, Valued, Varied, Verified, Vindicated, Vitalized, Vivified

Wakened, Was in unison, Wed, Wedded, Weighed, Welcomed, Went by the book, Went to bat for, Went flat out, Went for it, Went the extra mile, Went to work, Went to town, Were of one mind, Whet, Whipped out/up, Whished (sped), Widened, Withstood, Won, Won over, Wooed, Worked, Worked out, Wove, Wowed, Wrangled, Wrapped, Wrote

Yielded

POSITIVE NON-BUSINESS VERBS

Abide, Absterge, Acclaim, Accourage, Accoy, Acknowledge, Admire, Adore, Allure, Amuse, Applaud, Apricate, Arouse, Asseverate, Assoil, Aver, Awaken, Beatify, Befriend, Be smitten with, Bestow, Bless, Blow away, Bonify, Brighten, Buoy, Buss (kiss), Calm, Canoodle, Caper, Caress, Cavort, Celebrate, Charm, Cheer, Cherish, Chirk, Comfort, Complect, Compliment, Comport, Concrew, Condole, Conflate, Console, Content, Coruscate, Court, Crown, Cruise, Cuddle, Dance, Degust, Deosculate, Depurate, Dig, Dignify, Dine, Disport, Dote on, Dream, Effloresce, Elate, Enamour, Enchant, Endear, Enjoy, Enkindle, Enliven, Ennoble, Enrapture, Entrance, Epurate, Equiparate, Esteem, Exalt, Excite, Excogitate, Exculpate, Exhilarate, Exosculate, Extol, Fall for, Fascinate, Favour, Feast, Feel, Felicify, Fill, Flip over, Fly, Forgive, Frolic, Gambol, Giggle, Gladden, Glorify, Go over big, Grant respite, Gratify, Grok, Habilitate, Have been, Have fun, Have place, Hearten, Herald, Hold, Holiday, Homologate, Honour, Hospitate, Hug, Hypnotize, Impetrate, Incede, Indulge, Infatuate, Jest, Joke, Ken, Kiss, Kick up one's heels, Laud, Laugh, Like, Live, Love, Macarize, Maffick, Magnetize, Make merry, Massage, Mesmerize, Move (emotionally), Mundify, Nest, Nestle, Nobilitate, Nosh, Nurse, Nuzzle, Omnify, Osculate, Pacificate, Pacify, Pamper, Peacekeeping, Peak, Pet, Play, Praise, Prize, Rede, Refocillate, Regale, Reguerdon, Rejoice, Relish, Revalorize, Revel, Revere, Rollick, Romp, Sail, Salute, Salve, Sanctify, Sate, Satiate, Savour, Score, Skip, Slake, Smooch, Soften, Soothe, Still, Star, Stay, Stir, Suffice, Suit, Survive, Sweep off one's feet, Thrill, Tickle, Tickle pink, Titivate, Touch, Tower, Travel, Treasure, Trumpet, Uprear, Vacation, Vaticinate, Venerate, Warm, Whoop it up, Winnow, Wive, Worship

Chapter 6

HYPNOSIS
&
THE JEDI MIND TRICK

"Thus the purpose of each experience is that the entity may magnify and glorify that which is good." (Edgar Cayce Reading 2599-1)

HOW TO GET WHAT YOU WANT
VIA HYPNOSIS

Hypnotic practice is, in itself, morally benign but the intent of the hypnotist is paramount in a human continuum where intent means everything.

The decisive factor in hypnosis must always be the benefit of the hypnotized subject. Hypnotist intent can range from healing to crime or even acts of war. The interest for many seeking this information will be somewhere in between these extremes. How do sales, or other goal-oriented interactions, for example, honestly factor into this subject benefit imperative?

The efficacy rate is extremely high for hypnotherapy used for addiction/substance abuse issues as well as for treating phobias. It can also be used for pain relief, peace of mind, and performance enhancement of all kinds, bearing in mind that a single session often isn't enough to produce long term post hypnotic results.

The trick to self-hypnosis, in accordance with the *Laws of Attraction*, is to consistently henceforward visualize and feel the enjoyment of already having or being that which is desired.

Following are the four most effective hypnotic words to use to get what you want. Like hypnosis itself these words are, in themselves, benign. Care should be taken to ensure that they always benefit the subject.

1. **You** – The engagement of all of the interest and ability that you have to offer is critical in the world that you want to create for you and those close to you.

2. **Remember** – Remember the halcyon days of your childhood when you were peaceful, carefree and playing happily?

3. **Because** – This is what you want; what you've always wanted. 'Reason' ranks very high on the Power vs. Force spectrum, but not as high as 'Compassion'.

4. **Imagine** – Imagine the world of your dreams wherein everyone is eager to help each other.

When you awaken you'll feel fully refreshed and enjoy nothing but peace, love, joy and appreciation for the rest of your days...

SNAP!

Hypnosis in a Third Person
as a Diagnostic Modality

THE JEDI MIND TRICK
of Organizational Behaviour

More creative than reinforcement theory is the HR observation that, in at least two particular areas, an employee can be made to believe in the existence of positive attributes about themselves, and thereafter perform accordingly, even if these attributes weren't previously objectively true.

These two known areas are: 1. Quality of work. 2. Autonomy.

If a supervisor tells an under-performing employee "I'm glad that I can leave you to work alone and expect a job well done" it will become true thereafter whether or not this was previously objectively true. These are just like the Jedi mind tricks of Star Wars which famously include 1. "These aren't the droids you're looking for" and 2. "Go home and rethink your life."

This utterly simple enchantment is a powerful positive device for the betterment of both the subject and the organization. The active efficacy in this principle is likely due to the perceived authority of the supervisor and sometimes works with teachers as well. Teaching can even be a *Gift of the Spirit.*

The arena of 'quality of work' has an enormity of possibilities via the many positive nouns, adjectives, verbs and adverbs that can constitute 'quality'. How many of these words can authority figures make true instantly just by communicating them to someone with growth potential?

These 'are' the words you're looking for.

Edgar Cayce Vs. Yoda

Chapter 7

ALL THE LOVE IN THE WORLD

"Let no day pass that ye do not speak a cheery and an encouraging word to someone! And ye will find thine own heart uplifted, thine own life opened, thy love appreciated, thy purposes understood. " (Edgar Cayce Reading 1754-1)

Abidingness, Acceptance, Accord, Acknowledgement, Admiration, Adoration, Adulation, Aelurophilia (aka Ailurophilia), Affection, Affinity, Agape, Ailurophilia (aka Aelurophilia), Aerophilia, Allegiance, Alliance, Altruism, Amativeness, Americophilia, Amiability, Amiableness, Amicability, Amicableness, Amity, Amore, Amour-propre, Androphilia, Anglophilia, Appeal, Appraisal, Appreciation, Appreciativeness, Approbation, Approval, Ardour, Aroha, Asset, Astrophilia, Attachment, Attraction, Audiophilia, Avidity, Awareness, Beauty, Beguin, Benefaction, Beneficence, Benevolence, Benevolentness, Bigheartedness, Billet-doux, Bibliophilia, Biophilia, Bliss, Brightness, Brotherhood, Camaraderie, Care, Caritas, Cartophilia, Charitableness, Charity, Choice, Cinephilia, Cognizance, Comfort, Comity, Commiseration, Commitment, Communion, Community, Companionship, Compassion, Compassionateness, Compatibility, Completion, Comprehension, Concord, Condolence, Connection, Consideration, Consonance, Cooperation, Cynophilia, Deference, Delight, Devotedness, Devotion, Elevation, Emotion, Empathy, Enamouredness, Enchantment, Endearment, Enophilia (aka Oenophilia), Faithfulness, Fancy, Favour, Feeling, Fellowship, Fidelity, Fondness, Forbearance, Forgiveness, Francophilia (aka Gallophilia), Fraternity, Friendliness, Friendship, Gallophilia (aka Francophilia), Generosity, Geniality, Gentleness, Germanophilia, Givingness, Godliness, Good wishes, Goodness, Goodwill, Grace, Graciousness, Gynephilia, Harmony, Heart, Heartiness, Helpfulness, Henosis, Heliophilia, Hellenophilia, Hippophilia, Honour, Humaneness,Humanitarianism,Ideal,Idealism,Idealization,Increase, Indophilia, Infatuation, Innocence, Inspiration, Interest, Iranophilia, Kindheartedness, Kindness, Kinship, Law, Largeheartedness,

Largesse, Lenience, Leniency, Lenity, Like-mindedness, Loveableness, Loving, Magnanimity, Mercy, Mindset, Mood, Mutuality, Mycophilia, Neighbourlikeness, Neighbourliness, Nemophilia, Neophilia, Nourishment, Nurture, Nyctophilia, Oenophilia (aka Enophilia), Oneness, Pacifism, Pardon, Partiality, Pash, Passion, Penchant, Perception, Perfection, Persophilia (aka Iranophilia), Philalethia, Philanthropism, Philanthropy, Philocaly, Philogyny, Philology, Philomathy, Philonoism, Philosophicalness, Philosophy, Philoxenia, Pleasure, Pluviophilia, Pogonophilia, Potency, Preciousness, Predilection, Predisposition, Preference, Prize, Probity, Propensity, Purity, Rapport, Rapprochement, Rapture, Reciprocity, Recognition, Regard, Respect, Responsiveness, Retrophilia, Reverence, Romanticism, Sanction, Satisfaction, Selection, Sensation, Sensibility, Sensitivity, Sentiment, Sentimentality, Service, Sharing, Sheltering, Shielding, Sincerity, Sinophilia, Sisterhood, Slavophilia, Sociability, Sociality, Sodality, Softheartedness, Solidarity, Spark, Spirituality, Steadfastness, Support, Sweetness, Sympathy, Technophilia, Tenderheartedness, Tenderness, Theological virtue, Theophilanthropism, Togetherness, Tolerance, Treasure, Trust, Truthfulness, Turophilia, Understanding, Unfailingness, Union, Unison, Unity, Urge, Valuation, Value, Veneration, Videophilia, Virtue, Warmheartedness, Warmth, Welcome, Wholeheartedness, Wisdom, Xenophilia, Yen

The word Philosophy originates with the Greek:
'Philos' (In love with...) 'Sophia' (...Wisdom).

-Phile (one who loves) Suffix

Aelurophile, Aerophile, Ailurophile, Arctophile, Astrophile, Audiophile, Bibliophile, Biophile, Cartophile, Cinephile, Discophile*, Enophile, Ergophile*, Foodophile*, Galanthophile*, Heliophile, Hippophile, Iconophile*, Jazzophile*, Linguaphile, Logophile*, Musicophile*, Mycophile, Nemophilist, Neophile/ Neophiliac, Oenophile, Orchidophile*, Ornithophile, Pluviophile*, Pogonophile, Retrophile, Thalassophile*, Turophile, Typhlophile*, Videophile*, Xenophile

There are a great many large and powerful loves all around us for which there are no official English words including the identified 'phile' words* with no official '-philia' counterpart; a practical impossibility. There are also less than 20 legitimate regional loves (ex. Anglophilia) even though such feelings attracting us homeward have been strongly felt by most indigenous, transplanted and nostalgic people from every region in the world since the beginning of time.

In addition a paraphilia is a psychological focus on uncommon erotic interests which usurp the –philia suffix from many popular pure and innocent loves of the same thing. Other such known loves (ex. flowers) have been pre-empted by other sciences.

There must reasonably be many other great, powerful, and popular loves with no name, between retrophilia and eager anticipation, which occupy our minds and permeate our lives while having no official English name.

-Philia (the love of) Suffix
Reverse Lookup

Air-breathing and Flying - Aerophilia
Astronomy - Astrophilia
Audio; high fidelity sound reproduction and technology - Audiophilia
Beards - Pogonophilia
Books - Bibliophilia
Cats - Ailurophilia
Cheese - Turophilia
Dogs - Cynophilia*
Flying and Air-breathing - Aerophilia
Foreign people or culture - Xenophilia
Forests - Nemophilia
Horses - Hippophilia
Life - Biophilia
Maps and Cards - Cartophilia
Masculinity and/or men - Androphilia
Motion pictures - Cinephilia
Mushrooms - Mycophilia
New or novel things - Neophilia
Night - Nyctophilia*
Past, the - Retrophilia
Sunlight - Heliophilia
Technology - Technophilia
Teddy bears - Arctophily
Wine - Oenophilia/Enophilia
Women and/or femininity - Gynephilia & Philogyny

*words with no official '-phile' counterpart.

Lovers of Cultures and Regions

America - Americophile
China, and/or its people, and/or its culture - Sinophile
England/Britain, and/or the English, and/or their culture
        - Anglophile
Europe and/or its cultures, peoples, and/or the European union
        - Europhile
Foreign people or culture - Xenophile
France and/or its people and/or its culture
        - Francophile/Gallophile
Germany - Germanophile
Greece and/or Greek culture ancient or modern - Hellenophile
Hispanic countries - Hispanophile
India and/or its people and/or its culture - Indophile
Iran and/or its people and/or its culture - Iranophile aka.
        Persophile (Persia)
Japan and/or Japanese culture - Japanophile
Russia and/or its people and/or its culture - Russophile
Slavic Countries and/or their people and/or their culture
        - Slavophile
United States and/or their way of life - Americophile

Positive Adjectives in
Arabic, Chinese, German, Hindi, & Spanish

"I Love You" in Every Language
For when you want to say it in theirs

Afrikaans - 1. Ek het jou liefe 2. Ek is lief vir jou
Albanian - Unë të dua
Alsatian - Ich hoan dich gear
Amharic/Ethiopian - Afekrishalehou
Arabic - Ana behibak (to a male) Ana behibek (to a female)
Arabic - Ooheboka (to a male) Ooheboki (to a female) formal
Arabic - 1. Ana bahebbak 2. Nhebuk (regional dialects)
Armenian - Yes sirum yem k'ez
Aruban, Bonairian and Curacaoan - Mi stimabo
Assyr - 1. Az tha hijthmekem 2. Ana ki bayinakh
Australian Aboriginal - Kungkungullun Ngune
Azerbaijani - Mən səni sevirəm

Bari/Sudanese - 1. Nan nyanyar do (I love you) 2. Nan nyanyar do parik (I love you very much)
Basque - Maite zaitut
Batak - Holong do rohangku tu ho
Bavarian - I mog di narrisch gern
Bengali - 1. Ami tomaye bhalobashi (colloquial) 2. Ami tomake bhalobashi
Berber - Dakkm tirikh
Bhojpuri - Ham tahara se pyar karila
Bicol/Philippine dialect - 1. Namumutan ta ka 2. Padaba taka
Binary - 01001001 00100000 01101100 01101111 01110110 01100101 00100000 01111001 01101111 01110101 00101110
Bisaya/Cebuano - Nahigugma ko nimo
Bosnian - 1. Volim te (Volim te ja) 2. Ja te volim
Brazilian Portugese - Eu te amo
Bulgarian - Obicham te
Burmese - mainnkohkyittaal

Cambodian/Kmer - Khnhom sralanh anak
Catalan - 1. T'estim (Mallorcan) 2. T'estim molt (I love you a lot) 3. T'estime (Valencian) 4. T'estimo (Catalonian)
Cebuano - Gihigugma tika

Chamorro - Hu guiaya hao
Chinese/Cantonese - Ngo oi ney
Chinese/Mandarin - Wo ai ni
Croatian - 1. Volim te 2. Ja te volim
Czech - 1. Miluji te 2. Miluju te (colloquial)

Danish - Jeg elsker dig
Dhivehi/Maldivian - Aharen kalaa dheke loabivey
Dutch - Ik hou van jou

Esperanto - Mi amas vin
Estonian - 1. Ma armastan sind 2. Mina armastan sind

Faroese - Eg elski teg
Farsi/Persian - Dúset daram (coloquial) Man túra dúst daram
Filipino - Iniibig kita
Finnish - Minä rakastan sinua
Flemish/Vlaams - 1. Ik zie oe geerne 2. Ik hou van je
French - Je t'aime
Friesian/Frisian - Ik hâld fan dy

Gaelic - Tha gaol agam ort
Galician - 1. A'mote 2. Quérote
Georgian - Miq'varkhar
German - Ich liebe dich
Greek - Se agapó
Gujrati - Huṁ tanē prēma karuṁ chu

Hausa - Ina son ku
Hebrew - 1. Ani ohev otach (male to female) 2. Ani ohev otcha (male to male) 3. Ani ohevet otcha (female to male) 4. Ani ohevet otach (female to female)
Hindi - Main tumase pyaar karata hoon
Hmong - Kuv hlub koj
Hokkien - Wa ai lu
Hopi - Nu' umi unangwa'ta
Hungarian - Szeretlek

Icelandic - ég elska þig
Indonesian - Aku cinta kamu
Irish - Taim i ngra' leat
Italian - 1. Ti amo (for lover/spouse) 2. Ti voglio bene (for a friend or relative)
Ivatan - Ichaddao ku imu

Japanese - Watashi wa, anata o aishiteimasu
Javanese - Aku tresna sampeyan

Kashmiri - Tske chhuk myon jigur
Kazakh - Men seni jaqsı köremin
Kiswahili - Nakupenda
Klingon - 1. Qabang 2. QaparHa' (depends on location within galaxy)
Konkani - Hanv tuzo mog kortam
Korean/Koryese - Salanghae
Kurdish - Ez ji te hez dikim
Kyrgyz - Men seni süyöm

Lahu - Nga naw hta ha ja
Lao - Khony hak chao
Latin - 1. Te amo 2. Amo te 3. Vos amo
Latvian - 1. Es tevi mīlu 2. Es mīlu tevi
Lingala - Nalingi yo
Lithuanian - Aš tave myliu
Luganda/Ugandan - Nkwagala
Luo/Kenyan - Aheri

Macedonian - Te sakam
Malay - Saya sayang awak
Maldivian/Dhivehi - Aharen kalaa dheke loabivey
Maltese - Inħobbok
Mandarin - Wo ai ni
Mapuche/Mapudungun - Inchepoyeneimi
Mohawk - Konnorónhkwa
Moldovan - Te iubesc

Mongolian - Bi chamd khairtai
Myanmar - Mainnkohkyittaal

Navaho - Ayóó anííníshní
Ndebele/Zimbabwean - Ngiyakuthanda
Nepali - Ma timilai maya garchu
Norwegian - Jeg elsker deg

Ossetian - Äz dä uarzyn

Pakistani/Urdu - Mein ap say muhabat karta hoon (masc.) Mein ap say muhabat karti hoon (fem.)
Pashto/Afghanistani - Za ta sara meena kawom
Persian/Farsi - Dúset daram (coloquial) Man túra dúst daram
Polish - kocham Cię
Portuguese - Eu te amo
Punjabi - Maiṁ tuhānū pi'āra karadā hāṁ

Romanian - Te iubesc
Russian - Ya lyublyu tebya

Scot Gaelic - Tha gaol agam ort
Serbian - Volim te
Shona/Zimbabwean - Ndinokuda
Sinhalese - Mama oyāṭa ādareyi
Sioux - Thečhíȟila
Slovak - Ľúbim ťa
Slovenian - Ljubim te
Somali - Waan ku jeclahay
Spanish - 1. Te amo (I love you) 2. Te quiero (I really care for you)
Srilankan/Sinhala/Sinhalese - Mama oyāṭa ādareyi
Sudanese/Bari - Nan nyanyar do (I love you)
Swahili - Nakupenda
Swedish - Jag älskar dig
Swiss-German - Ch'ha Di Ga'rn
Syrian/Lebanese - Ana bəḥibbək (to a female) Ana bahibbak (to a male)

Tagalog - Mahal kita
Taiwanese - Góa ài lì
Tamil - Nāṇ uṇṇai kātalikkiṟēṇ
Telugu - Nēnu ninnu prēmistunnānu
Thai - Čhạn rạk khuṇ
Tibetan - Nga kayrâng-la gawpo yö (I like/have interest in, you)
Tigrinya/Eritrean - Yefkrekiye (to a female) Yefkrekaye (to a male)
Tunisian - Ana nhebbek
Turkish - Seni seviyorum

Ukrainian - Ya tebe lyublyu
Urdu/Pakistani - Mein ap say muhabat karta hoon (masc.) Mein ap say muhabat karti hoon (fem.)
Uzbek - Men seni Sevaman

Vietnamese - Tôi mến bạn
Vlaams/Flemish - 1. Ik zie oe geerne 2. Ik hou van je

Welsh - Rwy'n dy garu di

Xhosa - Ndiyakuthanda

Yiddish - Ikh hab dir lib
Yoruba - Mo nifẹ rẹ
Yugoslavian (Bosnian, Croatian, or Serbian) - Volim te

Zulu - Ngiyakuthanda
Zuni - 'Ho'doh'ee'cheht'mah

The Universe is permeated with love. Turn on the tap.

UNLIMITED LOVE

How can we acquire skill in experiencing more love? At least four ways; by increasing the intensity, frequency, and duration of the emotion as well as including more and greater targets. One day the frequency and duration may combine to form "All of the Time". Until then here's a good way to go:

Start by imagining all the love by, and for, our parents. The more slowly-paced the contemplation of these thoughts the better. Next, in addition to the thought of all our love to, and from, our parents let's add any and all affection for siblings, and then the love that we've had for any and all pets who have shared their lives with us. After sustaining that thought for a while add all the joyous love that we've enjoyed in friendships along the way...

...Now add to this already immense feeling, all of our romantic loves, from our first puppy love until our current, and thereby greatest, love...

...Now add all the love for any children.

Express and impress these feelings for a while. Then, while still maintaining the thought of all of this love, add in all of the love that we've ever felt for all of mankind, and all of the love that we've ever felt for God.

Overwhelming? There's so much more.

Now try to genuinely love everyone within a room somewhere, or on a bus with us, for example, and then everyone in the city or town, the overall region, the state or province, the country, the continent, and on the entire planet.... ...and then also contemplate what the similar loves of all those people have been.

Imagine all the love that has ever been felt by our fellow human beings. How long can this   'be   sustained?   A   minute?   Two minutes? Fifteen? An hour? A day? More? Now add to that all of the love that will be felt by everyone in the future into perpetuity. Then add to this all the love ever felt by every living creature and then add to this every particle of love ever felt by all creatures in the past and future until the end of time... and hold that thought. How long can this, now enormous, love be sustained?

Earth is but a drop in the immeasurable cosmic ocean so now multiply this earthly feeling of love exponentially to reflect all of the actual love existing in the universe in the past, present, and future, in every possible world in every possible dimension.

Now double it. How long can we hold that thought? Now double it again... and hold. Now multiply it by a factor of ten... and hold. Multiply this by a hundred, and hold, and then a thousand before making it the intensity of a sun going supernova... ...then billions of suns going supernova in an ever eternally increasing passion of immeasurably expanding white light of LOVE.

A mind, once stretched to accept a new thought or idea, never regains its original shape. As our love begins to include every living thing everywhere, with exquisite intensity, during every waking moment, then perhaps we'll be on our way to learning to love the way God loves.

It's Everywhere

Chapter 8

ONENESS

"The first lesson for six months should be One-One-One-One; Oneness of God, Oneness of man's relation, Oneness of force, Oneness of time, Oneness of purpose, Oneness in every effort-Oneness- Oneness!" (Edgar Cayce Reading 900-429)

The subject of wisdom isn't taught in schools but it's an elementary lesson.

Wisdom = Oneness.

From Oneness everything else is derived, most notably, *The Universal Laws.*

Wisdom is also one of the *Gifts of the Spirit*, which, remarkably, are characterized by increased supernatural ability thereby making wisdom not only wise, but, in the long run, truly magical as well. Oneness has its ubiquitous benefits.

The Gifts of the Spirit are granted as a result of *The Fruits of the Spirit* which are the personal application of *The Universal Laws.*

Wisdom is the opposite of the selfishness that presents a challenge to most people because selfishness is as insidiously smart, insightful, and desirous as its owner. Many sincerely spiritual people, for example, have succumbed to variations of "holier than thou".

Meditation is an excellent way to contemplate Oneness of consciousness.

UNIR1

DIVINE WORDS

"I am that I am" - Exodus 3:14

Looking at everything through the lens of a great Oneness is a wise world view and direction.

DIVINE ADJECTIVES

Contemplation of these can be mind-expanding keeping in mind that souls are eternal. Circle, highlight, tick, or underline all of the words that you know, for a certainty, are absolutely true, while mentally repeating the words...

... "I am..."

Abiding, Absolute, Abundant, Accepting, Acclaimed, Active, Actual, Acute, Adaptable, Adept, Admirable, Admired, Adorable, Adored, Adoring, Advanced, Advantageous, Adventurous, Advisable, Ae, Aeonian, Aesthetic, Affectionate, Affective, Affordable, Ageless, Airy, Alert, Alive, All-important, All-knowing[1] Altruistic, Amazing, Animastic, Anointed, Apodictic, Apposite, Apparent, Appealing, Applauded, Appreciated, Appreciative, Appropriate, Ascendant, Assertive, Associative, Astounding, Attentive, Attractive, Atypical/Typical, August, Auspicious, Authentic, Authoriative, Available, Aware, Awesome, Axiological, Axiomatic

Balanced, Beautiful, Belonging, Beloved, Benedictive, Benedictory, Beneficial, Beneficent, Benevolent, Benign, Best, Biggest, Blameless, Blessed, Blissful, Bold, Bright, Bulletproof, Busy

Calm, Capable, Captivating, Carefree/Determined, Caring, Catalytic, Categorical, Celebrated, Celestial, Central, Charismatic, Charmed, Charming, Cherishable, Clairvoyant, Clear, Climactic, Close, Coherent, Colorful, Colossal, Comfortable, Comforting,

---

1   Words like 'All-knowing' are humanly impossible because truth grows

Commendable, Committed, Compassionate, Compatible, Completed, Comprehensive, Concise, Concomitant, Concordant, Conducive, Confident, Congruent, Congruous, Conscientious, Conscious, Consecrated, Considerable, Consistent, Consolidated, Consonant, Constant, Constitutional, Constitutive, Constructive, Consubstantial, Contemplative, Contemporary, Content, Contiguous, Continuous, Cool, Cooperative, Coordinated, Copious, Correlative, Cosmic, Credible, Culminating, Cultivating, Curative, Current

Dapatical, Daring, Dazzling, Dear, Decent, Decisive, Dedicated, Deductive, Deep, Definite, Definitive, Deliberate, Delicate, Demonstrative, Dependable, Desired, Desirable, Determinant, Determined, Developed, Developing, Diehard, Diligent, Disciplined, Discovered, Diverse, Divine, Dominant, Doubtless, Durable, Dynamic/Finished

Easy/Hard, Ecstatic, Ecumenical, Effective, Effectual, Efficient, Effulgent, Electric, Elementary, Emerging/Eternal, Eminent, Empathetic, Empathic, Empirical, Empowering, Empyrean, Encouraging, Endearing, Endless, Endorsed, Enduring, Energetic, Energizing, Engaged, Engaging, Enkindling, Enlightening, Ennobled, Ennobling, Enraptured, Enrapturing, Enriching, Entertaining, Enthusiastic, Epididactic, Essential, Established, Eternal/Changeable, Ethereal/Material, Ethical, Evident, Eviternal, Evocative, Exact, Exalted, Exciting, Executive, Exhilarating, Expanding, Expectant, Experienced, Expert, Expressive, Exquisite, Extraordinary

Fair, Faithful, Famed, Familial, Familiar, Famous, Fantastic, Far-reaching, Far-sighted, Fascinating, Favourite, Fecund, Fertile, Fine, Firm, First class, First order, First rate, First, Flexible, Flourishing, Fluent, Forgiving, Formidable, Forthcoming, Fortifying, Forward thinking, Foundational, Foundationary, Frank, Free, Freestyle, Friendly, Fruitful, Full, Fulfilling, Fundamental, Futuristic

Genuine, Generous, Gifted, Giving, Glorious, Godly, Godlike, Good, Good-looking, Goodly, Graceful, Grateful, Gratifying, Great, Greatest, Greathearted, Grounded, Guaranteed, Guiding

Hallowed, Harmonic, Harmonious, Hearty, Henotic, High, High-class, High demand, High quality, Holy, Honest, Honored, Huge

Ideal, Idealistic, Idolized, Illuminated, Illustrious, Immaculate, Immarcescible, Immeasurable, Immediate, Immortal, Impartial, Important, Impregnable, Inclusive, Incorruptible, Indefatigable, Indestructible, Indispensable, Indisputable, Indivisible, Indomitable, Ineffable/Material, Inexhaustible, Infallible, Infinite, Influential, Informed, Inimitable, Innate, Inspirational, Instinctive, Integral, Integrated, International, Invincible, Inviolable, Invulnerable, Irrefutable, Irrevincible

Joyous

Knowable, Knowing, Known

Large, Largifical, Latitudinarian, Lavish, Liberal, Light, Live, Lively, Long-standing, Loving, Luciferous, Lush

Magical, Mainstream, Majestic, Marvelous, Massive, Masterful, Masterly, Maxed, Maximal, Maximum, Meditative, Merciful, Metaphysical (until known), Methodical, Meticulous, Mighty, Miraculous, Mirific, Moral, Most excellent, Most superior, Multifaceted, Mutual

Natural, Near to one's heart, Nearby, Necessary, Needed, Neutral, Noble, Noetic, Nondenominational, Normal, Normative

Objective, OK,

(Omni=All) Omniactive, Omniactual, Omnibenevolent, Omnicausal, Omnicompetent, Omnidirectional, Omnierudite, Omniessencial, Omnifarous, Omniferous, Omnific, Omniformal, Omnilingual, Omnilucent, Omnimental, Omniparental, Omnipatient, Omnipercipient, Omniperfect, Omnipotent, Omnipresent, Omniprevalent,

Omniproductive, Omniprudent, Omniregent, Omnirevealing, Omniscient, Omnisentient, Omnisignificant, Omnisufficient, Omnitemporal, Omnitonal, Omnivalent, Omnivisual,

One, Open, Optimistic, Orbific, Original, Overflowing

Paciferous, Pacific, Palmarian, Pansophical, Pansophistical, Parental, Participative, Participatory, Passionate, Patient, Peaceful, Penetrating, Perceptive, Perceptual, Perdurable, Perennial, Perfect, Perpetual, Persevering, Persistent, Philanthropic, Philodemic, Phlegmatic, Planetary, Plenary, Polite, Pollent, Positive, Powerful, Praised, Praiseworthy, Preponderant, Prevailing, Priceless, Primary, Prodigious, Prolific, Pure

Qualified, Qualitative, Quiet, Quintessential

Ready, Regular, Related, Relative, Relevant, Reliable, Replete, Reputable, Resilient, Resolute, Resounding, Respected, Respectful, Revered, Reverent, Revitalizing, Rewarding, Right, Righteous, Rooted, Rousing, Rugged, Ruling

Sacred, Sacrosanct, Salvific, Sanctiloquent, Sanctified, Savvy, Scholastic, Scientific, Scintillating, Scrupulous, Seasoned, Second to none, Self-assured, Self-governing, Selfless, Self-made, Self-starting, Self-sufficient, Service-minded, Set, Sheltering, Smart, Soothing, Soulful, Spacious, Special, Spectacular, Spirited, Spiritual, Splendorous, Spontaneous, Sthenic, Stoic, Strategic, Successful, Suitable, Superconscious, Superior, Supersensible, Supported, Supraliminal, Sweeping, Synergistic

Teaching, Thorough, Thriving, Timeless, Timeless/Becoming, Tireless, Top, Transformable/Eternal, Treasured, True, Trustworthy

Ubiquitous, Ultimate, Unassailable, Unbeatable, Unblemished, Unconditional, Unconquerable, Undaunted, Undeniable, Understanding, Undivided, Unequalled, Unified, Unisonous, Unisonal, Unisonant, Universal, Unstoppable, Updated, Uplifting

Vast, Vivifying, Volcanic

Welcome, Well arranged, Well built, Well done, Well established, Well founded, Well informed, Well intentioned, Well proportioned, Well received, Well suited, Well-meaning, Wholesome, Willing, Wonderful, Wonder-working, Wondrous, World(s) class, Worldly-wise, Worshipped, Worthy

Christmas Words

DIVINE NOUNS

"Father, God! Let me, as thy child, see in my fellow man the divinity I would worship in Thee."
(Edgar Cayce Reading 262-130)

"I am..."

Abidingness, Ability, Absolution, Absoluteness, Abundance, Acceptance, Accord, Achievement, Actuality, Actualization, Acuity, Acumen, Acuteness, Adaptability, Adeptness, Advancement, Advantage, Affinity, Agape, Agapism, Agelessness, Alertness, Aliveness, Altruism, Amativeness, Amazedness, Amazement, Amelioration, Amore, Amour-propre, Anticipation, Apogee, Apotheosis, Appetence/Appetency, Application, Appositeness, Appraisal, Appreciation, Appreciativeness, Aptitude, Aptness, Aroha, Ascension, Ascendancy, Assuredness, Astuteness, Ataraxia, Ataraxis, Ataraxy, Atonement, At-oneness, Attention, Attentiveness, Attraction, Authenticity, Authority, Authoritativeness, Autonomy, Awareness, Awe, Awesomeness

Backbone, Backing, Balance, Beauty, Belief, Belonging, Beneficence, Benefit, Benevolence, Benevolentness, Benison, Bestowal, Bestowment, Betterment, Big deal, Bigheartedness, Biophilia, Blessing, Blessedness, Bliss, Blissfulness, Blitheness, Blithesomeness, Boldness, Boost, Bounty, Bountifulness, Bounteousness, Brightness, Bright side, Brilliance, Broadmindedness, Brotherhood, Brotherliness

Caliber, Call forth, Calling, Calm, Calmness, Candor, Candour, Capability, Capacity, Care, Carefreeness, Carefulness, Caritas, Catalyst, Causality, Casualness, Certainty, Certitude, Character, Charge, Charitableness, Charity, Chemistry, Chill, Choice, Christmas, Clairvoyance, Clarity, Classic, (next to) Cleanliness, Clearness, Clemency, Closeness, Cloud nine, Clout, Cogency, Cognition, Cognizance, Coherence, Collaboration, Collectedness, Collectivism, Colourfulness, Comity, Command, Commitment, Communion, Compassion, Compassionateness, Compatibility, Competence, Competency, Complement, Completion, Completeness, Composedness, Composition, Composure, Comprehension, Conceivability, Concision, Concord, Concordance, Concurrence, Conduct, Confelicity, Confidence, Confirmation, Congruence, Congruity, Connectedness, Connection, Consecration, Conscience, Conscientiousness, Consciousness, Consideration, Consistency, Consonance, Constancy, Constructiveness, Contemporariness, Contentedness, Contentment, Continuity, Control, Conviction, Convincingness, Coolness, Cooperation, Coordination, Correctness, Cosmotheism, Courage, Courageousness, Creation, Creativeness, Creativity, Cred, Credence, Credibility, Creditableness, Creditability, Culmen, Culmination, Cultivation, Cure, Cure-all

Dearness, Decency, Decisiveness, Dedication, Deepness, Definiteness, Deity, Deification, Deliverance, Demand, Dependability, Deservingness, Desiderata, Desideratum, Desirability, Desirableness, Determination, Determinedness, Determinant, Development, Devotedness, Devotion, Devoutness, Dignity, Diligence, Direction, Directness, Discernment, Discovery, Diversity, Divinity, Durability, Dynamism

Earnestness, Earthiness, Earthliness, Ecstasy, Ectropy, Edification, Effectiveness, Effect, Effectualness, Effulgence, Elevation, Embrace, Emergence, Eminence, Empathy, Emphasis, Empowerment, Emulation, Empyrean, Enablement, Encouragement, Endearment, Endowment, Endurance, Energy, Engagement, Engagingness, Enlightenment, Enlivenment, Enough, Enrapturement, Enrichment, Entaxy, Entirety, Entrustment, Epinicion, Equability, Equality, Equanimity, Equipoise, Equipollence, Equiponderance, Equity, Equivalence, Esse, Essence, Eternity, Ethicality, Ethicalness, Ethics, Eudaimonia, Eudaimonism, Eupathy, Euphoria, Eutaxy, Euthenics, Even-handedness, Evenness, Evocativeness, Evolution, Evolvement, Exactitude, Exactness, Excellence, Excellency, Exceptionalness, Exemplariness, Existence, Expansiveness, Expectancy, Expergefaction, Experience, Expertise, Exploration, Exquisiteness, Extraordinariness, Extropy

Fact, Factuality, Factualness, Fairness, Faith, Faithfulness, Far-sightedness, Fearlessness, Feeling, Fellowship, Fertility, Fidelity, Flair, Flexibility, Flow, Focus, Fondness, Forbearance, Forgiveness, Foresight, Foreseeability, Forthrightness, Fortitude, Fortunateness, Fortune, Foundation, Fount, Frankness, Fraternity, Freedom, Freshness, Friendliness, Friendship, Fruitfulness, Fulfillment, Fulgor, Fullness

Generation, Generativity, Generator, Generosity, Genius, Gentleness, Genuineness, Giftedness, Givingness, Gladsomeness, Glorification, Glory, Gnosis, Go, God, Goddess, Godliness, Good, Good fortune, Good nature, Goodness, Good thing, Goodwill, Grace, Gracefulness, Graciousness, Gramercy, Grandeur, Gratefulness, Gratitude, Gratulation, Gravitas, Greatness, Great respect, Growth, Guidance

Happiness, Harmoniousness, Harmony, Health, Healthiness, Headway, Heart, Heartiness, Heartsease, Heartsomeness, Heaven, Heavenliness, Help, Helpfulness, Henosis, Heroism, Heuristic(s), Holiness, Honesty, Honour, Hope, Hopefulness, Humanism, Humaneness, Humanity, Humanitarianism

Iamatology, Icon, Ideal, Idealism, Idealization, Idol, Idolization, Illumination, Illustriousness, Immanentism, Immaculateness, Immensity, Immortality, Immunity, Impartiality, Impeccability, Imperative, Imperturbability, Imperturbation, Importance, Impressiveness, Incentive, Inception, Incisiveness, Inclusion, Inclusiveness, Incorruptibility, Incorruption, Indefatigability, Indestructability, Indispensability, Indomitability, Inducement, Infallibility, Infiniteness, Infinity, Influence, Inner peace, Insight, Insightfulness, Inspiration, Inspiritment, Instauration, Instinct, Instruction, Integration, Integrity, Intelligence, Intensity, Intentness, Interaction, Interconnection, Interdependence, Interestingness, Intertwinement, Intrigue, Intuition, Invigoration, Invincibility, Irrefragableness, Irrefutability, Irreplaceability, Irrepressibility, Irreproachability, Irreproachableness, Irresistibility, Isness, Isonomy, Izzat

Jnana, Joie de Vivre, Joy, Joyance, Joyfulness, Joyousness, Joy to the world, Jubilance, Jubilation, Judgement, Judiciousness, Jumboism, Justice

Kairos, Kalon, Key, Key resource, Kindheartedness, Kindliness, Kindness, Know-how, Knowledge

Largeheartedness, Largesse, Latria, Laudability, Lavishness, Law, Law & Order, Lead, Leadership, Learned optimism, Learning, Legitimacy, Legend, Legerity, Lenience, Leniency, Lenity, Levelheadedness, Liberation, Liberty, Life, Lifesaver, Lift, Likeableness, Like-mindedness, Liking, Lionheartedness, Living, Lodestone, Logic, Logos, Lollapalooza, Longanimity, Longevity, Lordliness, Lovability, Love, Loveableness, Loveliness, Loving, Loving-kindness, Lovingness, Loyalty, Luck, Lucubration, Luminosity, Lushness

Macarism, Magic, Magnanimity, Magnificence, Magnitude, Majesty, Malleability, Management, Manuduction, Marvel, Masterdom, Masterfulness, Mastermind, Mastership, Mastery,

Maximum, Meaningfulness, Meditation, Meliorism, Mercy, Merit, Metaphysics, Meticulousness, Mettle, Might, Mildness, Mindfulness, Mirabilia, Miracle, Monotheism, Morality, Morals, Motivation, Munificence, Mutuality

Naissance, Naturalness, Nature, Nascence/Nascency, Neighbourliness, Nemophilia, Nemophily, Ne plus ultra, Neutrality, Niceness, Nirvana, Nitency, Nobleness, Nonviolence, Noteworthiness, Nourishment, Novity, Nurture, Nutrication, Nutrition

Objectiveness, Omnism, Oneness, Oomph, Openness, Open-handedness, Open-heartedness, Open-mindedness, Optimism, Option, Order, Origin, Originality, Origination

Pacifism, Panacea, Pansophism/Pansophy, Pantheism, Paragon, Pardon, Patience, Peace, Peaceableness, Peace of Mind, Pedagogics, Perceptiveness, Percipience, Perseverance, Persistence, Perspicacity, Phenomena, Phenomenon, Philalethia, Philanthropism, Philanthropy, Pinnacle, Placidity, Placidness, Pleasantness, Plenitude, Plenteousness, Plenty, Poiesis, Positive, Positivity, Potency, Potential, Power, Powerfulness, Practicality, Praiseworthiness, Preciousness, Preciseness, Precision, Pre-eminence, Prefulgence, Premium, Prepollence, Presence, Prevalence, Prevision, Prevoyance, Principle, Principles, Probity, Proficiency, Profundity, Profoundness, Prolificacy, Prominence, Promise, Pronoia, Propinquity, Propitiation, Propitiousness, Prosperity, Protection, Protectorship, Providence, Pull, Purity

Qualifiedness, Quality, Quiescence, Quiescency, Quiet, Quietism, Quietness, Quietude, Quiety, Quintessence

Radiance, Rapport, Rapprochement, Rapture, Ratification, Ratiocination, Rationality, Reach, Readiness, Reaffirmation, Realism, Reality, Realm, Realness, Realization, Reason, Reasonableness, Reassurance, Reception, Receptiveness, Reciprocity, Recognition, Reconciliation, Recovery, Rectification, Rectitude, Redemption, Refinement, Regardfulness, Reinforcement,

Rejuvenation, Relevance, Relevancy, Reliability, Remedy, Remission, Renaissance, Renewal, Renown, Repletion, Rescue, Reserve, Reserves, Resilience, Resolution, Resource, Resources, Resourcefulness, Respect, Respectability, Respite, Responsibility, Responsiveness, Restfulness, Restoration, Retentiveness, Revelation, Reverence, Reverential regard, Reverential wonder, Right, Rights, Righteousness, Rightfulness, Rightness, Ruggedness, Rule

Sacredness, Safeness, Safety, Sagaciousness, Sagacity, Saintliness, Salience, Salubriousness, Salvation, Sanctanimity, Sanctification, Sanction, Sapience, Satori, Savvy, Scrupulousness, Security, Sedulousness, Seemliness, Selection, Self-acceptance, Self-assertion, Self-assurance, Self-composedness, Self-composure, Self-confidence, Self-control, Self-determination, Self-esteem, Self-expression, Self-forgiveness, Selflessness, Self-regard, Self-reliance, Self-respect, Self-restraint, Self-satisfaction, Self-sufficiency, Self-trust, Self-worth, Sense, Sensation, Sensibility, Sensitivity, Serendipity, Sereneness, Serenity, Service, Seventh heaven, Sharing, Sheltering, Shielding, Significance, Silence, Simplicity, Sincerity, Smartness, Smarts, Sociability, Sociality, Soft-heartedness, Solace, Solidity, Solidarity, Sooth, Soothingness, Soundlessness, Soundness, Source, Sovereignty, Space, Specialness, Spirit, Spiritedness, Spirituality, Splendidness, Splendour, Stability, Staidness, Stalwartness, Standards, Start, Staunchness, Steadfastness, Steadiness, Stick-to-itiveness, Stillness, Straightforwardness, Straightness, Strength, (right) Stuff, Sublimity, Substance, Subtleness, Succor, Suffisance, Sufficiency, Suitability, Suitableness, Superabilty, Superabundance, Superbness, Superiority, Supplement, Support, Supremacy, Sure-footedness, Sure-handedness, Sureness, Surety, Survival, Sustainability, Sustenance, Sway, Synergy, Syntropy

Telegnosis, Telergy, Temper (not "a" temper), Temperateness, Tenacity, Tenderheartedness, Tenderness, Thankfulness, Thanks, Thaumatogeny, Thaumatology, Thaumaturgy, Theanthropism, Theanthroposophy, Theocentrism, Theological virtue, Theopanism, Theopathy, Theophilanthropism, Theopsychism, Theosophy,

Theotherapy, Thinkableness, Thoroughness, Theurgy, Thoughtfulness, (next to) Tidiness, Timelessness, Tiptop, Tirelessness, Togetherness, Tolerance, Top, Tranquility, Tranquilness, Transcendence, Transcendentalism, Transformation, Transparency, True love, Trueness, Trust, Trustworthiness, Truth, Truthfulness, Tutelage

Uberty, Ubiquitousness Ubiquity, Ubuntu, Understanding, Unfailingness, Unicity, Unification, Uniqueness, Union, Unison, Unity, Universalism, Unreservedness, Unselfishness, Untroubledness, Upgrade, Uplift, Uprightness, Upside, Upstandingness, Upwardness, Utopia

Validity, Validation, Value, Values, Variety, Veracity, Veraciousness, Verdancy, Verity, Versatility, Vigilance, Virtue, Virtuousness, Vision, Vitalism, Vitality, Vitalization

Warmheartedness, Ways and means, Weal, Wealth, Weightiness, Welcome, Welcomeness, Welfare, Wellbeing, Wellness, What it takes, Wherewithal, Wholeness, Wholeheartedness, Wholesomeness, Whole-spiritedness, Wisdom, Wonder, Wonderfulness, Wonderment, Wonderwork, Wondrousness, Worldliness, Worship, Worthiness

Xenophilia, Xenophily

Zenith

Divine words aren't a shortcut. They must be applied

"For there are no shortcuts to knowledge, to wisdom, to understanding – these must be lived, must be experienced by each and every soul." (Edgar Cayce Reading 830-2)

Notwithstanding, *Divine Words*, when contemplated, integrally establish some momentum in that ubiquitous unisonous direction because 'mind is the builder' and thereby the crystallizer of positive things.

Chapter 9
THE POSITIVE EMOTIONS

"In the activities mentally, keep optimistic - even when everything goes wrong."
(Edgar Cayce Reading 3329-1)

The Positive Emotions embody attractive powers, provide the thought energy that drives us and, like *The Universal Laws, The Fruits of the Spirit* and *The Gifts of the Spirit*, they indicate both a good path and destination. All of the positive emotions provide an instant blessing by making us feel really good as well as widening our scope to BIG picture Oneness.

Dr. Barbara Fredrickson identifies the top 10 positive emotions as **Interest**, **Amusement**, **Inspiration**, **Hope**, **Pride**, **Serenity**, **Love**, **Joy**, **Awe**, and **Gratitude**. These emotions improve a person's physiology; the heart and immune system as well as mental health and ability and feel great the whole time.

Simple acknowledgement, and recollection thereafter, or contemplation, of these positive emotions, as they occur, is genuinely uplifting:

"I'm open to..."

HOPE
The whole range from Hope to Certainty.

Advancement, Advocacy, Aid, Aim, Ambition, Anticipation, Approach, Aspiration, Assumption, Assuredness, Attraction, Belief, Boost, Bright side, Buoyancy, Certainty, Certitude, Comfort, Commission, Conceivability, Confidence, Conjecture, Constancy, Conviction, Dearest wish, Dependence, Desiderata, Desideratum, Desire, Direction, Dream, Drive, Encouragement, Enkindlement, Enthusiasm, Envisagement, Expectancy, Expectation, Faith, Faithfulness, Fancy, Forecast, Foreseeability, Fortitude, Future, Gain, Goal, Goodness, Heaven, Helpfulness, Hopefulness,

Incentive, Inducement, Inspiration, Intent, Intention, Interdependence, Invigoration, Kindness, Likelihood, Love, Loyalty, Need, Objective, Opportunity, Optimism, Outlook, Paradise, Picture, Plan, Possibility, Possibleness, Potential, Potentiality, Prediction, Presumption, Prevision, Probability, Promise, Prospect, Purpose, Pursuit, Quality, Reinforcement, Reliance, Rosiness, Sanguineness, Sanguinity, Security, Speculation, Succor, Support, Supposition, Sureness, Surety, Thinkableness, Trust, Upwardness, Utopia, Virtuality, Vision, Want, Whole-spiritedness, Wish, Yen

INTEREST, AMUSEMENT & INSPIRATION

Absorption, Advantage, Affect, Affinity, Agacerie, Alliance, Allure, Allurement, Amusement, Animation, Appeal, Applicability, Appositeness, Ardency, Ardour, Arousal, Attendance, Attention, Attentiveness, Attraction, Attractiveness, Avidity, Avidness, Awakening, Beckon, Beguilement, Behoof, Belonging, Benefit, Boon, Call forth, Calling, Captivation, Care, Carrot, Chemistry, Choice, Compulsion, Connection, Consideration, Consonance, Craving, Curiosity, Curiousness, Dash, Dazzle, Delight, Demand, Desire, Desirableness, Destiny, Direction, Diversion, Dividend, Draw, Drive, Eagerness, Effectiveness, Elan, Enamouredness, Enchantingness, Enchantment, Encouragement, Endearment, Energization, Engagingness, Engrossingness, Engrossment, Enjoyment, Enlivenment, Enrapturement, Enthrallment, Enthusiasm, Entertainment, Enticement, Entrancement, Evocation, Exhilaration, Exuberance, Fancy, Fascination, Favourite, Fervor, Flirtation, Focus, Fondness, Grab, Gratification, Gravy, Heed, Hold, Hook, Hunger, Immersion, Impassionedness, Import, Impression, Impulse, Incentive, Incitement, Inclination, Inducement, Indulgence, Infatuation, Influence, Inquisitiveness, Inspiration, Inspiritment, Interest, Interestingness, Intrigue, Invitation, Invitingness, Involvement, Keenness, Kindling, Leaning, Liking, Livelihood, Lodestone, Longing, Lure, Magnetization, Matter, Merit, Mesmerization, Mission, Motivation, Motive, Newsworthiness, Notice, Oomph, Partiality, Participation, Passion, Patronage, Peculiarity, Perk, Persuasion, Persuasiveness, Pizazz,

Pleasure, Poignancy, Predilection, Preference, Preoccupation, Priority, Provocation, Purpose, Pursuance, Pursuit, Quality, Raise, Ravishment, Refreshment, Regardfulness, Relation, Relevance, Relevancy, Relish, Responsiveness, Revelation, Rivet, Search, Solicitude, Spellbinder, Spice, Spiciness, Spirit, Steering, Stimulant, Stimulation, Stimulus, Sweetener, Sweetening, Tantalization, Thoughtfulness, Thirst, Tickle, Titillation, Transfixion, Transportability, Turn on, Understanding, Use, Vehemence, Verve, Vigour, Vim, Vivacity, Want, Whim, Winsomeness, Wow, Yearning, Yen, Zeal, Zealousness, Zestfulness

PRIDE

Amour-propre, Aplomb, Assurance, Assuredness, Bloom, Blossom, Boldness, Cachet, Certitude, Character, Composure, Confidence, Congratulations, Contentedness, Cred, Credit, Decency, Elevation, Ethics, Excellence, Faith, Fullness, Gallantry, Gladness, Good thing, Grace, Graciousness, Gratification, Happiness, Honour, Identity, Inspiration, Integrity, Liveliness, Merit, Morale, Morality, Nobility, Nobleness, Peace of Mind, Pleasure, Poise, Prestige, Pride, Propriety, Proudness, Rectitude, Refreshment, Respect, Respectability, Righteousness, Satisfaction, Self-confidence, Self-esteem, Self-love, Self-regard, Self-reliance, Self-respect, Self-satisfaction, Self-trust, Self-worth, Sensibility, Significance, Sufficiency, Sureness, Surety, Trust, Upstandingness, Vigour, Virtue, Well-being, Worth, Worthiness

SERENITY

Accord, Agreement, Amity, Aplomb, Armistice, Assurance, Ataraxia, Ataraxis, Ataraxy, Atonement, At-oneness, Balance, Bed of roses, Blessedness, Breeze, Calm, Calmness, Capacity, Chill, Clarity, Clearness, Collectedness, Comfort, Comity, Composedness, Composure, Concord, Concordance, Consonance, Constancy, Contemplation, Contentedness, Contentment, Cool-headedness, Coolness, Detachment, Dignity, Dispassion, Ease, Easiness, Easygoingness, Effortlessness, Enlightenment, Enough,

Equability, Equanimity, Equilibrium, Evenness, Forbearance, Freedom, Fulfillment, Gentleness, Gladness, Goodwill, Gratification, Happiness, Harmony, Heart, Heartsease, Heaven, Humility, Impartiality, Imperturbability, Imperturbation, Indisturbance, Inexcitability, Insouciance, Juste-milieu, Justice, Law & order, Leisure, Leniency, Lenity, Levelheadedness, Liberty, Marmoreal repose, Middle way, Mildness, Moderateness, Moderation, Naturalness, Neutrality, Nirvana, Noiselessness, Nonaggression, Nonchalance, Nonviolence, Nothing in excess, Order, Orderliness, Pacifism, Paradise, Passiveness, Passivity, Patience, Peace and quiet, Peace of mind, Peace, Peaceableness, Peacefulness, Philosophicalness, Philosophy, Placidity, Placidness, Poise, Presence of mind, Quiescence, Quiescency, Quiet, Quietism, Quietness, Quietude, Relaxation, Relaxedness, Reliability, Relief, Repletion, Requiescence, Reserve, Rest, Restfulness, Sangfroid, Satiety, Satisfaction, Satori, Security, Sedateness, Self-assurance, Self-composedness, Self-control, Self-possession, Self-restraint, Sereneness, Serenity, Silence, Simplicity, Smoothness, Snugness, Sobriety, Soothingness, Soundlessness, Stability, Staidness, Steadiness, Stillness, Temperance, Temperateness, Tranquility, Tranquilness, Understanding, Unexcitability, Unflappability, Unison, Unity, Unreservedness, Unruffledness, Untroubledness, Wellbeing

JOY

Affability, Afterglow, Agreeability, Agreeableness, Alleviation, Amiability, Amusement, Appreciation, At-oneness, Avidity, Blast, Blessedness, Bliss, Blissfulness, Blitheness, Blithesomeness, Bonniness, Boost, Brightness, Bright side, Buoyancy, Celebration, Cheer, Cheerfulness, Cheeriness, Cloud nine, Congeniality, Congenialness, Contentedness, Contentment, Conviviality, Cordiality, Delectation, Delight, Delightedness, Delightfulness, Ease, Ebullience, Ecstasy, Effervescence, Elation, Elevation, Enchantment, Enjoyableness, Enjoyment, Enlightenment, Enlivenment, Enthrallment, Enthusiasm, Euphoria, Exaltation, Excitation, Exhilaration, Exuberance, Exultance, Exultation, Felicity,

Festivity, Fortunateness, Frivolity, Frolic, Fulfillment, Fun, Gaiety, Gas, Gayness, Gladness, Gladsomeness, Glee, Gleefulness, Glow, Good fortune, Good nature, Good spirit(s), Gratification, Gratulation, Gusto, Happiness, Hey-day, High, Hilariousness, Hilarity, Hoot, Humour, Hurrah, In seventh heaven, Intoxication, Jauntiness, Jocosity, Jocularity, Jocundity, Joie de vivre, Jollies, Jollification, Jolliness, Jollity, Joviality, Joy, Joyance, Joyfulness, Joyousness, Jubilance, Jubilation, Jubilee, Kick, Laughs, Laughter, Levity, Lift, Lightheartedness, Liveliness, Merriment, Merriness, Merrymaking, Mirth, Mirthfulness, Nirvana, Optimism, Pep, Peppiness, Play, Perkiness, Playfulness, Pleasantness, Pleasure, Rapture, Ravishment, Regalement, Rejoicing, Relish, Repletion, Revelry, Rhapsody, Rollick, Romp, Rosiness, Satiety, Satisfaction, Seventh heaven, Sociability, Sparkle, Spice, Spirit, Spiritedness, Sportiveness, Spree, Sprightliness, Sunshine, Tang, Thrill, Titillation, Transport, Treat, Uplift, Vim, Vitality, Vitalization, Vivaciousness, Vivacity, Vivification, Whimsy, Well-being, Zeal, Zest, Zing, Zip

Smile more - It alleviates pain

LOVE

Abidingness, Acceptance, Accord, Acknowledgement, Admiration, Adoration, Adulation, Aerophilia, Affection, Affinity, Agape, Ailurophilia, Allegiance, Alliance, Altruism, Amativeness, Amiability, Amiableness, Amicability, Amicableness, Amity, Amore, Amour-propre, Appeal, Appraisal, Appreciation, Appreciativeness, Approbation, Approval, Arctophilia, Ardour, Aroha, Astrophilia, Audiophilia, Attachment, Attraction, Avidity, Awareness, Beauty, Beguin, Benefaction, Beneficence, Benevolence, Benevolentness, Bigheartedness, Billet-doux, Bibliophilia, Biophilia, Bonhomie, Bliss, Brightness, Brotherhood, Camaraderie, Care, Caritas, Charitableness, Charity, Choice, Cinephilia, Cognizance, Comfort, Comity, Commiseration, Commitment, Communion, Community, Companionship, Compassion, Compassionateness, Compatibility, Completion,

Comprehension, Concord, Condolence, Connection, Consideration, Consonance, Cooperation, Cynophilia, Deference, Delight, Devotedness, Devotion, Elevation, Emotion, Empathy, Enamouredness, Enchantment, Endearment, Faithfulness, Fancy, Favour, Feeling, Fellowship, Fidelity, Fondness, Forbearance, Forgiveness, Fraternity, Friendliness, Friendship, Generosity, Geniality, Gentleness, Givingness, Godliness, Good wishes, Goodness, Goodwill, Grace, Graciousness, Harmony, Heart, Heartiness, Heliophilia, Helpfulness, Hippophilia, Honour, Humaneness, Humanitarianism, Ideal, Idealism, Idealization, Increase, Infatuation, Innocence, Inspiration, Interest, Joy, Kindheartedness, Kindness, Kinship, Largeheartedness, Largesse, Law, Lenience, Leniency, Lenity, Life, Like-mindedness, Logophilia, Loveableness, Loving, Magnanimity, Mercy, Mindset, Mood, Mutuality, Mycophilia, Neighbourlikeness, Neighbourliness, Nemophilia, Neophilia, Nourishment, Nurture, Nyctophilia, Oneness, Option, Pacifism, Pardon, Partiality, Pash, Passion, Penchant, Perception, Perfection, Philalethia, Philanthropism, Philanthropy, Philocaly, Philogyny, Philology, Philomathy, Philonoism, Philosophicalness, Philosophy, Philo-xenia, Pleasure, Pluviophilia, Polyamory, Potency, Preciousness, Predilection, Predisposition, Preference, Prize, Probity, Propensity, Purity, Quintessence, Rapport, Rapprochement, Rapture, Reaction, Reciprocity, Recognition, Regard, Respect, Responsiveness, Retrophilia, Revelry, Reverence, Romanticism, Sanction, Satisfaction, Selection, Sensation, Sensibility, Sensitivity, Sensuality, Sentiment, Sentimentality, Service, Sharing, Sheltering, Shielding, Sincerity, Sisterhood, Sociability, Sociality, Sodality, Softheartedness, Solidarity, Spark, Spirituality, Steadfastness, Support, Sweetener, Sweetness, Sympathy, Tenderheartedness, Tenderness, Theological virtue, Theo-philanthropism, Togetherness, Tolerance, Treasure, Trust, Truthfulness, Typhlophilia, Understanding, Unfailingness, Union, Unison, Unicity, Unity, Urge, Valuation, Value, Veneration, Virtue, Warmheartedness, Warmth, Welcome, Wholeheartedness, Wisdom, Xenophilia, Xenophily, Yen

See *All the Love in the World* Chapter 7 for more.

AWE

Acclaim, Acclamation, Admiration, Adoration, Adulation, Allegiance, Amazedness, Amazement, Apex, Apogee, Apotheosis, Appeal, Appreciation, Appreciativeness, Approbation, Approval, Astonishment, Astoundment, Awesomeness, Bedazzlement, Climax, Dazzlement, Deference, Deification, Delight, Devotion, Elevation, Esteem, Exaltation, Fascination, Favour, Fidelity, Flabbergast, Flabbergastment, Glorification, Glory, Greatness, Great respect, Height, Homage, Honour, Idolization, Impression, Inspiration, Love, Loyalty, Marvel, Ne plus ultra, Obeisance, Peak, Piousness, Pietism, Piety, Pinnacle, Quintessence, Recognition, Regard, Respect, Reverence, Reverential regard, Reverential wonder, Sensation, Stimulation, Sublimity, Surprise, Top, Tribute, Veneration, Vertex, Wonder, Wonderment, Worship, Zenith

GRATITUDE

Acknowledgement, Admiration, Adoration, Affection, Answer, Apperception, Appreciation, Appreciativeness, Approbation, Approval, Assimilation, Awareness, Benison, Blessing, Cognition, Cognizance, Comprehension, Conception, Consciousness, Credit, Favour, Glorification, Glory, Grace, Gramercy, Gratefulness, Gratitude, Hailing, Honour, Honouring, Idealization, Joy, Love, Nod, Notice, Perception, Praise, Realization, Recognition, Recognizance (archaic), Regard, Respect, Responsiveness, Reverence, Sanctification, Thankfulness, Thanks, Thanksgiving, Tribute, Understanding, Valuation, Verity

GRAMERCY (Grand Merci) This great appreciation is arguably the ultimate top single emotion ranking just above Love and Joy because it invites Ubiquity into the picture. Contemplate gramercy often.

Chapter 10

THANK-YOU WORDS

"Show due consideration as to how much ye owe the world, rather than as to how much the world owes you!" (Edgar Cayce Reading 2172-1)

The words in the following thankful lists are those with which an appreciative note might be written. Words directly related to food and drink are **bold**.

THANK-YOU ADJECTIVES

A-1, A-one, Abounding, Abundant, Acclaimed, Accommodating, Accommodative, Accomplished, Accordant, Acuminate, Acuminous, Adept, Admirable, Admired, Adroit, Adventuresome, Adventurous, Aesthetic, Aesthetical, Affable, Affined, Afflated, Afflating, **Aged**, Agreeable, Airy, Alacritous, Alfresco, **Alimental, Alimentary**, All there, Alluring, Amative, Amatory, Amazing, Ambrosial, Ambrosian, Amenable, Amiable, Amicable, Ample, Amoroso, Amusing, **Anamnestic**, **Aperitive**, **Aplenty**, Appealing, **Appetizing**, Applauded, Appreciated, Appreciative, Approbative, **Aromatic**, Artful, Articulate, **Artisanal**, Artistic, Ascendant, At ease, At hand, At leisure, At one's disposal, At the ready, Attentive, Attractive, Auspicious, Authentic, Avant-garde, Awaited, Awesome

Beautified, Beautiful, Becoming, Bee's knees, Benevolent, Best, Best-loved, Better, Better-than-before, Bewitching, Beyond compare, Big, Biggest, Big-hearted, Bijou, Blissful, Blithe, Blithesome, Blooming, Blossoming, Blue-ribbon, Bodacious, Boffo, Boisterous, Bold, Bonzer, Boss, **Bounteous**, **Bountiful,** Breathtaking, Bright, Brill, Brilliant, **Brimming**, **Bubbly,** Buoyant, **Bursting**, Bustling, **Buttery**

Calm, Calmative, Calming, Candescent, Cantier, Cantiest, Canty, Capital, Captivating, Cared for, Carefree, Careful, Caring, Casual,

Celebrated, Celebratory, Champion, Charmed, Charming, Cheerful, Cherishable, Cherished, Cherry, Chic, Chipper, Chirpiest, Chirpy, Chivalrous, **Chocolatey**, Choice, Choicest, Chummy, **Citrusy**, Civil, Civilized, Classic, Classical, Classy, Clean, Clear, Cohortative, Collaborative, Colourful, Comfortable, Comforting, Commanding, Commendable, Commendatory, Commodious, Commutual, Companionable, Compassionate, Compatible, Compelling, Complaisant, Complete, Composed, Comprehensive, Conceptual, Concordant, Confelicitous, Conferrable, Congenial, Conscientious, Considerable, Considerate, Contemporary, Content, Convenient, Conversant, Convivial, Cool, Coordinated, Copacetic, **Copious**, Cordial, Corking, Coruscant, Cosmopolitan, Cosy, Courteous, Courtly, Couthie, Cozy, Crack, Crackerjack, **Creamy**, Creative, **Crisp**, Crowd-pleasing, Cultivated, Cultured, **Curative**, Cute, Cutting-edge, **Crunchy**

Dainty, Dandy, **Dapatical**, Dapper, Daring, Darling, Dashing, Dazzling, Dear, Dearest, Debonair, Decent, Decorous, **Delectable**, **Delicate, Delicious,** Delighted, **Delightful**, **Delish**, Deluxe, Deserving, Designer, Desirable, Desired, Desirous, Dignified, Disarming, Discerning, Disciplined, Discreet, Discrete, Distinctive, Distinguished, Diverse, Diverting, Divine, Doted on, Doting, Doxological, Droll, Ducky, Dulcet, Dynamic, Dynamite

Easygoing,   Easy to talk to,   Easy to understand,   Ebullient, Effervescent, Efflorescent, Effortless, Effulgent, Elated, Elating, Electric, Electrifying, Elegant, Elevating, Eloquent, **Empyreal**, Enamouring, Enchanted, Enchanting, Endearing, Energetic, Energizing, Engaging, Engrossing, Enjoyable, Enjoyed, Enlightening, Enlivened, **Enlivening**, Enriching, Entertaining, Enthralling, Enthusiastic, Enticed, Enticing, Entranced, Entrancing, Epic, **Epicurean**, Esthetic, Esthetical, Eudaemonistic/Eudaemonistical, **Eupeptic**, Euphonious, Euphoric, Eventful, Evocative, Exceeding, Excellent, Excelling, Exceptional, Excited, Exciting, Exemplary, Exhilarated, Exhilarating, Exhortative, Exhortatory, Expansive, Expert, Expressive, Exquisite, Exotic, Extra-, Extraordinaire, Extraordinary, Exuberant, Eye-catching

Fab, Fabulous, Familial, Familiar, Family, Fancy, Fancy-free, Fanciful, Fantabulous, Fantastic, Far-out, Fascinating, Fashionable, Favourite, Feelgood, Felicitous, **Feracious**, Festal, Festive, Filled, **Filling**, Fine, Finer, Finest, **Finger-licking**, First-class, First-order, First-rate, Fitting, **Five-star**, **Flaky**, Flamboyant, Flashy, **Flavoured**, **Flavourful**, **Flavoursome**, Flawless, Flourishing, Flowing, Fluent, Fly (chiefly British), Fond, Foremost, Foresighted, Formal, Fortuitous, Fortunate, Forward-thinking, **Four-star**, Frabjous, Fraternal, Freethinking, **Fresh**, Friendly, Frolicsome, Front-page, **Fruity**, Fulfilling, Fulgent, Full, **Full-bodied**, Fun

Galore, Gamesome, **Gastronomic**, Gay, Gelastic, Gelogenic, **Generous**, Genial, Genteel, Gentle, Gentlemanly, Genuine, Gifted, Giving, Glad, Glamorous, **Glazed**, Gleaming, Gleeful, Glistening, Glorious, Glowing, Golden, **Good**, Goodhearted, Good-feeling, Good-humoured, Goodly, Good-natured, Gorgeous, **Gourmet**, Graced, Graceful, Gracious, Gradely, Grand, Grateful, Gratified, **Gratifying**, Great, Greatest, Greathearted, Gregarious, Groovy, Gumptious, **Gustatory**

Hale, Handsome, Happening, Happy, Happy-go-lucky, Harmonic, Harmonious, Healthful, Healthy, Heartfelt, Heart-to-heart, Heartsome, Heartwarming, Hearty, Heavenly, Helpful, Henotic, Hep, Heralded, Herbal, High calibre, High-class, High-quality, Highspirited, Highest, Highly regarded, Highly valued, Hilarious, Honeyed, Hortative, Hortatory, Hospitable, **Hot**, Humorous

Ideal, Illecebrous, Illuminating, Illustrious, Imaginative, Imitable, Immaculate, Immarcescible, Immeasurable, Immediate, Immense, Immortal, Immune, Impartial, Impassioned, Impavid, Impeccable, Imperturbable, Impish, Important, Impressive, Improved, Improvisational, In, In 7th heaven, Incandescent, Inclusive, Incomparable, Incredible, In demand, **Inebriating**, Ineffable, Infatuating, In fine fettle (good spirits), **Infused**, Inimitable, Innovative, In love, In seventh heaven, Insouciant, Inspired, Inspiring, Inspirited, **Inspiriting**, Interconnective, Intellectual, Intelligent Interactive,

Interesting, In the groove, In the swim, Intoxicating, Intrigued, Intriguing, Invigorated, **Invigorating**, Inviting, In vogue, Irenic, **Irresistible**

Jam-packed, Jaunty, Jazzy, Jestful, Jiggish, Jocose, Jocoserious, Jocular, Joculatory, Jocund, Jolif, Jolly, Jovial, Joyful, Joyous, Joysome, Jubilant, **Juicy**, Just right

Keen, Kind, Kind-hearted, Kindly, Kindred, Kingly, Knightly, Knowledgeable, Kooky

Ladylike, Laid-back, Lambent, Largifical, Lasting, Laudable, Laudatory, Lautitious, **Lavish**, **Lean**, Legendary, Liefly, Leisurely, Lepid, Liberal, Liberating, **Light**, Lightening, Likable, Liked, Like-minded, **Lip-smacking**, Lively, Lovable, Loved, Lovely, Loving, Luculent, Ludibund, Ludic, Luminous, **Luscious**, Lush, Lustrous, Lusory, Luxuriant, Luxurious

Magical, Magnanimous, Magnetic, Magnificent, Majestic, **Malty**, Mannerly, **Marinated**, Marvelous, **Mashed**, Masterful, Masterly, Matchless, Maximal, Maximum, Meaningful, Measured, **Meaty**, Meet, Mellifluous, Melliloquent, Mellisonant, Mellow, Melodious, Memorable, Meritable, Meritorious, Merry, Mesmerizing, Meticulous, Mild, Mind-blowing, Mindful, **Minty**, Mirthful, Modern, Modernistic, **Moist**, Momentous, **More**, **Morish**, Most excellent, **Mouthwatering**, Moving, Multidimensional, Musical

Natty, Near to one's heart, Neat, **Nectarous**, Neighbourly, Neoteric, Nice, Nifty, Nitid, Nonpareil, Notable, Noteworthy, **Nourished**, **Nourishing**, Novel, **Nurturing**, **Nutrimental**, **Nutritional**, **Nutritious**, **Nummy**, **Nutty**

"What foods these morsels be!" – William Shakespoon

Obliging, **Oenophilic/Enophilic**, Olympian, On, On cloud nine, On the ball, On the beam, Open-handed, Open-hearted, Open-minded, Optimal, Optimum, Opulent, Organized, Original, Ornamental, Outgoing, Out-of-sight, Out-of-this-world, Outstanding, **Over-**

flowing, Overjoyed

Pabulous, **Palatable**, Pally, Paradisaic, Paradisal, Paradisiacal, **Par excellence**, Peaceful, **Peachy**, Peachy keen, Peak, Peerless, Peppy, Perceptual, Perfect, Perfective, Perky, Personable, Phenomenal, Philoxenial, Picturesque, **Piquant**, Playful, Pleasant, Pleased, Pleasing, Pleasurable, **Plenteous**, **Plentiful**, **Plum**, **Plummy**, Pluperfect, Polished, Polite, Popular, Posh, Positive, Praised, Praiseworthy, Precious, Preferable, Preferred, Prefulgent, Premier, Premium, Prepared, Prepossessing, Prescious, Pretty, Priceless, Primal, Primary, **Prime**, Primed, Primo, Princely, Pristine, Privileged, Prized, Prize-winning, Procinct, Prodigious, Proficient, Profulgent, Prolific, Proper, Propitious, Prosperous, Provocative, Proud, Pukka, Pure, Purposeful

Quenched, Quenching

Rad, Radiant, **Rapturous**, **Ravishing**, Readied, Ready, Recherche', Receptive, Recommendable, Recuperative, Red-carpet, Redolent, Refined, **Refreshing**, Refulgent, Regal, Regnant, Rejuvenating, Rejuvenescent, Relaxed, Relaxing, Relieving, Relished, Relishing, Remarkable, **Renascent**, **Renewing**, **Replete**, Resourceful, Respectable, Respectful, **Resplendent**, Restful, Restorative, Revitalized, Revitalizing, Reviviscent, Revivifying, Rhapsodic, Riant, **Rich**, Rident, Ridibund, Right neighbourly, Risible, Risorial, Robust, Rollicking, Rosy, Rousing, Rutilant

Salubrious, **Salted**, **Salutary**, **Sapid**, **Saporific**, **Saporous**, **Satisfied**, **Satisfying**, **Saucy**, **Savoury**, Scintillant, Scintillating, Scintillescent, **Scrumptious**, **Seasoned**, Second-to-none, Selcouth, Sensate, Sensational, Sentimental, Serene, Shining, Silky, Sincere, **Slaking**, Smart, Smiling, Smooth, Snazzy, Snappy, Soaring, Sociable, Social, Societal, Sophisticated, **Sparkling**, Special, Spectacular, **Spicy**, Spirited, Splendid, Splendiferous, Splendorous, Spruce, Stellar, Sterling, Stimulating, Stimulative, Stimulatory, Striking, Strong, Stupendous, Stylish, Suave, Suaveolent, Sublime, Substantial, Successful, **Succulent**, **Sugary, Sumptuous**, Sunny, Super, **Superabundant**, Superb,

Super-civilized, Superior, Superlative, Surpassing, Swank, **Sweet**, **Sweet-smelling**, **Sweet-tasting**, **Sybaritic**

Talented, Tangible, **Tangy**, **Tantalizing**, **Tasteful**, **Tasty**, Tempestive, Tempting, **Tender**, Tender-hearted, Terrific, Thankful, Thankworthy, Thorough, Thoughtful, Thrilled, Thrilling, Tickety-boo, Tickled, Tidy, Tight, Timeless, Tip-top, Tireless, Titillating, Tonic, **Toothsome**, Top, Top drawer, Top-notch, Tops, Totally-tubular, To the max, Touching, Touted, Tranquil, Transcendent, Transporting, Treasurable, Treasured, Tremendous, Trim, Triumphant

Unassuming, Unbeatable, Uncompromising, Unconditionally loving, Understanding, Unequalled, Unfailing, Unforgettable, Unparalleled, Unrivalled, Unselfish, Unsurpassed, Untiring, Unwithdrawing, Upbeat, **Upbuilding**, Uplifted, Uplifting, Up to snuff, Uptown, Urbane, Usable, Utile dulci, Utmost, Utopian, Utopic

Valued, **Vegetarian**, Vegete, **Velvety**, Vibrant, **Vitalizing**, **Vitative**, Vivacious, Vivid, **Vivifying**, Vogue

Waggish, Wanted, Warm, Warm-hearted, Welcome, Welcomed, Welcoming, Weleful, Well-arranged, Well-built, Well-disposed, Well-done, Well-liked, Well-made, Well-planned, Well-received, Well-suited, Well-timed, Welsome, Whimsical, Whipped, Whizbang, Wholehearted, **Wholesome**, Winning, Winsome, With it, Without equal, Without limit, Witty, Wizardly, Wonderful, Wonderstruck, Wonder-working, Wondrous, World class, Worthwhile, Worthy

Xenial, Xenodocial

Yummy

Zany, Zazzy, **Zestful, Zesty,** Zero cool, **Zingy**, Zoetic

THANK-YOU NOUNS

Abidingness, Ability, Abundance, Acceptance, Accommodation, Accord, Adroitness, Adventure, Aesthetic, Affability, Affection, Affinity, Afflatus, Agreeability, Agreeableness, Aliveness, Alleviation, Allure, Amativeness, Ambrosia, Amelioration, Amenity, Amiability, Amiableness, Amicability, Amity, Amore, Amour-propre, **Aperitif,** Applause, Appeal, Appetence, **Appetizer,** Appreciation, Approbation, Aptness, Artistry, Attentiveness, Auspiciousness, Authenticity, Awesomeness

Badinage, Balance, Bash, Beauty, Benefaction, Beneficence, Benevolence, Benevolentness, Benison, Bigheartedness, Blessedness, Blessing, Blissfulness, Blitheness, Blithesomeness, Bonhomie, Bonniness, **Boost**, Bounce, **Bounty**, **Bounteousness**, **Bountifulness**, Brightness, Brilliance, Brio, **Brunch**, Buoyancy

Companionship, Company, Conversation, Conviviality, Cachet, Camaraderie, Care, Carefulness, Caritas, Character, Charisma, Charm, Cheer, Cheerfulness, Cheeriness, Civility, Class, Classiness, Cleanliness, Cleverness, Closeness, Cockaigne, Colourfulness, Comedy, Comfort, Comity, Commendation, Commitment, Companionship, Compassion, Compassionateness, Complement, Completeness, Composedness, Composition, Composure, Congeniality, Congenialness, Congratulations, Consanguinity, Conscientiousness, Consideration, Consistency, Consonance, Contemporariness, Contentedness, Contentment, Contribution, Conversance, Conversation, Conviviality, Coolheadedness, Coolness, Coordination, Cordiality, Cordialness, Correctness, Cosiness, Courteousness, Courtesy, Courtliness, Creation, Creativeness, Creativity, Culture, Cuteness

Dash, Dazzle, Dazzlement, Debonairness, Dearness, **Decency**, Decorum, Dedication, Deftness, **Delectableness, Delectations, Delicacies, Delicacy, Deliciousness**, Delight, **Delights**, Delightedness, Delightfulness, Dependability, **Desert**, Desiderata, Desideratum, Desirability, Desirableness, Dexterity, Dexterousness,

Dignity, Diligence, **Dinner**, Discernment, Discretion, Distinction, Drive, Dynamism

Earthliness, Ease, Easygoingness, Ebullience, Effectiveness, Effervescence, Efficacy, Efficiency, Efflorescence, Effortlessness, Effulgence, Élan, Elegance, Eloquence, Embrace, Eminence, Enablement, Enamouredness, Enchantingness, Enchantments, Encomium, Energy, Engagement, Engagingness, Engrossingness, Engrossment, Enhancement, Enjoyableness, Enjoyment, Enkindlement, Enlightenment, Enlivenment, Ennoblement, Enough, Enrapturement, Enrichment, Enterprise, Entertainment, Enthrallment, Enthusiasm, **Enticement**, Entrancement, **Epicureanism**, Equanimity, Esprit, Esse, Essence, Etiquette, Eudaimonia, Eudaimonism, Eunoia, Eupathy, Euphony, Eutaxy, Eutrapely, Event, Everything, Evocativeness, Exactly/Just what I needed, Excellence, Excellency, Exceptionalness, Excitation, Excitement, Exemplariness, Exhilaration, Existence, Expertise, Exploration, Expressiveness, **Exquisiteness**, Extraordinariness, Exuberance, Exuberancy

Fabulousness, Facilitation, Facility, Facundity, Family, Fancy, Favour, **Feast**, Feat, Felicity, Fellowship, Feminacy, Festival, Festiveness, Festivity, Fete, Fineness, Finesse, Flair, Flamboyance, **Flavour**, Fleetness, Flexibility, Flourish, Flow, **Foison**, Fondness, **Food**, **Foodophile**, **Food stuffs**, Fraternity, **Freshness**, Friendliness, Friendship, Frivolity, Frolic, Frolicsomeness, **Fruitfulness**, **Fulfillment**, **Fullness**, Fulgor, Fun

Gallantry, Gaiety, Gamesomeness, Gathering, Gayness, Gettogether, Generativity, **Generosity**, **Generousness**, Geniality, Genialness, Genius, Gentleness, Genuineness, Gift, Gifts, Giftedness, Givingness, Gladness, Gladsomeness, Glamour, Glee, Gleefulness, Good, Good cheer, Good company, **Good food**, Good nature, Goodness, Good spirit(s), Good thing, Good time, Goodwill, Good wishes, Grace, Gracefulness, Graciousness, Gramercy, Gratitude, Gratefulness, Gratulation, **Gravy**, Greatness, Grooviness, Gumption, **Gusto**

Happiness, Harmoniousness, Harmony, **Healthiness**, Heart, **Heartiness**, Heartsomeness, Heavenliness, Helpfulness, Highspiritedness, Hilariousness, Hilarity, Hipness, Hoot, Hospitableness, Hospitality, Humanity, Humdinger, Humour, Humourousness

Illustriousness, Imagination, Immaculateness, Impeccability, Impishness, Implementation, Impressiveness, Inclusion, Inclusiveness, Indispensability, Individuality, Indulgence, Indulgences, Industriousness, Ingenuity, Initiative, Innovation, Insight, Insightfulness, Inspiration, Inspiritment, **Instauration**, Instinct, Interaction, Interconnection, Interestingness, Inventiveness, Invigoration, Invitation, Invitingness, Irreplaceability, Irrepressibility, Irresistibility, Isness

Jauntiness, Jazziness, Jocosity, Jocularity, Jocundity, Joie de vivre, Jollies, Jollification, Jolliness, Jollity, Joviality, Joy, Joyance, Joyfulness, Joyousness, Jubilance, Jubilation, Jubilee, **Juice**, **Juiciness**

Kalon, Keenness, Kindheartedness, Kindliness, Kindness, Kinship, Knack, Know-how, Knowledge, Kudos

Largeheartedness, **Largesse**, Laudability, Laugh, Laughter, **Lavishness**, Lead, Leadership, Lenity, Lepidity, Levity, **Libation**, Liberation, Lift, Light-heartedness, Lightness, Likeableness, Like-mindedness, Liveliness, Living, Lollapalooza, Lovability, Love, Loveableness, Loveliness, Love object, Loving, Loving-kindness, Lovingness, Luminosity, **Lunch**, **Lusciousness**, Lushness, Lustre, Luxury, Luxuriousness

Magic, Magnificence, Majesty, Management, Manners, Marvel, Masterdom, Masterfulness, Mastermind, Masterpiece, Mastership, Mastery, **Meal**, Meaningfulness, Mellifluousness, Mellowness, Memories, Memory, Merriment, Merriness, Merrymaking, Meticulousness, Mindfulness, Mirth, Mirthfulness, Mischief, Mischievousness, Modernity, Morale, Moxie, **Munificence**

Naturalness, Neatness, Neighbourlikeness, Neighbourliness, Niceness, Nicety, Niftiness, Nimbleness, Nirvana, Noteworthiness, **Nourishment**, Novity, **Nurture**, **Nutrication**, **Nutrition**

Oblectation, Obligingness, **Oenomel**, Openness, Open-handedness, Open-heartedness, Open-mindedness, Opportunity, Opulence, Orderliness, **Or d'oeuvres**, Originality, Outgoingness, Ovation

Pabulum, Panacea, Panache, Panaesthesia, Panegyric, Paradise, Parage, Party, Pathopoeia, Patronage, Pep, **Pepper-upper**, Peppiness, Percipience, Perfectibilism, Perfectionism, Perfection, Perkiness, Perseverance, Personage, Personality, Pertness, Phenomena, Phenomenon, Philocaly, Philoxenia, **Pick-me-up**, **Piquancy**, Pizzazz, Playfulness, Pleasantness, Pleasantry, **Plenteousness**, **Plenitude**, **Plenty**, Plushness, Poise, Polish, Politeness, Positivity, Practicality, Praiseworthiness, Preciousness, **Preparation**, **Preparedness**, Present, Presentation, Pride, Proactiveness, Proactivity, Procinct, Proficiency, Pronoia, Propinquity, Propitiousness, Prowess

Quaintness, Quality, Quiescence, Quiescency, Quietness, Quietude, Quintessence

Radiance, Raillery, Raise, Rapport, **Ravishment**, Readiness, Realm, Realness, Reassurance, **Reception**, Receptiveness, Reciprocity, Recognition, Refinement, Reflation, Refresher, Refreshment, Regalement, Regality, Regardfulness, Regards, Rejoicing, Rejuvenation, Relaxation, Relaxedness, Release, Reliability, **Relish**, Remarkableness, Remedy, Renewal, Repast, Repletion, Reputation, Resources, Resourcefulness, Respect, Respectability, Respite, Responsiveness, Restfulness, Restoration, Revelry, Reverence, Revival, Rhapsody, **Richness**, Risibility, Rollick, Romanticism, Romp, Rosiness

Saintliness, **Salubriousness**, Salute, Sanguineness, Sanguinity, **Sapidity**, **Satiation**, **Satiety**, **Satisfaction**, **Sauciness**, Savoir-faire, **Savouriness**, Scintillation, **Scrumptiousness**, Scrupulousness, **Seasoning**, Selection, Self-composure, Self-confidence, Self-discipline, Self-expression, Selflessness, Sensation, Sensibility, Sentiment, Sereneness, Serenity, Service, Seventh heaven, Sharing, Sheltering, Shot in the arm, Simplicity, Sincerity, Skill, Smartness, Smile, Smoothness, **Snacks**, Snazziness, Sociability, Social grace, Sociality, Soiree, Solace, Soothingness, Sophistication, Soul, Soulfulness, Space, Spark, Sparkle, Specialness, **Spice**, **Spiciness**, Spirit, **Spirits**, Spiritedness, Splendidness, **Splendour**, Spontaneity, Sportiveness, Sprightliness, Spunk, Standard, Standards, Stateliness, Stature, Stick-to-itiveness, Stimulation, Stimulus, Straightforwardness, Style, Stylishness, Suavity, Sublimity, **Substance**, Subtleness, Success, Successfulness, Succor, **Succulence**, Sufficiency, **Suffisance**, Suitability, Suitableness, **Sumptuousness**, Sunniness, Sunshine, Superabilty, **Superabundance**, Superbia, Superbness, Superiority, **Supper**, Supplement, Support, Supremacy, Sure-footedness, Sure-handedness, Sureness, Surety, Surprise, **Sustenance**, Swankiness, **Sweetener**, **Sweetening**, **Sweetness**, Synergy

Ta!

Tact, Talent, **Tang**, **Tantalization**, **Taste**, Temper (not "a" temper), Temperateness, **Temptations**, Tenderheartedness, **Tenderness**, Thanks, Thank-you, Thaumaturgy, Therapy, Thoroughness, Thoughtfulness, **Threpsology,** Thrill, Thumbs-up, Tidiness, Timelessness, Timeliness, Tirelessness, Titillation, Togetherness, Touch, Tranquility, Tranquilness, Transcendence, **Treat**, **Treats**, Tribute, **Trophism**, **Trophology**

Uberty, Ubuntu, Unfailingness, Unflappability, Uniqueness, Unreservedness, **Unselfishness**, **Uplift**, Upstandingness, Utopia

Value, Values, Versatility, Verve, Vibrancy, Vigour, Vim, Virtu, Virtue, Virtuosity, Virtuousness, Vision, Vitality, **Vitalization**, Vivaciousness, Vivacity, Vivency, **Vivification**, Volition

Warmheartedness, Warmth, Ways, Ways and means, Welcome, Welcomeness, Wellness, What it takes, Wherewithal, Whimsy, Wholeheartedness, Wholeness, Wholesomeness, Whole-spiritedness,

Willingness, **Wine**, Winsomeness, Wit, Witticisms, Wittiness, Wonderfulness, Wonderment, Wonderwork, Wondrousness, Worldliness

Xenophilia, Xenophily

Yen

Zaniness, Zap, Zeal, Zealousness, **Zest**, **Zestfulness**, **Zestiness**, **Zing**, Zip, Zoomagnetism

THANK-YOU RECIPIENTS

BFF, Cohorts, Colleagues, Companions, Convive, Boy/Girl, **Epicure**, **Enophile (Oenophile)**, **Foodie**, Friends, **Gastronome**, Gentleman, Gentlemen, Gentlewoman, Gentlewomen, **Gourmet**, Host, Hostess, Ladies, My love, **Turophile**

THANK-YOU ADVERBS

Abundantly, Accommodatingly, Adeptly, Admirably, Admiringly, Adroitly, Adventuresomely, Aesthetically, Affably, Affectionately, Affirmatively, Agreeably, Alluringly, Amazingly, Amenably, Amiably, **Amply**, Amoroso, Amusingly, **Appetizingly**, Appreciatively, Approvingly, Aptly, Artistically, Attractively, Atypically, Auspiciously, Augustly, Authentically, Awesomely

Beauteously, Beautifully, Befriendingly, Beneficently, Beneficially, Benevolently, Blazingly, Blessedly, Blissfully, Blithely, Boisterously, Boldly, **Bounteously**, **Bountifully**, Brightly, Brilliantly, Brotherly, Buoyantly

Capably, Captivatingly, Carefully, Caringly, Casually, Charismatically, Charmingly, Cheerfully, Chicly, Chivalrously, Civilly, Cleanly, Colourfully, Comfortably, Comfortingly, Commendably, Companionably, Compellingly, Conamore, Confidently, Congenially, Conscientiously, Considerately, Contently, Conversantly, Convivially, Coolly, Cordially, Cozily, Courteously, Creatively

Dapperly, Dashingly, Dazzlingly, Dearly, Debonairly, Decorously, Deftly, **Delectably**, Deliberately, Delicately, **Deliciously**, Delightedly, Delightfully, Devotedly, Dexterously, Diligently, Disarmingly, Discerningly, Discriminatingly, Distinctively, Divinely, Dreamily, Dynamically

Eagerly, Ebulliently, Ecstatically, Effectively, Effectually, Effervescently, Efficiently, Effortlessly, Effulgently, Elaborately, Elatedly, Elatingly, Electrically, Elegantly, Elevatingly, Eloquently, Eminently, Enchantingly, Endearingly, Energetically, Energizingly, Engagingly, Engrossingly, Enjoyably, Enlighteningly, Enliveningly, Enrapturously, Enrichingly, Entertainingly, Enthrallingly, Enthusiastically, **Enticingly**, Entrancingly, Especially, Esteemingly, Eternally, Eudaemonistically, Euphorically, Evocatively, Exactly, Exceedingly, Excellently, Excellingly, Exceptionally, Excitingly, Executively, Exhilaratingly, Exotically, Expertly, Expressively, Exquisitely, Extraordinarily, Extravagantly, Exuberantly

Fabulously, Fain, Fantastically, Fascinatingly, Fashionably, Favourably, Felicitously, Festively, Fetchingly, Finely, Fitly, Fittingly, Flamboyantly, **Flavourfully**, Flourishingly, Fluently, Fondly, Forever, Formally, Fortuitously, Fortunately, Fraternally, Freely, **Freshly**, Frolicsomely, **Fruitfully**, Fully, **Fullfilingly**

Gaily, Gallantly, Gamefully, Gamesomely, **Gastronomically**, **Generously**, Genially, Gently, Genuinely, Gladly, Gleefully, Gloriously, Glowingly, Good-humouredly, Good-naturedly, Gorgeously, Gracefully, Graciously, Grandly, Gratefully, Gratifyingly, Greatly, **Gustatorially**

Handily, Happily, Harmoniously, Hauntingly, **Healthily**, **Heartily**, High-spiritedly, Highly, Hilariously, Hiply, Honestly, Hospitably, Humbly, Humorously, Hypnotically

Illustriously, Imaginatively, Immaculately, Immeasurably, Impassionedly, Impeccably, Impishly, Importantly, Impressively, Incisively, Indefatigably, Influentially, Ingeniously, Innovatively, Insightfully, Inspirationally, Inspiredly, Inspiringly, Intellectually,

Intelligently, Interactively, Interestingly, Intimately, Inventively, **Invitingly**, Irrepressibly, **Irresistibly**

Jestingly, Jocosely, Jocularly, Jovially, Joyfully, Joyously, Jubilantly

Keenly, Kindly, Kind-heartedly

Laudably, **Lavishly**, Liberally, Liberatingly, Lightly, Light-heartedly, Likably, Lively, Longingly, Lovably, Lovingly, Luminously, **Lusciously**, **Lushly**, Lustrously, Luxuriantly, Luxuriously

Magically, Magnanimously, Magnetically, Magnificently, Majestically, Majorly, Marvelously, Masterfully, Maternally, Meaningfully, Measurably, Melodiously, Mellowly, Merrily, Meticulously, Mindfully, Miraculously, Mirthfully, Mischievously, Modestly, Most deeply, Most fortunately, Most fully, Most highly, **Munificently**, Musically

Naturally, Neatly, Nicely, Niftily, Nimbly, Nobly, Notably

Obligingly, Openly, Openhandedly, Open-heartedly, Open-mindedly, Opportunely, Optimally, **Opulently**, Originally, Outstandingly

Passionately, Paternally, Patiently, Peaceably, Peacefully, Perceptively, Perfectly, Permissively, Personably, Personally, Persuasively, Pertly, Phenomenally, Philoxenially, Picturesquely, **Piquantly**, Placidly, Playfully, Pleasantly, Pleasingly, Pleasurably, Poetically, Politely, Popularly, Positively, Powerfully, Praiseworthily, Preciously, Preparedly, Prestigiously, Pristinely, Proactively, **Prodigiously**, Proficiently, Prolifically, Prominently, Promisingly, Properly, Propitiously, Proactively, Provocatively, Proudly, Purely

Quaintly, Qualitatively, Quick-wittedly, Quietly, Quintessentially

Radiantly, **Rapturously**, **Ravishingly**, Readily, Really, Receptively, **Refreshingly**, Regally, Relaxingly, Reliably, Remarkably, Reputably, Resourcefully, Responsibly, Respectably, Respectfully, **Resplendently**, Responsibly, Responsively, Restfully, Restively, **Restoratively**, **Rhapsodically**, **Richly**, Risibly, **Robustly**, Rollickingly, Rosily, Rousingly

Salubriously, Satisfactorily, **Saucily**, Sanguinely, Scintillatingly, **Scrumptiously**, Scrupulously, Sedulously, Selflessly, **Sensationally**, Sensitively, Sensuously, Serendipitously, Serenely, Significantly, Simply, Sincerely, Skillfully, Sleekly, Smartly, Smashingly, Smilingly, Smoothly, Sociably, Soft-heartedly, Solicitously, Solidly, Soothingly, Sophisticatedly, Soulfully, Specially, Spectacularly, Spellbindingly, Spiritedly, Splendidly, Splendiferously, Spontaneously, Sportingly, Sportively, Stunningly, Stupendously, Stylishly, Suavely, Sublimely, Substantially, Successfully, **Sumptuously**, Superabundantly, Superbly, Superiorly, Supportively, Supportingly, Supremely, **Sweetly**, Swimmingly, Synergistically

Tactfully, **Tantalizingly**, **Tastefully**, Tenderly, Terrifically, Thankfully, Thoroughly, Thoughtfully, Thrillingly, Tidily, Tirelessly, Together, Totally, Touchingly, Transcendently, Tranquilly, Tremendously, Triumphantly, Truly, Truthfully

Unbelievably, Unequivocally, Uniquely, Unstoppably, **Unselfishly**, Urbanely

Verily, Vibrantly, Visually, Vivaciously, Vively

Warmly, Warm-heartedly, Well, Whole-heartedly, **Wholesomely**, Wholly, With relish, Winningly, Wonderfully, Wondrously

Yearningly

Zanily, with Zeal, Zealously, Zestfully

THANK-YOU VERBS

Admire, Adore, **Allure**, Amuse, Anticipate, Apricate, Applaud, Appreciate, Arouse, Arrive, Articulate, Astound, Attend, Attract, Awaken, Become, Begin, Befriend, Beguile, Belong, Benefit, Blend in, Bless, Bloom, Blossom, Blown away, Buoy

Calm, Caper, Captivate, Cavort, Celebrate, Charm, Cheer, Cherish, **Comfort**, Commend, Compel, Compliment, Comport, Connect, Content, Convey, Cultivate, Dance, **Degust**, Dazzle, Dig, **Dine**

Effloresce, Elate, Electrify, Embrace, Enamour, Enchant, Energize, Engage, Engage in, Engross, Enjoy, Enliven, Entertain, Enthrall, Entice, Evoke, Exalt, Excite, Exhilarate, Experiment, Express, Extract, Fascinate, **Feast**, **Feed**, Felicitate, Feel, **Fill**, Fire up, Find, Frolic, Fulfill

Gambol, Gather, Get into, Giggle, Gladden, **Gratify**, Greet, Grow, Harmonize, Have, Hearten, Heighten, Holiday, Homologate, Hospitate, Impart, Impress, Indulge, Inspirit, Integrate, Interact, Interconnect, Interest, Interface, Interplay, Invigorate, Jest, Joke, Join

Kick up one's heels, Kindle, Laud, Laugh, Learn, Let you know, Liberate, Lift, Like, Lighten, Listen, Liven, Love, **Lure**, Maffick, Make merry, Normalize, **Nosh**, **Nourish**, **Nurture**, Pamper, Pass along, Play, Please, Plunge into, Prize

Quench, Quiet, Rack up, **Raise**, Rally, **Refocillate**, **Refresh**, Rejoice, **Rejuvenate**, Relate, Relax, **Relish**, **Restore**, Revel, **Revive**, **Revivify**, Rise, Rollick, Romp, Salve, **Sate**, **Satiate**, **Satisfy**, **Savour**, Score, **Slake**, Smile, Soothe, Spark, Sparkle, State, Still, Stir, **Suffice**, Suit, Sweep off one's feet, **Sweeten**

Temper, Thrill, Tickle, Titillate, Titivate, Touch, Treasure

Value, Voice, Welcome, Whoop it up, Wow

Thanks for making the world a better place!

Having hereby stated a most appreciative thanks to every soul, as well as to Ubiquity itself for holding these positive precepts in eviternal actuality forever, the only thing left to say is...

...Amen

1. certainty; truth *n.*
2. so it is; so be it *adverb*

Synonymous Nouns: Accuracy, Actuality, Certainty, Correctness, Exactitude, Fact, Factuality, Factualness, Precision, Rightness, Sooth, Trueness, Truth, Truthfulness, Veraciousness, Veracity, Veriloquence, Verity

Synonymous Adverbs: Absolutely, Certainly, De facto, Definitely, Exactly, Forsooth, Indeed, Positively, Really, Surely, Truly, Truthfully, Unequivocally, Veraciously, Veritably, Without a doubt...

...Verily.

DICTIONARY OF
EXTRAORDINARY WORDS

Absterge *v.* to cleanse or wipe clean *olde word*

Accession *n.* 1. an achievement of rank or dignity 2. an acquisition, addition, or increase 3. agreement or assent 4. admittance; access

Acclamation *n.* 1. an exclamation or salute of vigorous approval 2. a vote of approval without formal ballot

Accordant *adj.* agreeing and compatible like music and dance

Accourage *v.* to encourage or give encouragement to *olde word*

Accoy *v.* 1. to calm or pacify 2. to bring under control by overwhelming *olde word*

Acculturate *v.* to assimilate cultural traits from another group

Acculturation *n.*1. the alteration of the culture of an individual or group resulting from contact with a different culture 2. the process by which a society's culture is instilled from infancy onward

Aceology *n.* the science of remedies, or of therapeutics aka. **Iamatology** *olde word*

Acumen *n.* accuracy, judgment, keenness, quickness, or insight

Acuminate, Acuminous *adj.* characterized by acumen

Adept *adj.* very skilled; proficient *n.* a highly skilled expert

Adonic *adj.* handsome; like Adonis

Adroit *adj.* clever or skillful in using the hands or mind

Adroitness *n.* quickness and skill in mind and body

Advantage *n.* 1. a beneficial factor or circumstances 2. benefit; gain; profit 3. a comparatively favourable position; asset or superiority *v.* to assist to favourable effect   **Advantageous** *adj.* affording advantage; beneficial or favourable   **Advantageousness** *n.* benefit to **take Advantage of** *idiom*; to avail oneself of or put to good use

Ae *adj.* One *Scottish*

Aegis *n.* a particular person's, or organization's, backing, protection, or support; from a protective mantle in ancient Greek mythology

Aelurophile, Ailurophile *n.* one who loves cats **Aelurophilia,** *n.* love of cats

Aeonian *adj.* of eons; everlasting; eternal

Aerophile *n.* one who loves aviation (yet aerophilic refers to organisms that thrive on air) **Aerophilia** *n.* 1. air-breathing organism 2. the love of aviation or flight

Aesthete *n.* someone who cultivates an uncommonly high sensitivity to beauty, as in nature or art

Aficionada *n.* female aficionado; one who is very enthusiastic and knowledgeable about an activity, pastime or subject

Affine *adj.* allowing for, or preserving, parallel relationships

Affined *adj.* connected or related

Afflated *adj.* inspired; having inspiration **Afflating** *adj.* inspiring

Afflation *n.* the inspiration of someone or something **Afflatus** *n.* a strong creative urge; particularly if from divine inspiration

Agacerie *n.* allurement; coquetry; enchantment; enticement

Agape, Agapism *n.* the love of man for God and vice versa

Agapeistic *adj.* of the love of God for man and man for God *Christian Greek*

Ailurophile, Aelurophile *n.* one who loves cats **Ailurophilia, Aelurophilia** *n.* love of cats

Alacritous *adj.* brisk; eager; lively; quick **Alacrity** *n.* 1. eagerness, cheerful willingness 2. celerity; quickness; speed

Alannah *n.* my child *Irish endearment*

Alaudine *adj.* like a skylark

Alfresco *adj.* outdoors; in the fresh or open air

Alimental, Alimentary *adj.* of nourishment or sustenance

Alpenglow *n.* the light of the rising or setting sun on high mountains

Amaranthine *adj.* 1. immortal; undying; unfading; of a mythical flower 2. a dark purplish reddish colour

Ambrosial, Ambrosian *adj.* extraordinarily enjoyable to smell or taste; particularly delicious or fragrant

Ameliorate *v.* to improve or make better **Amelioration** *n.* 1. an instance, or the act of ameliorating; improvement 2. the state of being improved **Ameliorative, Amelioratory** *adj.* of improving; making better

Amenity *n.* the quality of being agreeable, attractive or pleasant 2. a thing that adds to material or physical comfort 3. a feature that adds to value or attractiveness 4. a social courtesy

Americophile *n.* one who loves the United States of America and/or its people and/or its culture **Americophilia** *n.* the love of all things related to the United States of America

Amoroso *adj.* of a tender loving manner

Amour-propre *n.* appropriate self-esteem or self-respect

Anamnestic *adj.* of recollecting, remembering or reminiscing about the past

Androphile *n.* one who is attracted to men

Androphilia *n.* attraction to men

Angelocracy *n.* government by angels **Angelology** *n.* the study of angels

Angelus *n.* 1. a devotional Christian prayer at morning, noon, and night 2. the bell rung to call the recitation of this prayer

Anglophile *n.* one who loves England and/or its people and/or its culture **Anglophilia** *n.* the love of all things English

Animastic *adj.* of a nonphysical animated nature re. animation of a mental or spiritual nature

Anodyne *adj.* of relieving pain

Anthophilous *adj.* 1. of loving flowers 2. frequenting or feeding on flowers *Zoology*

Aperitive *adj.* serving to open as one's appetite

Aplomb *n.* assured, self-confident poise

Apodictic *adj.* of absolute certainty

Apogee *n.* 1. the highest point possible 2. the furthest point from Earth in a celestial object's orbit

Apollonian *adj.* 1. like the god Apollo 2. relating to the ordered, self-disciplined, and rational aspects of human nature

Apotheosis *n.* 1. deification; evolution to become divine 2. elevation to a preeminent position; glorification 3. a glorified or exalted example 4. the greatest event or time

Apperception *n.* 1. fully aware conscious perception 2. the process of cognition via which newly observed qualities of a thing are connected to past experiences

Appetence, Appetency *n.* 1. a strong desire or craving 2. a natural affinity or propensity **Appetent** *adj.* having eager desire or longing

Apposite *adj.* apt in the circumstances; appropriate; perfect; the opposite of 'opposite' **Appositeness** *n.* appropriateness, aptness, or relevance for the occasion

Approbate *v.* to approve, authorize or sanction officially **Approbation** *n.* 1. an expression of warm approval; praise 2. official approval **Approbative** *adj.* approving **Approbate** *v.* to approve

Apricate *v.* 1. to bask in the sun or sunbathe 2. to introduce to sunlight

Arcadian *adj.* pastoral; peaceful; rustic; simple

Arctophile *n.* one who loves, or collects teddy bears

Arctophily *n.* the collection of teddy bears

Argus-eyed *adj.* vigilant

Aroha *n.* affectionate regard, compassion, or love *Maori*

Aromatic *adj.* of a distinctive and pleasant smell

Artisanal *adj.* of skilled craftwork made by hand

Ascendant *adj.* 1. moving or inclining upward; rising 2. superior; dominant in influence or position **Ascendancy** *n* the act or state of upward movement **Ascendant** *n.* 1. the top position in control 2. an ancestor

Aspirant *adj.* having ambitions to achieve something, typically in a career *n.* a person with ambitions to achieve something

Asseverate *v.* to declare positively and resolutely; affirm

Assiduous *adj.* showing great care and perseverance

Assimilation *n.* the act or process of assimilating or the state of being assimilated used in Physiology, Linguistics, and Sociology

Assoil *v.* 1. to pardon or absolve 2. to atone for *olde word*

Assurgent *adj.* rising, or tending to rise, upward **Assurgency** *n.*

Astrophile *n.* one who loves stars **Astrophilia** *n.* the love of stars, planets and all outer space

Ataraxia, Ataraxis, Ataraxy *n.* calmness; peace of mind; tranquility

Atticism *n.* 1. characteristic Attic Greek feature 2. conciseness and elegance in expression

Au fait *adj.* experienced, proficient, or familiar with something *French* 'to the fact'

Aubade *n.* a poem or piece of music appropriate to the early morning or dawn

Audiophile *n.* one who loves high fidelity sound reproduction

Audiophilia *n.* the love of high fidelity sound reproduction

Aureole *n.* 1. an oval light surrounding the body or head of a holy person or deity 2. corona in astronomy

Auriferous *adj.* bearing or containing gold

Auroral *adj.* 1. like an aurora 2. of the dawn

Auspicious *adj.* favourable; conducive to success

Auspiciousness *n.* the quality of being auspicious

Autodidact *n.* one who is self-taught **Autodidactic** *adj.* self-taught

Avant-garde *adj.* of an innovative group esp. in the arts *n.* a group that promotes or creates techniques or ideas esp. in the arts

Axiological *adj.* of the philosophical study of value; of ethics, and aesthetics

Axiomatic *adj.* self-evident

Baconian *adj.* like Sir Francis Bacon esp. the belief that truth is knowable via empirical observation and induction

Badinage *n.* playful light banter

Baisemain *n.* the act of kissing someone's hand and thereby a sign of respect *olde word*

Balmy *adj.* pleasantly warm; summery

Basorexia *n.* the erotic urge to kiss

Beamish *adj.* beaming with anticipation, happiness or optimism

Beatific *adj.* blissfully happy; conveying Holy bliss

Beatitude *n.* 1. the highest blessedness or happiness 2. any of the blessedness declarations in the Sermon on the Mount made by Jesus

Beatify *v.* 1. to make superlatively happy 2. to announce someone's sainthood in the Roman Catholic Church 3. to glorify; exalt

Beatus *n.* one who is beatified (one step before sainthood)

Beau ideal *n.* 1. the concept of perfect beauty 2. an ideal model or type

Bedizenment *n.* dressing or ornamentation of a gaudy or showy manner

Bee's Knees *n.* excellent person or thing

Beguin *n.* infatuation

Behoof *n.* advantage; benefit **Behooves** *pl. legal*

Bel-esprit *n.* 1. a cultivated highly intelligent person 2. a witty or clever person

Benedicite *n.* 1. a blessing or grace 2. an expression of surprise *arcane*

Benedictive, Benedictory *adj.* of a blessing or benevolent wish

Benediction n. 1. a blessing 2. the invoking of a divine blessing at the end of a church service 3. a Roman Catholic service that includes blessing the congregation with the host. 4. an expression of good wishes

Benefaction *n.* aid or a charitable deed or gift

Beneficence *n.* 1. a beneficial, charitable, or kind act 2. the quality or state of being charitable

Beneficent *adj.* of generosity or doing good

Benefic *adj.* beneficent *olde word*

Benignant *adj.* benevolent and kindly **Benison** *n.* a spoken blessing *olde word*

Besotted *adj.* drunk with love

Bibelot *n.* 1. a small decorative item 2. a finely crafted miniature book

Bibliophile *n.* one who loves books **Bibliophilia** *n.* the love of books

Bijou *adj.* small, elegant and tasteful

Billet-doux *n.* a love letter

Biophile *n.* one who loves the living world **Biophilia** *n.* an innate love for the natural world **Biophilic** *adj.* of loving the natural world

Blithesome *adj.* carefree; light-hearted; happy

Bodacious *adj.* 1. impressive; remarkable 2. physically attractive, primarily regarding women

Bonafide *adj.* 1. good faith; the sincere intent of being honest and law-abiding as in contract negotiation; in accord with standards of honesty, sincerity, and trust

Bon ton *n.* 1. a sophisticated style or manner 2. the proper thing to do 3. high society

Bonhomie *n.* an affable and pleasant disposition; geniality

Bonify *v.* to convert into, or render, good

Bon vivant *n.* someone with refined taste especially regarding food and drink

Bonzer/Bonza *adj.* excellent; first-rate

Boolean *adj.* of a logical deductive system

Boomlet *n.* a small spurt of interest or growth as in birth rate, business, or politics

Bravura *n.* 1. a) masterful style or technique in musical performance b) a musical passage or piece that displays a performer's virtuosity 2. a showy display or manner

Breviloquent *adj.* of concise speaking **Breviloquence** *n.* abrupt speech

Brill *adj.* short for brilliant

Brio *n.* vigour; vivacity

Brobdingnagian *adj.* gigantic *n.* giant

Buccal *adj.* of the mouth or cheek (romantic)

Bucolic *adj.* of the pleasantness of country life and countryside

Cachet *n.* 1. appeal; distinction; prestige 2. a document seal

Callista *n.* most beautiful *Greek feminine*

Camelot *n.* of no known location, it's symbolic of the virtues of the castle and court of the legendary King Arthur

Candescent *adj.* glowing with heat

Canorous *adj.* melodious or resonant of voice

Canorousness *n.* the musical quality of being richly tuneful and melodious

Canty *adj.* brisk; in good spirits; lively; spritely **Cantier** *adj.* more canty **Cantiest** *adj.* most canty

Caritas *n.* charity

Cartophile *n.* one who loves maps or cards **Cartophilia** *n.* the love of maps or cards

Celeritous *adj.* swift; speedy; fast **Celerity** *n.* swiftness; speed

Cerebration *n.* the act of considering; thinking; thought

Chamberlain *n.* an officer who manages the household of a noble or sovereign; an official of high rank in royal courts; a chief steward

Chaplinesque *adj.* like Charlie Chaplin

Chirk *v.* to make or become cheerful - used with up

Christmastide, Twelvetide *n.* twelve days of the Christmas season commencing Christmas eve

Cinephile *n.* one who loves motion pictures **Cinephilia** *n.* the love of motion pictures

Clemency *n.* 1. leniency, mercy, or an act thereof 2. mildness, especially of the weather **Clement** *adj.* 1. mild (of weather) 2. merciful (of a person)

Clerisy *n.* educated people aka. the literati

Coadjutant *adj.* of helping others **Coadjutant, Coadjutor** *n.* aide; helper; assistant

Coadjuvancy *n.* joint cooperation or assistance

Cock-a-hoop *adj.* visibly happy and excited about something

Cockaigne *n.* a utopia where ease and luxury prevail

Cogitabund *adj.* deeply thoughtful; meditative

Cognoscente *n.* someone with superior specialized knowledge or highly refined taste **Cognoscenti** *pl.*

Cohort *n.* 1. a banded together group or regarded as such 2. an ancient military unit of Rome = 6 centuries = 1/10th of a legion

Cohortative, Cohortatory *adj.* mutually encouraging ex. "Let's..."

Collegial *adj.* of shared responsibility among a group of colleagues

Coltish *adj.* like a colt; energetic; frisky; playful; possibly awkward

Columbine *adj.* dovelike

Comity *n.* 1. social harmony 2. executive or legal cooperation between nations

Communion *n.* 1. an instance of sharing as in feelings or thoughts 2. spiritual or religious fellowship 3. a group of Christians, such as a denomination, with the same faith and rites 4. an Ecclesiastical sacrament

Compendious *adj.* concise and comprehensive

Compendiousness *n.* the state or quality of being compendious

Complaisant *adj.* agreeable; obliging; willing to please others

Complect *v.* entwine; to join by interweaving

Complement *n.* 1. something that completes; brings to perfection by comprising a whole 2. also found in colour, grammar, immunology, logic, mathematics and music

Comport *v.* to behave or conduct oneself in a particular manner 2. to harmonize or agree often with dignity

Comportment *n.* personal bearing; behaviour; conduct; demeanour

Conamore *adv.* 1. with love *Italian* 2. lovingly; with tenderness or enthusiasm *musical direction*

Conception *n.* 1. fertilization; formation of a viable zygote by the union of sperm and ovum or the entity formed 2. the ability to comprehend abstract mental concepts 3. a concept or thought; something mentally conceived and believed 4. the start of formation of an idea or plan

Concrew *v.* to grow together *olde word*

Condolatory *adj.* of sympathy for one who is suffering grief, misfortune, or sorrow

Confelicitous *adj.* of pleasure in another's happiness

Confelicity *n.* pleasure in another's happiness

Conferrable *adj.* worthy of bestowment of an honour for example

Conflate *v.* 1. to fuse or meld: bring together 2. to combine into one whole 3. to confuse in distinction between

Confrere *n.* a colleague; a fellow member of a profession or fraternity

Conjugate *adj.* connected, coupled, or related

Consanguinity *n.* 1. a blood relationship or from a common ancestor 2. a close connection or affinity

Consentaneous *adj.* 1. well suited; expressing agreement 2. of the consent of all **Consentaneity** *n.* the quality or state of being consentaneous

Consentient *adj.* unanimous; united in harmonious agreement

Consonant *adj.* 1. in harmony or agreement with 2. of a consonant sound or letter

Constitutional *adj.* 1. relating to, or of, a constitution 2. consistent with, permissible, or sanctioned by, a constitution 3. operating under, or established by, a constitutional government 4. inherent in the nature, or basic structure, of a person or thing 5. of a person's physical makeup *n.* a regular walk taken for a person's health

Constitutive *adj.* 1. that which is essential to making a thing what it is 2. having the power to enact, establish, or institute

Consubstantial *adj.* of the same essence, nature, or substance

Convictive *adj.* having power, or serving, to convince

Convive *n.* one who drinks or feasts together

Coruscant *adj.* glittering; shimmering   **Coruscate** *v.* 1. to flash, sparkle, glitter or shimmer 2. to display shimmering virtuosity in one's art

Cosmocrat *n.* a ruler of the world

Cosmolatry *n.* worship of the cosmos

Cosmopolitan *adj.* 1. relevant to the whole world 2. comprised of elements from around the world 3. comfortable and familiar with many different worldly cultures **Cosmopolitan, Cosmopolite** *n.* a person or organism of the whole world

Cosmotheism, Pantheism *n.* identification of God with the universe and its phenomena

Couthie *adj.* sociable; genial; agreeable

Crackerjack *adj.* especially good *n.* an especially good person or thing

Credence *n.* plausibility; credibility; acceptance as true

Crepuscular *adj.* of the twilight

Credential *adj.* 1. that which entitles one to authority; confidence, or credit 2. evidence regarding one's right to authority, confidence, or credit

Culmen *n.* summit

Cynophilia *n.* the love of dogs

Cynosure *n.* the center of attention or admiration

Daedal *adj.* ingenious and complex in design or function; intricate

Dapatical *adj.* sumptuous in cheer

Definitive *adj.* complete and reliable; absolute

Degust *v.* to savour or taste with relish

Deipnosophist *n.* a master of dinner table conversation

Delectation *n.* delight; enjoyment; pleasure

Demulcent *adj.* of a soothing or softening caress

Demophilia *n.* fondness for crowds **Demophile** *n.* one who loves crowds

Deosculate *v.* to warmly kiss

Depurate *v.* to purify or cleanse, or become purified or cleansed

Desiderata *n.* something needed or desired **Desideratum** *pl.*

Dialectical *adj.* of the art or process of finding the truth via an exchange of logical arguments

Didactic *adj.* intended to teach, particularly with moral instruction as a motive

Didascalic *adj.* of education or teaching sometimes a moral lesson

Digerati *n.* those skilled in technology, especially in computers and programming

Dilly *n.* someone or something that is extraordinary in quality or size

Dinkum *adj.* genuine; true; honest

Discophile *n.* one who loves phonograph records or CDs

Dispassionate *adj.* uninfluenced by strong feeling so able to be more impartial and rational

Disport *v.* to amuse oneself in a frolicsome, light manner

Dithyramb *n.* 1. a wildly enthusiastic speech or written piece 2. an irregular poetic expression suggestive of the frenetic dithyramb of ancient Greece

Doozy *n.* an impressive, extraordinary, or unique thing

Doughty *adj.* brave and persistent **Doughtiness** *n.* the quality or state of being doughty

Doula *n.* a woman who assists another during childbirth and provides support for the mother and her family afterward

Doxological *adj.* of giving praise to God **Doxology** *n.* an expression of praise to God, particularly a short hymn

Doyen *n.* the man who is a group's senior member **Doyenne** *n.* the woman who is a group's senior member

Droll *adj.* whimsically comical or amusingly odd **Drollness** *n.* the quality of being whimsically comical or amusingly odd

Dulcet *adj.* sweet and soothing, especially of sound

Ecclesiastical *adj.* 1. of the church especially as an organization 2. belonging to, or for use in, a church

Echt *adj.* authentic and typical

Eclectic *adj.* of combined elements from a variety of sources, styles, or systems

Ecstatic *n.* one who experiences times of intense trancelike joy

Ecumenical *adj.* 1. of unity among churches or religions 2. of worldwide applicability or scope

Ectropy, Entaxy, Extropy, Negentropy, and **Syntropy** *n.* negative entropy

Edification *n.* intellectual, spiritual, or moral enlightenment

Edified, Edifying *adj.* improved or instructed intellectually or morally

Effloresce *v.* to bloom, blossom, develop or flourish

Efflorescence *n.* 1. time or state of flowering *Botany* 2. a. gradual developing or unfolding b. time of greatest vigour; culmination

Effulgence *n.* brilliant radiance   **Effulgent** *adj.* brightly shining; radiant

Eirenicon *n.* a proposition to harmonize conflicting viewpoints

Élan *n.* 1. liveliness and vigour 2. distinctive flair or style **Electuary** *n.* pulverized medication mixed into a honey or sugar paste; *olde word*

Eleemosynary *adj.* of charity

Elemental *adj.* 1. basic; primordial; rudimental 2. of nature's powers

Eleutherian *adj.* of giving, or protecting, freedom

Elysium *n.* a place or state of complete happiness *Greek mythology; Elysian Fields*

Emmanuel, Immanuel *n.* the name of Jesus Christ when prophesied as the Messiah

Empyreal *adj.* celestial; of the highest part of heaven

Empyrean *adj.* of, or from, heaven *n.* 1. the highest reaches of heaven and realm of pure light or fire 2. the paradise of God and the angels

En règle *adj.* according to the rules; correct; in order

Encomium *n.* 1. glowing, warm praise 2. a formal expression of praise

Enophile, Oenophile *n.* one who loves wine **Enophilia** *n.* the love of wine.

Entaxy, Ectropy, Extropy, Negentropy, and **Syntropy** *n.* negative entropy

Epi- *prefix* on; upon

Epicurean *adj.* of sensual pleasure especially via food and drink

Epicureanism *n.* 1. the philosophy that happiness, or pain avoidance, is the highest good and advocates the pursuit of pleasures in moderation 2. devotion to pleasure and luxury

Epideictic *adj.* designed to display rhetorical oratory of a speaker

Epididact *n.* person given to, or engaged by, ultra moral instruction **Epididactic** *adj.* above or beyond moral instruction

Epigram *n.* 1. concise, clever, sometimes paradoxical statement 2. short, witty poem expressing a single observation or thought

Epigrammatic *n.* of the nature of an epigram; concise, amusing and clever

Epimyth *n.* the moral of a story

Epinician *adj.* of celebrating triumph **Epinicion** *n.* a victory song

Epithalamion *n.* an ode in honour of a bride and groom *olde word*

Epurate *v.* purify **Epuration** *n.* purification

Equable *adj.* calm; even-tempered **Equableness** *n.* the quality or state of being equable

Equanimity *n.* the quality of being composed and calm

Equanimous *adj.* calm; collected; poised **Equanimousness** *n.* the quality or state of being equanimous

Equiparate *adj.* equal or level *v.* to regard as equal or level or to compare **Equiparation** *n.* the act of regarding as equal or comparing

Equiparent *adj.* of a mutual or level relationship

Equipoise *n.* 1. equality in distribution of relationship, emotional forces or weight; balance; equilibrium 2. a counterpoise or counterbalance

Equipollence *n.* equivalence **Equipollent** *adj.* 1. of equal effectiveness, force, power, or significance 2. equivalent

Equiponderance, Equiponderancy *n.* equality of weight; balanced **Equiponderant, Equiponderate** *adj.* of equality of weight

Equity *adj.* 1. of an ownership interest 2. of, or about, stocks n. 1. the quality of being fair and just 2. something that is fair and just 3 ownership interest in a holding, property, or corporation 4. the value of the reputation of a brand

Ergophile *n.* one who loves work or exercise

Ergophilia *n.* the love of work or exercise *neologism*

Erudite *adj.* of great knowledge or learning **Erudition** *n.* the quality or state of being erudite

Esprit *n.* liveliness of spirit or mind; sprightly wittiness

Esse *n.* 1. existence 2. essence; essential nature

Ethography *n.* a description of ethical and moral systems

Ethonomics *n.* the discipline of defining and recording the prioritization of values within value systems, their relationships to each other, and their affect

Eudaemonistic, Eudaemonistical *adj.* of evaluating actions via their capacity to produce happiness **Eudaimonia** *n.* a contented state of happiness, health, and prosperity

Eudaimonism *n.* the evaluation of actions based on their capacity to create happiness **Eudaimonist** *n.* one who evaluates actions based on their capacity to create happiness

Eunoia *n.* 1. the sympathetic and benevolent good will that a speaker cultivates with an audience 2. well mind or beautiful thinking

Eupathy *n.* right feeling

Eupeptic *adj.* 1. of good digestion 2. cheerful; happy

Euphonic, Euphonious *adj.* of pleasant sound **Euphony** *n.* pleasant sound particularly regarding the phonetic quality of words

Europhile *n.* one who loves Europe and/or its peoples and/or its cultures **Europhilia** *n.* the love of all things European

Eurythmic *adj.* of harmonious proportion

Eutaxy *n.* a condition or state of good order *olde word*

Euthenics *n.* the study of improvement of living conditions to improve human functioning and well-being **Euthenist** *n.* one who studies the improvement of living conditions to improve human functioning and well-being

Eutrapelia, Eutrapely *n.* the quality of skilled conversation; eloquence; facundity; urbanity

Eutaxy *n.* good or established arrangement, management, or order

Eviternal *adj.* eternal; everlasting

Excelsior *adj.* higher

Excogitate *v.* to think out, or consider, thoroughly and carefully **Excogitation** *n.* thoroughly considered thought

Excogitative *adj.* thoughtful, careful, and thorough **Excogitate** *v.* to think about something thoroughly and carefully or to consider

Exculpable *adj.* innocent; free of blame or guilt **Exculpate** *v.* to exonerate or clear of blame or guilt **Exculpation** *n.* the act of freeing from blame or guilt

Exhortative, Exhortatory *adj.* strongly encouraging; also Hortative and Hortatory *n.* encouraging advice

Exosculate *v.* to kiss repeatedly and fondly

Expergefacient *adj.* of awakening **Expergefaction** *n.* awakening

Explicate *v. t*o explain or make clear

Exponent *n.* 1. someone who expounds or represents 2. someone who advocates, represents, or speaks for 3. a number or symbol place above right another number, expression, or symbol denoting the power to which it is to be raised *Mathematics*

Extropy, Entaxy, Ectropy, Negentropy, and **Syntropy** *n.* negative entropy

Eyesome *adj.* visually attractive

Facund *adj.* fluently persuasive and forceful **Facundious** *adj.* full of words; eloquent **Facundity** *n.* of eloquence

Faith *n.* confidence in, or unquestioning expectation, of the truth

Feateous *adj.* handsome, neat, shapely, well-made

Fecund *adj.* 1. fruitful; 2. capable of producing abundant offspring 3. very intellectually or creatively productive

Felicify, Felicitate *v.* to make happy **Felicitous** *adj.* 1. well-chosen or suited; apt 2. fortunate and pleasing

Feminacy *n.* femininity; a feminine nature

Feracious *adj.* fruitful; prolific

Festal *adj.* of a celebration or festival

Fettle *n.* 1. sound or proper condition 2. of emotional or mental condition or state; spirits

Filial *n.* of a son or daughter; of offspring

Fleek *adj.* 1. of perfectly trimmed eyebrows 2. of perfection

Florescence *n.* the quality of blooming

Foison *n.* 1. physical power or strength *Scottish* 2. an abundant harvest; plenty *olde word*

Foodophile *n.* one who loves food

Forbearant, Forbearing *adj.* patient; restrained; self-controlled; tolerant **Forbearance** *n.* the quality or state of being forbearing

Frabjous *adj.* delightful; extraordinary; wonderful

Francophile, Gallophile *n.* one who loves France and/or its people and/or its culture **Francophilia, Gallophilia** *n.* the love of all things French

Fulgent *adj.* brightly shining   **Fulgor** *n.* brightness; splendour, brilliant or dazzling light

Furbelow *n.* 1. a flounce or a ruffle 2. a piece of showy ornamentation *v.* to decorate with trimmings

Furtherance *n.* 1. the act of advancement; furthering 2. something that advances or furthers

Funny Definitions

Gabriel *n.* strong male archangel

Galanthophile *n.* one who loves snowdrop flowers

Gallophile, Francophile *n.* one who loves France and/or its people and/or its culture **Gallophilia, Francophilia** *n.* the love of all things French

Galvanize *v.* 1. to shock or stimulate with electric current 2. to arouse to action or awareness 3. to coat metals with rust-resistant zinc **Galvanized** *adj.* 1. stimulated, or shocked, with electricity 2. aroused into action or awareness 3. coated with rust-resistant zinc **Galvanizing** *adj.* 1. of galvanizing, or shocking, with electricity 2. of arousal into action or awareness 3. coating with rust-resistant zinc

Gambol *v.* to caper; frolic; or skip about in play or dance

Gelasin *n.* a dimple that appears with a smile **Gelastic** *adj.* relating to, or causing, laughter **Gelogenic** *adj.* inducing, producing, or provoking laughter

Generativity *n.* The sense of connection between generations

Germanophile *n.* one who loves Germany and/or its people and/or its culture **Germanophilia** *n.* the love of all things German

Glabrous *adj.* of skin; free from hair; smooth

Glistering *adj.* having brief glinting flashes or points of light

Gnarly *adj.* gnarled *slang:* 1. cool (good) 2. dangerous (less good)

Gnomic *adj.* 1. of gnomes or aphorisms 2. of writers of aphorisms

Gnosis *n.* intuitive apprehension of spiritual truths

Gracile *adj.* of slender, slight, graceful build (of a hominid species)

Gradely *adj.* desirable, fine and good

Graith, Graithly *adj.* prepared; ready *olde Scottish*

Gramercy *n.* great appreciation; from 'Grand Merci'

Grandee *n.* 1. the top ranking nobleman in Portugal or Spain 2. a person of high rank or eminence

Gratulation *n.* expression and/or feeling of joy

Gravitas *n.* gravity or seriousness in treatment or demeanour

Grok *v.* 1. to intuitively know or understand something with no intellectual thought 2. to thoroughly understand something in intricate detail "to become one with the observed" *Martian* from 'drink' as to 'drink something in'

Gruntled *adj.* funny version of contented; pleased; satisfied

Gustatory *adj.* of taste or tasting

Gynephilia *n.* attraction to women

Habilitation n. 1. The act of clothing someone 2. The act of equipping or outfitting (a mine) for operation

Halcyon *adj.* 1. of past time that was idyllically tranquil or happy 2. a golden, prosperous time *n.* a fabled bird, related to the kingfisher, that could calm waves and wind when nesting on the sea during the winter solstice

Haloed *adj.* 1. of a luminous disk, nimbus, or ring encircling the heads of sacred figures 2. of a feeling of admiration, glory or reverence associated with a person or thing

Hardihood *n.* 1. daring and boldness 2. insolence or impudence

Harmony *n.* 1. agreement in accord, action, feeling or opinion 2. congruity or order to one another and the whole 3. the art and science of musical chord combination and structure

Heartsome *adj.* 1. encouraging or cheering 2. cheerful; joyful

Heliophile *n.* one who loves sunlight **Heliophilia** *n.* the love of sunlight

Hellenophile *n.* one who loves Greece and/or its people and/or its culture **Hellenophilia** *n.* 1. the love of all things Greek 2. the theory that modern science began in Greece

Henosis *n.* oneness, union, or unity **Henotic** *adj.* of or pertaining to producing peace and harmony, unifying, One

Heuristic *adj.* 1. of enabling someone to discover, investigate, and learn for themselves 2. of a speculative formulation that guides the investigation or solution of a problem

Heuristic *n.* 1. a speculative formulation, method, or process, often self-taught, that guides the investigation of, or solution to, a problem 2. in computer science a problem-solving technique via which the most appropriate solution of several found, by alternative methods, is selected, at each stage of a program to use in the next step of the program

Heuristics *pl.* (with a sing. verb) the study and application of heuristic methodologies

Hippophile *n.* one who loves horses **Hippophilia** *n.* the love of horses

Hispanophile *n.* one who loves Hispanic countries

Homologate *v.* to officially approve or confirm

Homologation *n.* official approval or confirmation

Honorificabilitudinitatibus, Honorificabilitudinity *n.* the state of being able to achieve honours *Shakespeare's longest word*

Hortative, Hortatory *adj.* strongly encouraging; also Exhortative, Exhortatory *n.* encouraging advice

Hospitate *v.* to receive hospitality as a gracious guest

Humdinger *n.* something remarkable or extraordinary

Hygeian *adj.* of or about health

Hygiastics, Hygiantics, Hygienics, Hygiology *n.* a branch of medicine studying, or system of principles promoting health and its preservation

Iamatology *n.* the medical study of remedies

Iconophile *n.* one who loves images or icons

Ideal *n.* 1. a concept of something in its perfection 2. something regarded as a standard model of excellence or perfection 3. a worthy or ultimate object of endeavour *adj.* conforming to a standard of excellence or perfection

Idolizer *n.* 1. one with great devotion or uncritical admiration 2 one who worships an idol

Idoneous *adj.* appropriate; fit; proper; suitable

Idoneity, Idoneousness *n.* the quality or state of being idoneous

Illecebrous *adj.* enticing; alluring; attractive

Illuminati *n.* people, often of religious or philosophical groups, who believe themselves, or profess, to be uncommonly enlightened about their subject

Immanentism *n.* a component of many religious philosophies wherein God, mind, and/or Spirit are said to be immanent in each individual and the world

Immanuel, Emmanuel *n.* the name of Jesus Christ when prophesied as the Messiah

Immarcescible *adj.* unwithering

Impavid *adj.* fearless; undaunted

Impeccancy *n.* the quality or state of being impeccant **Impeccant** *adj.* blameless, faultless, sinless or error free

Impetrate *v.* 1. to pray or entreat 2. to obtain by prayer

Impetrative, Impetratory *adj* tending to get, or getting, by entreaty.

Impetration *n.* the act of impetrating, or receiving via entreaty or petition **Impetrator** *n.* one who impetrates

Inamorata *n.* a female lover **Inamorato** *n.* a male lover

Inaurate *adj.* gilded or gleaming as if gold covered *v.* to cover in gold

Incede *v.* to march onwards or advance in a measured or stately way

Inception *n.* the start of something, like a commencement; or an undertaking

Incomplex *adj.* simple

Indefatigable *adj.* untiring; persistent; relentless

Indefatigability *n.* the capability of persistent effort; unrelenting; untiring

Indifferentism *n.* the belief that all religions are equally valid

Indophile *n.* one who loves India and/or its people and/or its culture

Indophilia *n.* the love of all things Indian

Indubitable *adj.* not doubtable; unquestionable

Indubitability *n.* the quality or state of being indubitable

Ineffable *adj.* qualitative beyond words

Innate *adj.* inborn; instinctive; intrinsic; natural **Innateness** *n.* the quality or state of being innate

Innocuous *adj.* safe; harmless

Innoxious *adj.* safe; not noxious

Insouciant *adj.* carefree; without anxiety, concern, or worry

Instauration *n.* 1. restoration; renovation 2. the establishment or institution of something

Intelligentsia *n.* the intellectual upper class of society

Intemerate *adj.* chaste, pure, undefiled

Iranophile, Persophile *n.* one who loves Iran and/or its people and/or its culture

Iranophilia, Persophilia *n.* the love of all things Iranian

Irenic *adj.* promoting peace

Irenology *n.* the study of peace

Iridine *adj.* iridescent

Irrefragable *adj.* indisputable

Irrefragableness, Irrefragablility *n.* the quality or state of being indisputable; not refutable or disprovable; trueness

Irrevincible *adj.* incontrovertible; invincible

Isness *n.* existence as something; the quality of being

Isonomy *n.* 1. equality before the law of citizens of a state 2. equality of civil or political rights **Isonomic, Isonomous** *adj.* of isonomy

Isopolity *n.* equality of political rights *Law*

Izzat *n.* honour or prestige *Islam*

Jazzophile *n.* one who loves jazz music

Jiggish *adj.* 1. of jig dance/music 2. frolicsome; playful

Jimp *adj.* delicate; elegant; handsome; neat; slender; spruce; trim

Jnana *n.* knowledge that is recognized when experienced and inseparable from total reality *Indian philosophy*

Jocose *adj.* 1. merry; given to joking 2. of joking: humorous

Jocoserious *adj.* of both a jocose and serious nature

Jolif *adj.* jolly; joyful; merry; pleasant

Jollification *n.* act or acts of merrymaking or lively conviviality

Joyance *n.* exulting gladness; a festive or joyful feeling *olde word*

Jumboism *n.* worship of, or admiration for, bigness

Junoesque *adj.* stately and regal; like the goddess Juno

Juste Milieu *n.* golden mean; happy medium; judicious moderation

Juvenescent *adj.* of being young or youthful

Kairos *n.* a fleeting propitious moment for action or decision

Kalon *n.* ideal perfect and moral beauty

Ken *n.* 1. understanding; perception 2. range of vision, view, or sight *v.* 1. to know; to have knowledge or an understanding 2. to recognize *kenned or kent, kens, kenning Scot.*

Lagniappe *n.* 1. a small free gift with a purchase in retail 2. an unexpected extra benefit or gift

Lambent *adj.* flickering, gleaming, or glowing with a soft radiance

Largesse *n.* 1. gifts or money given 2. generosity in giving gifts or spirit **Largifical** *adj.* generous; liberal; ample

Latitudinarian *adj.* of allowing latitude, notably in religion *n.* of a person who is latitudinarian

Latria *n.* the adoration that is exclusive to loving God

Laureate *adj.* worthy of great distinction or honour *n.* one who is awarded for the highest achievements in their field

Lautitious *adj.* sumptuous

Legatee *n.* inheritor of a legacy

Legator *n.* testator; one who makes a will

Legerity *n.* agility or quickness of body and/or mind

Lenity *n.* an act or quality of tolerance; leniency

Lepid *adj.* amusing; jocose; pleasant **Lepidity** *n.* facetiousness; humour; wit *olde word*

Lexicon *n.* the vocabulary of a language, person, or field of knowledge **Lexicology** *n.* study of words **Lexicography** *n.* compiling of dictionaries

Liberal *adj.* 1. open to new ideas, reform and tolerant of others 2. broad-minded and unbounded by tradition 3. generous

Libertarian adj. of advocating, or conforming to principles, of liberty or observing a doctrine of free will **Libertarian** *n.* 1. an advocate of maximizing individual rights and minimizing the role of the state. 2. believer in free will **Libertarianism** *n.* 1. advocacy of freedom, especially in conduct or thought 2. advocacy of the doctrine of free will *from Liberty*

Librocubicularist *n.* someone who reads in bed

Lief, Liefly *adj.* delightful, lovable or pleasant

Limpid *adj.* clear; unclouded

Linguaphile *n.* one who loves languages and words

Lissome *adj.* graceful, supple and thin; lithesome

Literary *adj.* 1. of, or concerning, literature 2. of, or concerning, writers or their profession 3. fond of, or knowledgeable about, literature

Littoral *adj.* of, or on, the seashore or lake shore

Lodestone *n.* 1. magnetite piece that attracts iron or steel 2. one that strongly attracts

Logophile *n.* one who loves words

Logos *n.* 1. the creative word of God in Christianity and Judaism 2. philosophically a) the principal, or human reasoning, governing the cosmos b) the active, material, rational principle of the cosmos identified with God; the Source of all creation and movement as well as the power of reason within the human soul

Lollapalooza *n.* something exceptionally good of its kind

Longanimity *n.* endurance, forbearance, patience and restraint

Longanimous *adj.* restrained, forbearing; enduring; patient

Long-suffering *n.* a *Fruit of the Spirit* related to tolerance, patience, compassion, and love

Luciferous *adj.* light bringing

Lucriferous *adj.* gainful; profitable

Lucubration *n.* arduous and intense thought or study

Lucubrations *pl.* written works created via laborious and pedantic effort or study

Luculent *adj.* of 1. shining brightly 2. clearly expressed

Ludibund *adj.* frolicsome; playful; recreational; sportive

Ludic *adj.* of undirected and spontaneous playfulness

Lusory *adj.* 1. of playing or used in play 2. playfully composed

Mabsoot *adj.* glad; happy; joyful; pleased; satisfied *Arabic*

Macarism *n.* a blessing; an ascription of blessedness

Macarize *v.* to call, or identify as, blessed

Macrobian *adj.* of an exceptionally long life span

Maffick *v.* to celebrate or rejoice in boisterous public demonstration *British*

Magistral *adj.* of a master or mastery

Magnanimous *adj.* showing forgiveness or kindness as in ignoring insults or dismissing the thought of vengeance

Magnanimity *n.* generousness of spirit

Majordomo/Major-domo *n.* 1. the head steward or butler in a noble household 2. a butler or steward 3. someone who directs affairs or makes arrangements for someone else

Mansuetude *n.* mildness; gentleness in manner

Manuduction *n.* hand guidance

Manumission *n.* being freed from slavery or the act of freeing from slavery

Margaric *adj.* of a pearl or pearls

Margaritiferous *adj.* of wearing or yielding pearls

Marmoreal, Marmorean *adj.* made of, or like, marble

Materfamilias *n.* the mother of the family or female head of the household

Maven *n.* an expert in any particular field

Mediagenic *adj.* attractive to news media

Meet *adj.* proper; right; suitable

Meliorism *n.* 1. the belief that the human condition can be improved through concerted effort 2. the belief that there is an inherent tendency toward progress or improvement in the human condition

Meliorist *n.* 1. one who believes that concerted effort can improve the human condition 2. one in whom there is a tendency toward improvement in the human condition **Melioristic** *adj.* of the doctrine that the world can be improved by human effort

Mellifluous *adj.* having a pleasant, flowing, or honey-like dulcet sound

Melliloquent *adj.* speaking harmoniously or sweetly

Mellisonant *adj.* pleasing to the ear

Mesmerism *n.* 1. fascination; spellbinding appeal 2. hypnotism

Metropolitan *n.* a citizen of a metropolis especially an apparently urbane one

Mettlesome *adj.* spirited; courageous; plucky **Mettlesomeness** *n.* high-spirited courage

Mickle *adj.* very large *olde word*

Minikin *adj.* small and delicate

Mirabilia *n.* miracles; wonders

Mirific *adj.* of wonderful things or working wonders

Moonstruck *adj.* loony in love

Muliebral, Muliebrile, Muliebrous, *adj.* womanly

Muliebrity *n.* femininity; being a woman

Multifarious *adj.* of great variety; diversity

Mundify *v.* to purify or cleanse a thing

Munificence *n.* 1. very generous of giving 2. an exhibition of great generosity **Munificent** *adj.* of great generosity **Munify** *v.* fortify

Munity *n.* a granted privilege or right

Musicophile *n.* one who loves music

Mycohphile *n.* one that loves mushrooms **Mycophilia** *n.* the love of mushrooms **Mycophilic** *adj.* of loving hunting, harvesting, and eating mushrooms

Nabob *n.* 1. in the past a governor in India 2. a person of prominence and wealth

Naissance *n.* the birth or origin of an idea, movement, organization, or person

Nascence/Nascency *adj.* the quality of birth and future potential *see Naissance* **Nascent** *adj.* emerging; coming into existence

Natalitial *adj.* of a birth or birthday

Negentropy, **Entaxy**, **Ectropy**, **Extropy**, and **Syntropy** *n.* negative entropy

Nemophile, Nemophilist *n.* one who loves forests and woodlands

Neonate *n.* a newborn

Neophile/Neophiliac *n.* one who loves new or modern things

Neophilia *n.* the love of new or modern things

Neoteric *adj.* modern; new; recent *n.* one who likes new ideas or things

Nepenthe *n.* drug mentioned in *The Odyssey* as a remedy for grief; it induces forgetfulness of sorrow and eases pain

Ne plus ultra *n.* 1. the ultimate highest pinnacle of achievement or excellence 2. the highest degree in quality or condition

Nirvana *n.* 1. an enlightened state of mind regarding the illusory nature of the self which transcends suffering and attains peace *Buddhist* 2. a state of mind regarding the relinquishment of individual attachments and recognition of identity with Brahman; escaping samsara *Hindu* 2. an ideal condition of harmony and/or joy, rest, and stability

Nisus *n.* a striving or endeavour to achieve a goal

Nitency *n.* brightness; fulgor; or lustre in endeavour or effort

Nitid *adj.* bright; glistening, lustrous

Nobiliary *adj.* of the nobility

Nobilitate *adj.* of nobleness, distinguished *v.* 1. to make someone a noble 2. to dignify or exalt someone or something

Nobleness *n.* the quality of having, or expressing, high moral character such as honour, generosity, or courage

Noctiflorous *adj.* flowering at night

Nocturne *n.* a musical composition inspired by, or evocative of, the night

Noegenesis *n.* the acquisition or creation of new knowledge combining experience and observation to infer new relationships

Noetic *adj.* of, or based in, mental activity or intellect

Nonesuch *n.* person or thing regarded as excellent or perfect

Nonpareil *adj.* unparalleled; having no match or equal

Normalism, Normism *n.* 1. the condition of being normal; adherence to, or belief in, a norm 2. a belief system and philosophy that each new experience enhances our understanding of reality aka. *Realism*

Novity *n.* 1. something new; a novelty 2. newness, novelty

Nubigenous *adj.* cloud-born; produced from clouds

Nutrication *n.* the act or type of feeding

Nutrimental *adj.* anything that nourishes or sustains the existence of life; nourishing

Nutritional *adj.* relating to food necessary for growth and health

Nyctophilia *n.* the love of night or darkness

Obeisance *n.* 1. a gesture, like a bow or curtsy, that demonstrates deference or homage 2. an attitude of deference or homage

Oblectation *n.* the act of greatly pleasing or the state of delight; of being highly pleased

Oecumenical *adj.* 1. of unity among churches or religions 2. of worldwide applicability or scope

Oenomel *n.* 1. a drink made of honey and wine 2. a source of sweetness and strength

Oenophile, Enophile *n.* wine lover **Oenophilia, Enophilia** *n.* the love of wine

Om *n.* elongated syllable expressed as the mantra used to 'home in'

Omnifarious *adj.* consisting of, or producing, all kinds of things

Omnify *v.* to make universal

Omnism *n.* respect and recognition of all religions

Omnist *n.* one who recognizes and respects all religions

On the qui vive *adj.* on the lookout or alert

Oneiric *adj.* of dreams or dreaming

Oneirocriticism *n.* dream analysis

Oneness *n.* 1. wisdom 2. the state or quality of being one in wholeness or in singleness 3. a state of perfect accord and harmony; a fundamental universal law 4. uniqueness; singularity 5. sameness of attributes 6. agreement; unison

Ophelimity *n.* the economic concept of a purely economic measure to relate to other dimensions of human utility to determine 'wantability'

Opinable *adj.* thinkable or able to be an opinion
Orbific *adj.* world-making *olde word*
Orison *n.* prayer **Ornithophile** *n.* one who loves birds
Orphean *adj.* 1. of Orpheus 2. enchanting or melodious
Osculate *v.* to kiss **Oscular** *adj.* of kissing
Pabulous *adj.* 1. affording food or nourishment 2. edible
Pabulum *n.* food; a substance for nourishment
Paciferous *adj.* bringing peace
Paean *n.* 1. a song of exultation 2. an ardent expression of praise or joy
Paladin *n.* 1. an icon of chivalry and heroic championship; a paragon 2. a strong defender or supporter of a cause
Palmarian, Palmary *adj.* worthy of praise or bearing the palm
Panacea *n.* a cure-all; the remedy for all challenges or diseases
Panaesthesia *n.* one's general consciousness; perception; awareness
Panaesthetism *n.* the hypothesis that consciousness may exist in all matter
Panegyric *n.* 1. a formal eulogistic public compliment 2. elaborate laudation or praise; an ecomium
Pangloss *n.* someone who's optimistic regardless of the circumstances **Panglossian** *adj.* optimistic; from a character in Voltaire's *Candide*
Pansophical *adj.* all-wise **Pansophist** *n.* one who has, or believes in, the possession of universal knowledge **Pansophistical** *adj.* of belief in the possession of universal knowledge
Pansophism/Pansophy *n.* the concept of having universal knowledge beyond human capacity
Pantheism *n.* 1. identification of God with the universe and its phenomena 2. belief in all gods
Pantisocracy *n.* a government or social group in which all rule equally
Paraclete *n.* the Holy Spirit
Paradigm *n.* 1. a model or pattern 2. assumptions, concepts, practices and values shared by a group of people particularly those in an intellectual discipline
Paradisaic, Paradisiacal *adj.* like paradise; heavenly
Parage *n.* 1. equity by virtue of birth or family 2. equality in status or rank *olde word*
Paragon *n.* 1. the peerless perfect example of excellence of its kind 2. a flawless diamond of at least 100 carats or a very big round pearl

Paramount *n.* one that has the highest authority, power, or rank
Parnassian *adj.* of poetry; poetic **Parousia** *n.* the second coming
Parthenian *adj.* of, or about, a virgin
Pash *n.* a romantic infatuation; crush
Patefaction *n.* open declaration; the act of disclosing, manifesting, or opening something
Paterfamilias *n.* the male head of the family or house
Pathopoeia *n.* an idiom, phrase, or speech intended to stimulate passions
Pecuniary *adj.* relating to, or consisting of, money
Pedagogics, Pedagogy *n.* the art and/or science of teaching
Peerage *n.* 1. the title or jurisdiction of those who govern a barony, county, duchy, marquisate, or viscountcy 2. a book listing the families of such peeresses and peers
Pellucid *adj.* 1. easily understood; lucid 2. (of sound) clear or pure in tone 3. reflecting light evenly from all surfaces
Penchant *n.* a strong liking or inclination
Pepper-upper *n.* something that provides temporary alertness or energy
Percipience *n.* 1. skill in discrimination; judgement; perception 2. psychic ability **Percipient** *adj.* perceptive; having a good understanding of things *n.* 1. someone with psychic ability 2. one that perceives
Perdurable *adj.* extremely durable; permanent
Peregal *adj.* fully equal
Perfectibilian *n.* perfectionist

The Positive Word of the Day

Perfectibilism *n.* the belief that something, especially human nature, is perfectible **Perfectibilist** *n.* someone who believes that something, especially human nature, is perfectible
Perfectibility *n.* the ability to become perfect or more perfect
Perfectionism *n.* the quality or state of the perfection standard
Pertinacity/Pertinacity *n.* the state or quality of being pertinent or relevant
Persophile, Iranophile *n.* one who loves Persia and/or its people and/or its culture **Persophilia, Iranophilia** *n.* the love of all things Persian
Perspicacious *adj.* of having a ready insight into, and understanding of, things
Perspicacity *n.* acute discernment; perception; understanding **Perspicuity** *n.* 1. clearness and lucidity. a verbal consequence of perspicacity
Perspicuous *adj.* 1. of clear expression; easy to understand 2. of one who expresses themselves well
Pharaonic *adj.* 1. of a pharaoh or the pharaohs 2. enormous in magnitude
Philalethia *n.* love of truth **Philalethist** *n.* one who loves the truth
Philocaly *n.* the love of beauty
Philodemic *adj.* of loving the people
Philogynist *n.* one who loves women **Philogyny** *n.* love of women
Philology *n.* the study of a language or languages
Philomath *n.* 1. one who loves knowledge 2. one who loves mathematics **Philomathy** *n.* 1. love of learning new facts and knowledge 2. love of mathematics
Philonoism *n.* love of knowledge **Philonoist** *n.* one who loves knowledge
Philoprogenitive *adj.* 1. of having many children 2. of showing love for one's children
Philoxenia *n.* 1. acts of hospitableness and welcome 2. love of strangers **Philoxenial** *adj.* of acts of hospitableness
Phlegmatic *adj.* of a calm, peaceful, relaxed and stolid disposition
Pierian *adj.* 1. of the muses or artistic or poetic inspiration 2. of Pieria
Pietism *n.* 1. emphasis on the personal and emotional aspects of religion 2. exaggerated or affected piety 3. a German Lutheran reform

movement in the 17th century which promoted the Protestant devotional ideal

Pigsney *n.* 1. a darling or sweetheart 2. the apple of someone's eye

Pip or Pippin *n.* an excellent person or thing

Piquant *adj.* of a pleasantly sharp taste or appetizing flavour especially spicy; tangy

Plaudit *n.* hearty expression of approval or praise

Plenary *adj.* 1. absolute; unqualified 2. of attendance by all participants of otherwise smaller groups (of a meeting)

Pluperfect *adj.* 1. an expression of appreciation for an action completed before its due time 2. ideal; beyond perfection; surpassingly accomplished

Pluviophile *n.* one who loves rain

Pogonophile *n.* one who loves beards **Pogonophilia** *n.* the love of beards

Poiesis *n.* 1. poetry 2. a poem

Pollent *adj.* strong

Polymath *n.* someone of considerable or varied learning

Polymathy *n.* having learning or knowledge in many fields

Postulant *n.* One submitting an application, petition or request 2. religious order candidate

Potable *adj.* drinkable; clean; pure; safe to drink

Potentate *n.* a monarch or ruler of unlimited power

Practicable *adj.* achievable, attainable; feasible, workable

Pragmatic *adj.* of or about actual occurrences or facts

Preceptor *n.* 1. an instructor or teacher 2. an expert or specialist who gives practical training especially in medicine

Precocious *adj.* of aptitude, development, or interests considered advanced for a given age **Precociousness, Precosity** *n.* uncommonly early development of mental ability or sexual characteristics

Prefulgent *adj.* shining the brightest **Prefulgence** *n.* the quality of shining the brightest

Prepollence *n.* predominance; prevalence

Prepossessing *adj.* appealing or attractive in appearance; beautiful; enchanting; handsome; pretty

Prepotent *adj.* greater than others in power or influence

Prescient *adj.* of foresight

Prevenient *adj.* 1. preceding; coming before 2. anticipatory; expectant

Prevision *n.* 1. foresight 2. a forecast or prediction

Prevoyance *n.* foresight; the ability to foresee

Prevoyant *adj.* foreseeing; prescient

Primitivism *n.* 1. the state or quality of being primitive 2. a simple style of art 3. a belief that it's best to live simply in a natural environment

Primo *adj.* of top importance or quality *n.* the upper or leading part in a duet

Primogenitor *n.* 1. one's earliest ancestor 2. any ancestor

Pro *adj.* in favour of *n.* short for 'professional'

Probative *adj.* tending to prove

Probity *n.* honesty; integrity; uprightness

Procinct *adj.* prepared *n.* a state of preparedness

Proconsul *n.* a high rank in the Roman and colonial empires

Proctor *n.* the supervisor of an examination or school dormitory *v.* to supervise an examination

Pro forma *adj.* 1. formally done, perfunctory 2. provided in advance so as to describe items and/or prescribe form

Profulgent *adj.* brilliant; shining forth

Progenitor *n.* 1. direct ancestor 2. an originator of a family line 3. a founder or originator

Proleptic, Proleptical *adj.* anticipatory

Promulgator *n.* one who makes something known to the public; one who advocates or popularizes **Promulgate** *v.* 1. to advocate, publicize, or popularize 2. to make law by formal public announcement

Promulgation *n.* 1. a public statement, or formal announcement of that statement, informing that an event is going to happen or has happened.

Pronoia *n.* the philosophy that the world is set up to secretly benefit people and/or a neologism that there exists a conspiracy to help one

Propinquity *n.* 1. close proximity 2. kinship 3. a similar nature

Propitious *adj.* 1. advantageous; benevolent; favourable 2. auspicious; of a good omen **Propitiable** *adj.* appeasable; capable of being propitiated **Propitiative** *adj.* inclined to propitiate or grant advantage **Propitiate** *v.* to appease, conciliate, or make well disposed; to gain or regain the favour or goodwill of **Propitiation** *n.* 1. conciliation 2. a thing that propitiates **Propitiator** *n.* one who grants advantage; benevolence; favour **Propitiousness** *n.* the quality of having a favourable outcome **Propitiously** *adverb*

Propriety *n.* 1. conformity to conventional standards of behaviour or morality 2. appropriateness, being proper **Proprieties** *pl.*

Protean *adj.* of the ability to change easily and frequently; multi-talented

Proto- *prefix* first

Pudicity *n.* chastity; chasteness; modesty

Puissant *adj.* of great influence or power

Pukka *adj.* 1. genuine 2. first-class; superior 3. socially correct

Pulchritudinous *adj.* of great physical appeal and beauty

Pundonor *n.* a point of honour

Purposive *adj.* 1. having or showing intention 2. serving a purpose 3. resolute; determined

Qualtagh *n.* the first person one sees outdoors on New Year's day

Quemeful *adj.* kindly; merciful

Quickening *n.* 1. increasing the speed; accelerating. 2. the showing signs of life process 3. the act of enlivening someone 4. the act of exciting or stimulating **Quicken** *v.* to cause a quickening

Quiescent *adj.* 1. inactive; quiet; still 2. characterized by an absence of discord or upheaval **Quiescence, Quiescency** *n.* the state of being quiescent

Quietism *n.* 1. the combining of passive contemplation and saintly annihilation of the will 2. a state of passive quietness **Quietist** *n.* one who practices Quietism

Quiety *n.* quietness; tranquility

Quintessence *n.* 1. the highly concentrated and pure essence of something 2. the most pure and typical instance

Quixotic *adj.* exceedingly idealistic; utopian; romantic **Quixotism** *n.* 1. the state of being swept up in the romance of noble deeds and unreachable goals 2. an impulsive or capricious quality

Raconteur *n.* someone who tells stories or anecdotes with wit and skill **Raconteuse** *n.* female raconteur

Raillery *n.* banter; good-natured teasing

Rapport *n.* a harmonious and sympathetic relationship of emotional affinity

Rapprochement *n.* a reestablishment, or state of, cordial relations as between two countries

Rara avis *n.* a rare person or thing; from 'rare bird'

Rathe *adj.* 1. (of a person or their actions) eager and prompt 2. (of fruit or flowers) ripening or blooming early in the year
Ratheness *n.* the quality or state of being rathe
Ratiocination *n.* logical and methodical reasoning **Ratiocinative** *adj.* of logical and methodical reasoning
Realism *n.*1. the quality of pragmatism or literal truth 2. representation in art or literature of things as they really are 3. the doctrine that the universe exists independent of being perceived or thought
Recherche' *adj.* exotic; obscure; rare
Recipient *adj.* open to receiving; receptive   *n.* one who receives something **Recipience** *n.* the quality or state of being recipient
Rectitude *n.* 1. righteousness; moral uprightness 2. being correct in judgement 3. being straight
Rede *n.* 1. council or advice 2. narration *v.* 1. to advise or counsel 2. explain or interpret *olde word*
Redintegrate *v.* 1. make complete or whole again; restore to perfect condition; renew 2. engage the process of redintegration *Psych.*
Redolence *n.* distinctive or characteristic odour
Redolent *adj.* 1. evocative; reminiscent; suggestive 2. fragrant
Reflation *n.* 1. increase in economic activity 2. an increase in credit and money supply intended to increase economic activity
Refocillate *v.* to revive, refresh, or give new life
Refulgent *adj.* brightly shining
Reguerdon *n.* reward *v.* to reward
Reinfund *v.* to flow or pour in again
Remissive *adj.* of bringing about, or granting, pardon or remission
Renascent *adj.* becoming active or popular again
Replete *adj.* 1. well-supplied or filled with something 2. sated by, or very full of, food
Repletion *n.* the condition of being filled, satisfied, or supplied
Requiescence *n.* repose
Retrocognition *n.* the extrasensory ability or occurrence of seeing into the past
Retrophile *n.* one who loves the past **Retrophilia** *n.* love of the past
Revalorize *v.* 1. to change, esp. higher, the valuation of assets 2. to replace a currency unit by another
Revivescence, Revivescency, Reviviscence *n.* restoration, or animation, to life; revival **Reviviscent** *adj.* of reviving; reanimation

Riant *adj.* mirthful; cheerful

Rident *adj.* gay; laughing; smiling

Ridibund *adj.* inclined, and easily brought, to laughter; happy

Ripsnorter *n.* exciting person or thing

Risibility *n.* 1. a tendency to laughter 2. laughter; hilarity

Risorial *adj.* pertaining to, or producing, laughter

Russophile *n.* one who loves Russia and/or its people and/or its culture

Rutilant *adj.* glittering or glowing with red or golden light

Sagacious *adj.* having keen discernment, farsightedness, and sound judgement **Sagaciousness/Sagacity** *n.* the quality of being sagacious

Sageship *n.* the wisdom and status of being a sage

Salad days *n.* a time of innocent, inexperienced, youthful summer days

Salient *adj.* 1. important; noteworthy 2. conspicuous; prominent 3. jutting, projecting or protruding beyond a line or surface 4. jumping; springing n. a projecting part or angle **Salience** *n.* 1. the quality or condition of being salient 2. a highlight or noteworthy part or feature

Salubrious *adj.* healthy; favourable to health

Salubrity, Salubriousness *n.* the quality or state of being salubrious

Salutary *adj.* 1. effecting or designed to effect an improvement; remedial 2. favourable to health; wholesome **Salutariness** *n.* the quality or state of effecting an improvement 2. the quality or state of being wholesome or favorable to health **Salutatory** *adj.* of the nature of a salutation

Salutiferous *adj.* favourable to safety or health

Salvific *adj.* leading to salvation

Salutary *adj.* 1. designed to effect, or effecting, an improvement; remedial 2. wholesome; favorable to good health

Sanative *adj.* of the ability to cure physically; or spiritually; healing; restorative **Sanatory** *adj.* of healing or health

Sanctanimity *n.* holiness of mind

Sanctified *adj.* 1. of consecration or setting apart for sacred use 2. of purification or making holy 3. of giving religious sanction such as a vow or oath 4. of giving moral or social sanction **Sanctification** *n.* the religious ceremony of making something sacred **Sanctify** *v.* to consecrate or isolate for sacred use

Sanctiloquent *adj.* speaking on sacred or holy things, or in a holy manner

Sanctum *n.* 1. a holy or sacred place 2. a private place

Sangfroid *n.* composure and coolness especially under challenging circumstances

Sanguine *adj.* 1. positive; optimistic, especially under challenging circumstances 2. blood red **Sanguineness, Sanguinity** *n.* 1. a state of cheerfulness; confidence; optimism 2. acceptance; ease 3. a rosy, ruddy complexion

Sapid *adj.* 1. a) having perceptible taste; flavour b) having pleasant strong flavour; savoury 2. engaging; mentally pleasing

Sapidity *n.* 1. having a strong pleasant flavour; savoury taste 2. an engaging, or pleasant to think about, thing

Sapience *n.* the quality of great discernment or wisdom

Sapient, **Sapiential** *adj.* having much discernment and wisdom

Sapor *n.* flavour; a quality perceptible to the sense of taste

Saporific, Saporous *adj.* flavourful; a quality perceptible to the sense of taste

Sartorial *adj.* of a tailor, tailored clothing, or tailoring

Satiety *n.* the state of being full or gratified beyond satisfaction

Sative *adj.* sown; cultivated; not wild

Satori *n.* an often sudden spiritual awakening *Buddhist*

Savoir faire *n.* ability to do or say the graceful or appropriate thing in social situations.

Schatzi *n.* German for 'girlfriend'; literally 'treasure'

Scholarch *n.* the head of a school

Scintillant *adj.* sparkling

Scintillescent *adj.* sparkling; glinting

Scion *n.* an heir or descendant

Sedulous *adj.* assiduous; constant; diligent; perseverant

Sedulousness *n.* assiduous attention and diligent work at one's occupation**Selcouth** *adj.* marvelous; rare; strange; unusual; unfamiliar; wondrous *olde word*

Sempiternal *adj.* enduring forever; eternal

Sensate *adj.* perceived or perceiving via the senses

Sesquipedalian *n.* a long word *adj.* 1. characterized by, or given to the use of long words 2. long and polysyllabic

Seraphic *adj.* of a seraph; one of a high order of celestial beings or angels

Serendipitous *adj.* fortunate in pleasant unexpected discoveries
Serendipity *n.* the instance, occurrence, or faculty of making lucky discoveries
Seva *n.* selfless service
Sinophile *n.* one who loves China and/or its people and/or its culture
Sinophilia *n.* the love of all things Chinese
Skookum *adj.* 1. brave, large, and powerful 2. excellent   *Canada and Northwest U.S.*
Slake *v.* 1. a) to quench a thirst or satisfy a craving b) to moderate or lessen the intensity or force of something (olde use) 2. to add moisture to, and thereby crumble, as lime
Slamin' *adj.* 1. cool; hip; hot: in; with the times 2. as loud and striking as a slamming door
Slavophile *n.* one who loves Slavic countries and/or Slavic people and/or their culture   **Slavophilia** *n.* the love of all things Slavic
Snod *adj.* 1. neat and tidy (of a person) 2. evenly cut; smooth (of flora) *Scot. and N. England*
Socius *n.* associate; consort; partner
Sockdologer *n.* 1. something exceptional or outstanding 2. a decisive blow or finisher
Sodality *n.* 1. fellowship 2. a devotional or charitable association or society
Soigne *adj.* 1. very elegantly attired 2. well-groomed
Solacious *adj.* giving solace
Solicitude *n.* care or concern
Solon *n.* 1. a wise lawgiver 2. a legislator
Sonsy *adj.* of an attractive healthy appearance
Sooth *n.* truth
Soothfast *adj.* 1. honest; truthful 2. real; true
Soul mate *n.* someone for whom one has deep affection and affinity; one person of a pair of people who are ideally compatible together in outlook, disposition, sensibility or perspective
Sophic *adj.* of teaching wisdom
Sovereign *adj.* 1. independent; self-governing 2. of having supreme power or rank 3. supreme; paramount   n. someone with supreme permanent governmental authority
Splendent *adj.* 1. glossy; shining 2. brilliant; illustrious
Sponsal *adj.* spousal

Sportive *adj.* 1. frolicsome; playful 2. interested in, or related to, sports

Sprauncy *adj.* of a showy or smart appearance

Staid *adj.* 1. of sedateness often with strait-laced propriety 2. permanent; fixed; set

Stalwart *adj.* 1. resolute and loyal 2. imposing and strong

Steward *n.* 1. someone who manages the finances, property or affairs of another 2. someone in charge of household affairs for a club, estate, hotel, or resort 3. a ship's officer 4. an airplane or ship attendant 5. someone who manages an event 6. a shop steward

Sthenia *n.* bodily strength, vigour, or vitality **Sthenic** *adj.* of having sthenia; active, strong, or vigorous

Stipendiary *adj.* 1. of getting a stipend 2. of compensation via stipend *n.* stipend recipient

Stoic *n.* 1. one who appears unaffected by pleasure, pain, grief or joy 2. follower of an ancient Greek philosophy that maintains that virtue is sufficient for happiness and God determines everything for the best; later it advocated the acceptance of all things as inevitable via natural order **Stoicism** *n.* the endurance of hardship or pain without complaint **Stoic, Stoical** *adj.* 1. seeming unaffected by pain or pleasure 2. of the stoic philosophy

Stonking *adj.* of extraordinary size or quality; an intensifier

Suasive *adj.* of the ability to convince or persuade; persuasive

Suaveolent *adj.* sweet-smelling or fragrant

Suaviloquent *adj.* sweetly speaking; using agreeable speech

Substant *adj.* 1. substantial; firm

Succor *n.* 1. assistance; relief or stress 2. one that gives assistance or relief

Suffisance *n.* enough; fulfilment; fullness; satisfaction; sufficient ability or supply

Sui generis *adj.* of its own kind; unique

Supercalifragilisticexpialidocious *adj.* 1. extraordinarily good or wonderful 2. atoning for educability through delicate beauty (from word roots: super- "above", cali- "beauty", fragilistic- "delicate", expiali- "to atone", and -docious "educable")

Superconscious *adj.* transcending normal human consciousness

Superlative *adj.* of the highest degree or quality

Supernal *adj.* 1. celestial; heavenly 2. of the sky or high above

Supersensible *adj.* above or beyond perception by the senses

Supraliminal *adj.* of stimuli above the threshold of consciousness or sensation

Surety *n.* the state of being certain or sure

Sustentative *adj.* 1. of something that supports or sustains 2. of maintenance or sustenance such as money

Swain *n.* 1 a young man from the country esp. a shepherd 2. a young male caller, suitor or lover

Sweven *n.* a dream or vision *olde word*

Sybaritic *adj.* 1. of luxury and pleasure 2. of the former Italian city of Sybaris **Sylph** *n.* 1. a graceful, slim girl or woman 2. an ancient forest nymph

that has air as its element

Sylvan *adj.* 1. of the forest or woods 2. located, or residing, in a forest or woods 3. abundant with trees; wooded

Synergy *n.* 1. the interaction of two or more components so that, when combined, the effect is more than the sum of their individual effects 2. cooperation between groups, often among subsidiaries of a corporation, that creates an enhanced overall effect 3. the occurrence of such interaction

Syngenesis *n.* sexual reproduction

Syntropy, Entaxy, **Ectropy**, **Extropy**, and **Negentropy** *n.* negative entropy

Tachytelic *adj.* of evolution at a faster rate than standard

Technophilia *n.* the love of new technology **Technophile** *n.* one who loves technology

Telegenic *adj.* appealing to television viewers

Telegnosis *n.* knowledge of remote events obtained without normal use of the five senses

Teleorganic *adj.* vital

Telergy *n.* the energy used in telepathy

Tempean *adj.* of a temple

Tempestive *adj.* occurring at the appropriate season or time

Tenable *adj.* 1. defensible rationally 2. defensible against physical assault 3. endurable or tolerable **Tenability** *n.* the quality or state of being tenable

Testamur *n.* a certificate verifying qualification via examination

Testator *n.* one who is deceased having left a valid legal will

Thaumatogeny *n.* the belief that life's origin was a miracle

Thaumatography *n.* a description or treatise about the world's natural wonders

Thaumatological *adj.* of the study of miracles

Thaumatologist *n.* one who studies miracles

Thaumatology *n.* the study of miracles **Thaumaturgy** *n.* the working of miracles or magic feats

Theanthropic *adj.* both human and divine in quality or nature

Theanthropism *n.* 1. giving human characteristics to God 2. the union of divine and human natures in Jesus

Theanthroposophy *n.* a belief system about theanthropism

Theocentricity, Theocentrism *n.* the hypothesis that God is the center of all truth in the universe

Theodidact *n.* student, or taught, of God

Theopanism *n.* the belief that the universe is a projection of, or emanates from, God

Theopathy *n.* the feeling of contemplating, or meditating on, God

Theophilanthropism *n.* a religion based on the immortality of the soul, personal virtue, and the belief in God **Theophilanthropist** *n.* one who practices theophilanthropism **Theophilanthropic** *adj.* of the qualities of theophilanthropism

Theopneustic *adj.* of the inspiration from, and of, the Spirit of God

Theopsychism *n.* the belief that the soul has a divine nature

Theosophy *n.* the system of beliefs and teachings of the *Theosophical Society* incorporating belief in reincarnation and spiritual evolution

Theotherapy *n.* the treatment of disease or illness via prayer and other religious procedures

Theotokos *n.* the Virgin Mary literally 'God bearer'

Therapeutic *adj.* 1. exhibiting or having healing capacity 2. of medical treatment of a condition or disease n. a therapeutic agent such as a drug

Theurgy *n.* divine or benevolent supernatural intervention in human matters

Threpsology *n.* a treatise on, or doctrine of, nutrition *Medical*

Timeous *adj.* timely; in good time

Titivation *n.* the act of decoration; sprucing up; from 'tidying + elevation' **Titivate** *v.* to adorn; spruce up

Tony *adj.* fashionable among the stylish or wealthy

Toothsome *adj.* 1. delicious; luscious 2. attractive; pleasant 3. physically attractive

Traditive *adj.* of tradition; cultural customs from one generation to the next

Transcendentalism *n.* 1. a philosophical and literary movement asserting that there's a perfect spiritual reality transcending the empirical world attainable via intuition 2. the state or quality of being transcendental

Transpicuous *adj.* easily transparent or understood

Transvolation *n.* flying across or beyond

Tretis *adj.* long and well-proportioned; nicely built; pretty *n.* treaty or treatise

Trophism *n.* the nourishment of the tissues

Trophology, Alimentology *n.* the study of nutrition

Trouvaille *n.* a windfall

Trustee *n.* 1. one who is given control of property in trust and is responsible to administer it exclusively for the purposes specified 2. a state that the United Nations makes responsible for the government of an area Thalassophile n. one who loves the ocean/sea

Tucket *n.* a trumpet flourish

Turophile *n.* one who loves cheese **Turophilia** *n.* the love of cheese

Tutelage *n.* the activity or capacity of, or state of being under, a guardian or tutor

Tutelary *n.* one who serves as a protector or guardian *adj.* of being a guardian or protector; guardianship

Twitterpated *adj.* 1. infatuated or romantically overcome 2. of a nervous excited state originated in the movie *Bambi*

Typhlophile *n.* one who loves the blind

Uber, Ueber *adj.* 1. prefix for over-the-top or super 2. German for above, about, and across

Uberty *n.* abundance; fruitfulness *olde word*

Ubiquity/Ubiquitousness *n.* the quality of being everywhere at once

Ubiquitous *adj.* being everywhere at once; omnipresent

Ubuntu *n.* generosity of spirit and social unity; the best of humanity *Zulu*

Ueber, Uber *adj.* prefix for over-the-top or super 2. German for above, about, and across

Unabashed *adj.* 1. not embarrassed or disconcerted; poised 2. not concealed; apparent; obvious

Unequivocable *adj.* unambiguous and clear; allowing no misunderstanding or doubt **Unequivocal** *adj.* another, more common, word for unequivocable

Unicity *n.* of being, or consisting of, one; unique and/or being united as a whole unique entity

Unisonous, Unisonal, Unisonant *adj.* in unison; in unity; One

Universalism *n.* 1. the doctrine that all people eventually will be saved 2. the condition of being universal rather than affiliated in outlook

Univocal *n.* a word with only one meaning

Univocal *adj.* meaning only one thing; unambiguous

Unwithdrawing *adj.* 1. not giving up or pulling back, 2. generous

Upbuild *v.* build up, enlarge, or increase

Upbuilder *n.* one who builds up, increases, or enlarges **Upbuilding** *adj. v.* of building up by creation, enlargement, fortification or increase

Uprear *v.* to lift or raise up or to rise up

Utile Dulci *adj.* of the useful with the pleasant

Uxorial *adj.* of, or befitting, a wife

Vatic, Vaticinal *adj.* oracular; of a prophet; prophetic **Vaticination** *n.* prediction; foretelling **Vaticinator** *n.* a prophet **Vaticinate** *v.* 1. to foretell; prophesy 2. to be a prophet

Vegete *adj.* active; lively; vigorous

Velocious *adj.* fast; rapid

Venial *adj.* pardonable; easily forgiven or excused

Ventorious *adj.* venturesome *olde word*

Venust *adj.* attractive; beautiful; elegant; graceful

Veraciousness *n.* the quality of accuracy; honesty; truth and truthfulness

Veracity *n.* 1. accuracy, adherence, or conformity to fact or the truth 2. a true statement

Verdant *adj.* green with grass or other vegetative growth

Verdurous *adj.* 1. flourishing or fresh 2. of lavish greenness and proliferate vegetation

Verecund *adj.* modest or shy

Veridical, Veridicous *adj.* 1. truthful 2. in accordance with future events or unknowable reality **Veridicality** *n.* the quality or state of being veridical

Veriloquent *adj.* of speaking truth; truthful

Verisimilitude *n.* the quality of appearing to be real and true

Verity *n.* 1. the condition or quality of being real or true 2. an enduring truth **Verities** *pl.*

Vernal *adj.* 1. of the, or like, spring 2. fresh and young

Vernality *n.* the quality or state of being spring-like

Vertex *n.* the highest point

Verve *n.* 1. enthusiasm and energy expressing ideas, artistic composition or performance 2. vigor; vitality; liveliness

Vespertine *adj.* of the evening

Vibratile *adj.* adapted to being vibrated or vibrating

Victor *n.* 1. one, or a team member, who defeats an adversary; the winner in a battle, contest, fight or struggle 2. 'V' is for victory

Victoria *n.* 1. Roman goddess of victory 2. exclamation of victory

Videophile *n.* one who loves video recordings and/or its technology

Viparious *adj.* life renewing *olde word*

Virtu *n.* 1. a knowledge, love, or taste for fine art objects 2. fine art objects, especially antiques as a group

Vitalism *n.* the theory that life proceeds from nonmaterial vital forces that cannot be entirely explained via physics or chemistry

Vitative *adj.* of vitality, fondness for life, and resistance to decline

Vivat *n.* long live! *expression*

Vively *adv.* in a lively manner

Vivency *n.* a manifestation of physical or mental energy

Volable *adj.* nimble-minded

Volant *adj.* flying or having the power of flight

Volitional *adj.* 1. by choice or with intention 2. of the capacity to choose; of the will

Votary *n.* 1. someone bound by vows to a life of religious service or worship 2. a committed devotee or worshiper of a religion

Vraisemblance *n.* appearance of truth; verisimilitude

Vulnerary *adj.* of healing or treating wounds **Vulnerary** *n.* something used to heal or treat wounds

Waggish *adj.* humorous in a facetious, playful, or mischievous way

Warranted *adj.* justified

Weal *n.* public happiness, prosperity, well-being

Weleful *adj.* 1. blessed 2. producing happiness or prosperity

Welsome *adj.* prosperous; well

Wight *adj.* (pronounced 'wit') brave; valorous   *n.* a creature; a living being *olde word*

Winnow *v.* to separate grain from chaff or good from bad

Wisdom *n.* Oneness

Woke *adj.* politically woken; awoken; awakened *v.* past of wake

Woodnote *n.* 1. the single call or song of a woodland bird 2. a natural spontaneous verbal expression

Xenial *adj.* genial or hospitable to guests especially strangers

Xenodocial *adj.* hospitable; friendly to strangers

Xenophile *n.* one who loves foreigners **Xenophilia** *n.* affection for unknown foreign objects or people

Yare *adj.* 1. agile; lively 2. manoeuvrable; responsive *nautical*

Yern *adj.* active; brisk; eager; quick

Younker *n.* 1. a young man 2. a child

Youthquake *n.* meaningful social, political, or cultural change resulting from the influence or actions of young people **Zazzy** *adj.*1. shiny or flashy 2. energetic, cool; stylish

Zenith *n.*1. the highest point above the observer's horizon reached by a celestial body 2. the culmination or peak of something

Zoetic *adj.* of life; living; vital

Zoomagnetism *n.* animal magnetism

Some Extraordinary Word
Graphic Definitions

END

Home

www.ingramcontent.com/pod-product-compliance
Lightning Source LLC
Chambersburg PA
CBHW050214270326
41914CB00003BA/408